PSYCHOANALYSTS AT WORK

Psychoanalysts at Work

More Selected Papers by Arnold D. Richards
Vol. III

Arthur A. Lynch, Editor

IPBOOKS.net
International Psychoanalytic Books

International Psychoanalytic Books (IPBooks)
New York • http://www.IPBooks.net

Psychoanalysts at Work

Published by IPBooks, Queens, NY
Online at: www.IPBooks.net

Copyright © 2020 Arnold D. Richards

ISBN: 978-1-949093-70-4

Dedicated to Stephen L. Richards
who taught me how to write

Table of Contents

Section 4. Views and Reviews

Section 5. Conclusion

AN APPRECIATION

by Judith Logue, Ph.D.

ARNOLD D. RICHARDS, M.D.—A MAN FOR ALL SEASONS

I met Dr. Arnold Richards more than ten years ago. He is progressive, principled, and persistent. To say that he is passionate, accomplished, and energetic is an understatement.

My introduction to Dr. Richards was when I developed and moderated the grand finale for his annual "Future of Psychoanalytic Education" symposium in New York City in 2007. This "Roundtable" was an interdisciplinary forum of representatives of 10 major U.S. psychoanalytic organizations to analyze the challenges and propose some changes for psychoanalytic education. It was a difficult task: negotiate with leaders of the major psychoanalytic organizations in the United States, allowed to speak for only ten minutes, on why we should collaborate, and all get along.

Throughout the year of planning for the symposium, he and I went back and forth and forth and back: about people, places, and policies. His direct style led me to understand how Arnie—as he is called by those who work closely with him—gets things done efficiently and successfully. Moreover, he does this in half the time it takes most ordinary people.

This introductory experience led to my understanding him, and respecting him for his intellect, insight and vision. And, it led to my caring for him deeply as a professional, colleague and friend.

Dr Richards is a determined and rebellious reformer fed up with the "Iron Law of Oligarchy." He is a brilliant intellectual, scholar, prolific author, traditionally educated, with numerous awards and certifications, whose passion was to end the control of the American Psychoanalytic Association by the Board on Professional Standards, BoPS. Though considered a hero by some, and a pariah by others, for his part in this achievement, there is no question that his influence has changed the politics of American psychoanalysis today and for the future.

Dr. Richards is a devoted and beloved physician, psychoanalyst, scholar, teacher, publisher, editor, and social activist with more creative energy than anyone I know. He extends the thinking and practice of Freud with his views on immortality. He proposes that wishes for longevity and immortality are among the most universal of human desires. Without apology or doubt, he takes Freud to task for dismissing what he knows to be true. And, in his many self-disclosing articles he acknowledges, with humility, that his ideas and theories also reflect his belief that the psychology of the analyst is represented in his or her theories.

Dr. Richards persists in a dogged and dedicated fight for diversity and progress in psychoanalysis which he has been doing since he was a young man: questioning injustice and rigid tenets and practices that make no sense. He continues to march for civil rights all over the world. He established an international psychoanalytic website and a publishing business at a time in life when many people retire.

He now travels to China at least three times a year to teach and supervise. He is beloved by his Chinese students, who praise his work, and teaching. They celebrate him at parties with music, dance, and joy.

With his wife, Dr. Arlene Richards, Arnie started a psychoanalytic psychotherapy program in Wuhan, China. In the second year of a three-year program with more than 200 students, they have assembled a faculty of psychoanalysts from the United States and Australia. They supervise and teach courses to more than 300 students which include more than 50 essential papers.

Arnold Richards is a very special man who is charming, generous, and passionate. He consistently directs for success—for others, not just for himself.

I have had the opportunity to work as a psychodynamic business coach with an ongoing analysand of Dr. Richards. Decades of excellent analysis saved this man's life. This patient's capacity for understanding and insight are testimony not only to a successful psychoanalysis, but especially to the competence and experience of his psychoanalyst. It is a unique and rare experience. Most importantly, it reflects Arnie's creativity and never-ending curiosity to explore new ways to apply psychoanalytic thinking and practice anywhere and everywhere.

Arnie stimulates dialogue and controversy daily on our listservs, in his prolific articles and books, and in personal and professional relationships. Count on Dr. Richards to test the limits of whatever and whomever he encounters, and to expand your horizons and enlighten you with his writing, teaching, and practice.

The Dynamic Evolution of Freudian Theory: An Introduction

Arthur A. Lynch, Ph.D.

Psychoanalysts at Work is the third volume of Arnold Richards's selected papers. In this volume, Richards continues to follow and elaborate on a particular transcending Freudian line in the evolution of psychoanalytic theory. The broad strokes of this track were spelled out earlier by Richards (2015, chapters 14 through 18).

The transcending Freudian line begins with Freud's Topographical model and the pursuit of the unconscious. It then evolves, by the 1920s, into the structural model, which placed a heavier emphasis on unconscious conflict between the instinctual forces and the ego and superego's efforts to manage them.

After Freud's death, this theoretical line blossomed into Ego Psychology under the guidance of Anna Freud, Heinz Hartmann, Rudolph Loewenstein and Ernst Kris. These early pioneers along with many others developed the theory from the 1940s on. In North America, Ego Psychology became the preeminent psychoanalytic theory. During its course, however, this theory was not without objection, or challenge. Critiques were delivered from both external

1

and internal sources. One prominent internal critique came from Arlow and Brenner (1964) as they began to address Freud's theoretical inconsistencies. These inconsistencies were due to Freud's neglect of reformulation after new findings and the absence of theoretical integration, which characterized his theories as his thinking progressed. Arlow & Brenner, (1964) reached the initial conclusion that many of the principles of the topographical model were unnecessary and even incongruous with the new structural model. Although they attempted to resolve some of these contradictions, they ultimately decided that the models were irreconcilable and that the topographical model should be discarded.

This process of assessing a concept's place in psychoanalytic theory was based on data evaluation and ultimately led to another major theoretical revision. This time it was the structural model that was overshadowed by contemporary conflict theory (Brenner, 1982). In this volume and elsewhere, Richards (2015) has discussed, in detail, the psychoanalytic contributions that lay at the foundation of contemporary conflict theory. Using this theory Richards then went on to evaluate other alternative contemporary psychoanalytic theories, including: the self psychologies, hermeneutic science and dialectical constructivism, and various relational models. After critiquing these theories, he (with A.K. Richards) explored the technical impact of the competing psychoanalytic models. Here the Richards ask the ever-present question: What are the technical consequences of different psychoanalytic theories?

In the chapters of Volume III, Richards returns to his "views" on the broad spectrum of clinical and theoretical issues. The title of the volume, "Psychoanalysts at work," reflects the premise that Contemporary Conflict Theory provides the everyday psychoanalytic practitioner with clinical and technical guidance that is based on "science" (Brenner, 2005), and falls within the structure of an evolutionary 'total composite psychoanalytic theory" Rangell, (2007). This guidance has been developed in every generation since Freud in much the same way that guilds have worked and shared their knowledge. All the current psychoanalytic traditions can be viewed as thought collectives (Fleck,1935) that follow a similar course: obtaining training, forming study groups and private supervision, and participating in the ongoing dialogue of their specific thought collective.

The elements of this premise are developed in the book's five sections, encompassing Richards' views on: antecedents, clinical data, clinical theory, reviews and conclusions.

The findings of Richards explorations in these five sections repeatedly demonstrate the enduring nature of "psychic conflict," as well as its dynamic manifestations both in a behavioural presence (i.e., "compromise formations), and in the universal influence of unconscious fantasy, whose narrative is defined by the individual's unique boundaries of pleasure and pain (Jacobson, 1964 and Arlow, 1980). These findings also demonstrate the individual's unique dynamic character and identity (Abend, 1974) that accompanies the motivational components of desire and fear,[1] the protective functions of defense, and the adaptive response of morality.

Section1, "Antecedents," covers four theoretical positions that contribute to a contemporary Freudian theory. These theorists include: Jacob Arlow, Charles Brenner, Ernst Ticho, and Leo Rangell.

The section begins with a discussion of the essential aspects of psychoanalytic theory that guide clinical technique. These essential aspects include: the sustained nature of unconscious fantasy, the dynamic characteristics of unconscious conflict and compromise

---

1 This is what Freud was referring to in his discussion of "wishes and worries" as early as 1900 (Freud, 1900, p.550).

formation, the technical consequences of the enduring impact of object relations, and the growth of a science within a specific professional culture—Total Composite Psychoanalytic Theory.

This particular group of theorists are aligned with conflict theory. Arlow and Brenner[2] more directly involved from their work on the structural theory. Ticho and Rangell who (like Jacobson, Fenichel, Mahler, & Kernberg) share a tradition of blending ego psychology and object relations theory. Perhaps the one most conscious of this identifier was Leo Rangell who considered himself as coming from "a developed Freudian approach". This over all group of contemporary Freudian analysts diverge along the lines of how the conflict manifests itself and how it secures other mental functions in its pursuit of gratification. Even with these differences the members of this group are more alike than not.

Richards (with Goodman) begins this section with an account of the life and contributions of one of the leading architects of both Structural Theory and Contemporary Conflict Theory—Jacob A. Arlow, M.D. In this brief biographical review, the authors bring together a professional life that was mostly private. Here they describe Arlow's experience growing up in his family, his education and particular passion for learning, and his experience in love, marriage and family, all before turning to his psychoanalytic training and career.

Arlow commuted daily from the suburbs to his Manhattan office. As his professional commitments increased and became more demanding, his time at home was diminished. He shares a quote with the authors from Lowell reflecting the regret this left: "He sings to the wide world and she to her nest. In the nice ear of nature which song is best?"

---

2 Brenner's work has been discussed in greater detail in Volume I(Richards, 2015).

Arlow's career was long and distinguished. He was on the faculty at 10 medical or psychoanalytic institutions. He won over a dozen medical or psychoanalytic awards for his work. He published 5 books and 140 papers, including 6 presentations to the International Psychoanalytic Association Congresses, plus an additional 30 book reviews. In organizational life he was just as busy. Holding the presidencies of both his local institute and the American Psychoanalytic Association, he also served as Treasurer of the International Psychoanalytic Association (1963–1967). He was always sought after as an analyst and supervisor. But perhaps the most remarkable aspect of this chapter is the clear description offered by the authors of Arlow as an analyst. To paraphrase this: 'He maintained a clear, firm view of the patient's struggles unclouded by "sentimentality or intellectual prejudice." His comments were unequivocal yet simple, consoling and genuine, humble but void of self-importance. He was always wary about what could be clinically anticipated. These qualities characterized Arlow's professional activity, and this more then anything else defined him as a man deeply committed to his craft.

In chapter 12, Richards, provides an introduction to Arlow's significant theoretical and technical contributions (e.g., unconscious fantasy, the genesis and dynamics of interpretation, and theory of pathogenesis).

Arlow's contributions, like Brenner's, have slowly replaced the older metapsychology with a more dynamic psychoanalytic theory. His contributions can be seen as evolving around three transitions (Kramer, 1988). Over the course, Arlow continues to shift in emphasis his point of view from structure to meaning.

The first transition, as noted, involves a conceptual shift from instinct theory, with its emphasis on the economic point of view, to conflict theory, emphasizing a more dynamic point of view.

This shift was initially identified in "Psychoanalytic Concepts and the Structural Theory" (Arlow & Brenner, 1964). Its impact freed clinicians to discard the more restrictive terminology that impeded fully grasping the early childhood derivatives, which fueled symptoms and behavior. This shift also led clinicians to a new appreciation of the dynamic unconscious.

The second major transformation concerns a shift of emphasis from unconscious content to the analysis of defense. Conflict remains central to all human functioning. Arlow sees defense as continuously attempting to mitigate the most painful effects of intrapsychic conflicts (i.e., anxiety and depressive affect). Defense remains central to the entire range of normal and pathological phenomena. This shift affects the way analysts think about and perform their work.

Finally, Arlow's third and perhaps most significant transformation is found in his efforts to centralize the concept of unconscious fantasy to clinical thinking and practice. The fundamental idea is that people's lives are affected by childhood wishes expressed in fantasies that have both individual and universal features. Arlow postulates a hierarchy of fantasy formations in the mind, which reflects the fluctuations of the individual's experience and psychic development. The hierarchy of fantasy organizes around universal infantile wishes. These fantasies mature with development but the wishes remain constant.

In its most natural form, unconscious fantasy is given to both external reality and psychic reality, to fantasy and trauma. A dynamic relation is posited between wishes and imperatives of childhood and childhood experiences. This dynamic relation continues through development and is what one observes in the analytic situation. This is not to say that the dynamic relation becomes pathogenic due to a traumatic event. Turning to Arlow's (1981) "Theories of Pathogenesis" paper, Richards clarifies the process by paraphrasing Arlow noting that: "the material of actual occurrences... is constantly subjected to selective scrutiny of memory under the guide of the inner constellation.... They are molded into patterns and it is with these rather than with the events... the analyst deals" (p. 333). "What constitutes trauma," Arlow points out, "is not inherent in the actual real event... but rather in the individual response to the disorganizing, disruptive combination of impulses and fears integrated into a set of unconscious fantasies" (Kramer, 1988, p. 34). Richards notes, "... this more nuanced view of fantasy, memory, and experience is part of a more general move beyond the ego psychology formulated by Hartmann and his colleagues"[3]

In Chapter 2, Richards turns to two major contributions by Charles Brenner and assesses the clinical value of "Conflict and Compromise Formation." Richards frames these two essential concepts in the ongoing state of theoretical pluralism. He elaborates on the dynamic impact "theoretical pluralism" has had on several emerging theories. He supports the benefits of disagreement and debate of differences but remains concerned about the destructive fragmenting consequences of theoretical pluralism, which include the devaluing and diminishing of other theories without adequate data. He then turns to the two essential concepts of conflict and compromise formation. Some believe that these two concepts, plus the concept of unconscious fantasy, provide the basis for a comprehensive science of mind. Others believe that the two terms are contradictory. They are conceptual opposites. (Kafka, E., "Is Psychoanalysis A Conflict Theory?" unpublished panel paper). There are challenges to all theoretical revisions and these should be welcomed.

---

3 Chapter 14 also takes on particular relevance at this point in Vol. III. This is a review of Loewenstein's "Practice and Precept in Psychoanalytic Technique: the Selected Papers of Rudolph M. Loewenstein." These are transitional papers bridging Ego Psychology and the Structural period (1964) written with the intent to update the theory while keeping the clinical practice vital and dynamic.

In the next chapter, Richards (with Ticho) reports on a panel that looked at the technical consequences of Object Relations Theory. Richards begins by framing the panel as an integrated ego psychology object relations theory based on the works of Mahler, Jacobson and Kernberg, with some reference to Winnicott, Fairbairn and Balint. On the panel there were two presenters (Selma Kramer and Otto Kernberg) and two discussants (Heinz Lichtenstein and James T. McLaughlin). The presenters both take the position of an integrated object relations ego psychological theory with different emphases in technique. From her clinical material, Krammer emphasizes the continuity between the two theories, showing how Mahler's work clarifies for the analyst the effect of rapprochement conflicts on the transference of superego precursors stemming from this preoedipal subphase. Kernberg examines four specific applications to the psychoanalytic situation. The first is the nature of the conflicts to be interpreted. Second is the shifting relationship between genetic history and early development and transference. Third is the regressive communicative process in the analytic situation. Finally, there is the question of empathy and regression in the transference. Severe distortion of the patient's ego does not require that the analyst abandon his position of technical neutrality; such a requirement entails the view that it is the therapist's empathic presence rather than his interpretation, which is really helpful. Kernberg reminds us that empathy is a precondition of interpretive work, not a replacement for it.

The last chapter of the section brings to conclusion the theoretical advances. Richards (with Lynch and Bachant) reviews the theoretical contributions of Leo Rangell, with attention to his concept of the Total Composite Psychoanalytic Theory. This chapter was originally written as the Afterword for the text "The Rangell Reader (2013)." It provides a concise outline to Rangell's extensive clinical theorizing.[4] Rangell did not consider himself a "Contemporary Conflict Theorist" by name, even though he privileged unconscious intrapsychic conflicts as the center of what he called the "human core"—the hub of unconscious mental processes. Rather, he viewed himself as a "Developed Freudian." In that way, his prolific contributions overlap much of the work forged by the analysts who have asserted the boundaries of psychoanalysis through Contemporary Conflict Theory. Rangell's contributions included different solutions for understanding mental processes; plus a different method for answering the overall question of how to define a unified, scientific, psychoanalytic theory (i.e., "total composite psychoanalytic theory"). Rangell's conclusion on this unified theory agrees with those who see theoretical pluralism as the central corrosive element to developing this scientific theory. His conclusions followed a method of unification similar to the method used, together and separately, by Brenner and Arlow (Arlow and Brenner, 1964; C. Brenner, 2006). This is a method of review and evaluation based on careful consideration followed by revision where the facts differ from Freud's original contributions. In addition, a similar 'review and revise' process is necessary for those who came after Freud in developing the theories of Ego Psychology and Object Relations. Finally, his conclusions were somewhat different than those drawn by many of his colleagues.

Within this framework the authors divide Rangell's psychoanalytic legacy into four domains of investigation: the human core, the psychoanalytic process, models of theory, and Political and Applied writings. As mentioned, Rangell (1967) placed unconscious intrapsychic conflicts at the center of what he identified as "The

---

4 His works include: 9 books; 438 professional publications; 25 reprints in other languages; 23 written, delivered but as yet unpublished articles.

Human Core." As the authors explore the human core they focus in on five basic dimensions: anxiety, the "intrapsychic process," a new ego function of "unconscious decision making," the syndrome of the "compromise of integrity," and the exercise of "free will" as an aspect of ego autonomy.

This synopsis is enhanced in Chapter 13 in a detailed review, by Richards, of The Human Core: Vols. I (Action within the Structural View & II (from Anxiety to Integrity), by Leo Rangell. Richards begins this review by noting that Rangell like Arlow and Brenner, has effected major revisions in Freudian theory by extending psychoanalytic theory into new areas. His contributions are proposed solutions to important psychoanalytic problems. After an exhaustive review Richards ends with a quote from Rangell: "Psychopathology stands on a base, not a point." It is aphorisms like this that stymie the progression of shallow revisionists.

Section 2 Offers Views on Clinical Data and clinical theory. It includes reflections on the case of a narcissistic patient treated in a classical psychoanalytic treatment, discussion of an expanded view of the replacement child syndrome, a careful investigation of the regressive phenomena of the Isakower Experience during a psychoanalytic treatment, and a treatment of a young woman for episodes of self-mutilation and suicide attempts as a consequence of father-daughter Incest.

The Narcissistic Patient Chapter 5 (with Arlene Kramer Richards, Ed.D.) reviews the existing definitions of Pathological Narcissism and compares the theories of Kernberg and Kohut with Conflict Theory. The authors begin this study with a historical review of the diagnostic criteria and clinical description of pathological narcissism based heavily in the work of Otto Kernberg and Heinz Kohut. They add Bach's (1994) two-sided description of the narcissistic personality by organizing emotional traits of grandiosity, ambition, feelings of entitlement, insecurity, inadequacy, and hypersensitivity within two major personality types the "overinflated narcissistic type" and "depleted narcissistic type."

The authors go on to describe the major differences between Kohut and Kernberg in their models of: aetiology, pathogenesis, development, the mind and treatment. Simply put Kohut sees the pathology as reflecting a faulty development. It is a psychological deficit leading to a developmental arrest. Kernberg sees trauma and mistreatment at the base of this pathology, which leads to the internalization of pathological objects and the intense expression of rage, hate and other forms of aggression.

The authors offer the case of Ms. V, a 45-year-old female who had an exaggerated sense of self-importance. After a failed start in psychotherapy and a 6-month hiatus the patient returned and began a four-times-per-week analysis, which lasted for 6 years. The authors provided a detailed description of this case and note that the treatment was a classic psychoanalytic technique yielding no special empathy, advice or education oriented interventions. Interpretations of transference and affect clarifications were well balanced.

Chapter 6 is the Replacement Child: Variations on a Theme in History and Psychoanalysis (with Leon Ainsfeld, D.S.W.). In this chapter the authors explore a number of variations on the theme of the replacement child. In the strictest sense of the term, a replacement child "is a child born to parents who have experienced the death of a child and then conceive a second child in order to fill the void left by the loss of the first." This central theme holds several configurations: a) when a sibling dies and another is expected to fulfill parental expectations; b) or a couple unable to conceive and choose adoption. The adopted child may be expected to fulfill the fantasies the parents retain for the unborn biological child; c) or for a couple whose child has severe limitations due to physical or mental special needs the other siblings can be affected by shifting familial expectations. Often, the authors' point out, that parents struggle with preoccupations regarding their sick child, leaving the healthier children feeling discounted. Or, they may focus intensely on the healthy children expecting them to excel and compensate for their sibling's inabilities in ways that mitigate the parents' feelings of guilt or failure. Arlow (1972) proposed that even an only child could experience survivor guilt or sibling rivalry. This spectrum of possibilities shows a wide range of circumstances affected by a similar dynamic constellation. The authors follow three clearly defined pathways of investigation: "(1) a reflection on Freud's life and work as inexhaustible sources of psychoanalytic knowledge; (2) an examination of the theme of the replacement child as it occurs in a more or less typical contexts; and (3) a meditation on the Holocaust as a collective tragedy that defies comprehension, against the backdrop of which the issues of survival and replacement take on their most urgent meaning." Here they believe what confronts us in any of these contexts "also lies in wait in each of the other two." Tying these three contexts together provides a powerful perspective to understand and intervene, in a number of professional ways.

The authors show that this dynamic is not only intrapsychic but is also actualized from familial and cultural systems. Staying close to Freud's writings throughout the paper the authors make a strong case demonstrating that these internalized struggles, also, haunted Freud. The authors have used self-disclosure, clinical illustrations, and a wide range of professional literature to help us grasp the depth of what Selma Fraiberg, (1975) called the "ghosts in the nursery".

In Chapter 7, Richards examines in detail, four Isakower-like experiences of a patient on the couch. Isakower phenomena have been viewed as primitive experiences involving maternal breast, womb, and face imagery. This case report draws attention to the

12

little known hypothesis behind the Isakower phenomena, that: certain perceptual experiences are related to childhood Oedipal masturbatory fantasies at the time of going to sleep. Richards presents data from four session of an analysis in its fourth year. He attends to the dynamic context in which the Isakower-like phenomena unfold and identifies six findings from the clinical material. One finding reveals that regressive Isakower-like phenomena served as a defense against Oedipal conflict.

In Chapter 8 Richards describes a case of self-mutilation and father-daughter incest. This case traces the analytic treatment of a young woman suffering from substance abuse, sexual acting-out, and repeated suicide attempts all reflecting severe and complex trauma; which were symptomatic from a history of parental physical and sexual abuse. Subjectively these were accompanied by fears of abandonment, isolation, and unlovability. The patient had a variety of self-mutilation activities: cutting, burning, and aggravating wounds. Maternal care in her childhood had been bleak. After a period of hospitalizations and outpatient psychotherapy the patient entered a five time a week analysis on the couch. The treatment uncovered the incestuous memory of intercourse with her father during late adolescence. This memory was expressed along with other memories and reconstructions of various forms of sexual experiences with her father. Together these proved to be central to the multiply determined understanding of her self-mutilation behavior, other symptoms and recovery. Richards concludes that the case strengthens the findings in the literature of a significant link between self-mutilation in adolescent girls and earlier sexual experiences.

Section 3 contains 4 papers on Richards' Views on Core Clinical Theory. This section includes: the evolution of drive in contemporary psychoanalysis; a commentary on reclaiming metapsychology, on psychoanalytic theories of the self and on unconscious fantasy.

The section begins with Chapter 9, a paper (with Bachant and Lynch), which was in response to Merton Gill regarding the authors' view of Relational Psychoanalysis. In his response to this earlier paper (Bachant Lynch and Richards, 1995a) Gill offers certain misconceptions of the contemporary classical tradition that required clarification.

In Chapter 10 Reisner's (1991) article and Holt's (1992) commentary seem seriously misguided in their understanding of relational considerations both in the Freudian corpus and beyond. This needs to be challenged. Especially the arguments that ego psychologists narrowed and systematized a rendition of Freud as a drive theorist for whom endogenous, biological, nonpsychological force is central and relational dynamics are peripheral. The contributions of these theorists are highlighted and compared with Reisner's and Holt's contentions.

Chapter 11 is a paper based on a 1980 panel. The panellists included: Harold P. Blum, William I. Grossman, Otto F. Kernberg, Leo Rangell, Arnold D. Richards, and Ernst A. Ticho.

Ernst A. Ticho presented the opening paper, "The Alternate Schools and the Self." He chose this topic because of its relevance to new psychoanalytic therapeutic approaches. He focuses on four schools of thought represented by Adler, Jung, Horney, and Sullivan. These points of view on the Self differ widely although they have a common thread that was confident, compelling and inspiring. They share an emphasis on the importance of the subjective, living, creative, experiencing, spontaneous aspects of the mind searching for meaning and the purpose of life. They stood opposed to Freud's emphasis on inner conflict and the role of sexuality. During this period of revision the dynamic unconscious was downgraded and replaced by the collective unconscious and technically, synthesis reigned over analysis. Freud differs from these theorists and uses the German term "Ich" for self in three ways. First, the term is use to signify the individual. Second, it is a component of the psychic structure. Finally, it is experienced as a state of subjectivity, a subjective self. In considering the respective approaches of each of the alternate schools Richards and Ticho reviews their models of the pathogenesis and technique.

Section 4 consists of Views and Reviews. In this section there is a review of psychoanalysis in the 21st century, Mazli's attempt to use Applied Psychoanalysis to define leadership types in "The Revolutionary Ascetic; and, reviews of Masterson's Psychotherapy of the Borderline Adult, and Psychoanalytic Treatment: An Intersubjective Approach by Brandchaft and Stolorow.

In Chapter 15, Richards reviews The Second Century of Psychoanalysis: Evolving Perspectives on Therapeutic Action. The editors of the volume are members of the Los Angeles Institute and Society for Psychoanalytic Studies (LAISPS). The book is a compendium of original papers on therapeutic action in Psychoanalysis. Richards begins by noting that Perlman, the series editor, reframes the age old question that dichotomized the options of therapeutic action into a more useful form. Perlman asks: How does each of the curative factors[5] interact to promote cure? He begins with Leo Rangell's chapter "the aims and method of psychoanalysis a century later." Richards identifies Rangell's central point: "as the American psychoanalytic mainstream referred to itself as representing ego psychology, in fact it was dedicated to what he calls "total composite theory". From this view Rangell identifies himself as a "developed" Freudian working with a theoretical frame where discoveries add to the knowledge base but don't replace it. Rangell rejects the idea that there is "authoritarianism, hegemony, or arrogance

---

5 Interpretation, therapeutic relationship

in this view." Richards agrees as far as theory goes but notes that this disclaimer breaks down particularly around the issue of lay analysis and the law suit. The discussion diverges slightly into the history and politics of the APsaA on this issue. The other 2 contributions in this the section include a brief history of therapeutic action by Christian and Diamond and a third chapter on the Enlightenment vision (know thyself) by Morris Eagle. To this Eagle also adds the impact of the postmodernists (especially Rorty) supporting the idea that "the truth (via interpretation) may not set one free.

Section two focuses on "Conflict, Fantasy and Insight in Therapeutic Action". Richards highlights the central points of the four chapters. Portuges and Hollander discuss Paul Gray's technique. Gray argues against an authoritarian stance and Richards notes that they also make a strong case for considering the role of social factors and social reality. Richards, with Arlene K. Richards, have put forth the idea that a psychoanalyst develops a theory of technique to counter his/her anti-therapeutic proclivities. Several examples are given. In another contribution Christopher Christian presents an "excellent overview for the transition from the structural model to Modern Conflict Theory. Richards faults Christian, however, for omitting Brenner's view of analytic change. Richards also wished Christian had included Arlow's role of unconscious fantasy and some mention of the therapeutic optimism modern conflict theory promotes, especially by Arlow, Brenner, Rangell and Beres. In this light Richards recognizes that several of the contributors were breaking new ground by thinking "outside the box. Richards highlight this in Kalish's chapter: "On movement thinking and therapeutic action in psychoanalysis."

Wolson, too, follows this thread in section III when he adds that the best account of therapeutic action is "analytic love." Wolson considers this from 8 distinct traditions in psychoanalysis.

Richards found it fitting that the volume should conclude with an interview with Hedda Bolgar whose life span was close to the entire twentieth century.

In Chapter 16 Richards reviews "The Revolutionary Ascetic. Evolution of a Political Type by Prof. Bruce Mazlish. This was Mazlish's third attempt to us a psychobiographical lens historically. The first was on Nixon and lacked sufficient developmental data. The second on James and John Stewart Mill corrected for the lack of biographical data but the application for this data to the broader historical trends was unconvincing. Richards begins by pointing out that The Revolutionary Ascetic was more psychohistorical then psychobiographical. In this volume Mazlish attempts an understanding of the revolutionary process by identifying personality types. Specifically he suggests that "ascetics" make revolutions and that "revolutionary ascetics" can be considered an "ideal personality type" Richards wonders if this is actually a personality type or an individual adapting to circumstance. "Do ascetics make revolution," or does revolution elicit "a certain amount of self-denial and self-discipline as well as a singular sense of purpose and devotion to a cause?"

Mazlish makes his case using as subjects Lenin and Mao. Richards questions the grounds on which the case is made for both subjects. Overall he finds the book at times lively and interesting but the argument is based on inadequate data which undermines its value.

Richards, in chapter 17, reviews James F. Masterson's book entitled "Psychotherapy of the Borderline Adult: A Developmental Approach." This approach presents an active technique primarily using interventions of confrontation and limit setting focused on pre-oedipal conflicts in the treatment with adult borderline patients. This approach is based on an object relations theory. Masterson's work is contrasted with a model that derives treatment recommendations from a conflict-drive psychoanalytic theory.

Masterson pitches his program from his own experience and the more than one hundred psychiatrists trained in this technique. In making his case for the "widespread application," of his approach Masterson promotes his success with patients who had previously been treated by other approaches with little or no benefit.

Richards believes a closer look at this theory and technique is needed. He begins by outlining Masterson's theory. Throughout his descriptions he poses simple questions and/or comments when pointing out the program's theoretical inconsistencies, gaps or unsupportable leaps of conjecture. Richards raises two fundamental questions:

First, although conflicts relating to separation, autonomy, and independence are clearly important in human development, what evidence is there that these issues are exclusively related to the pathology of one definable diagnostic group?

Second, is a treatment approach based on a consistent focus on separation-individuation themes more helpful and effective in treating some patients than a more open-ended, investigative therapeutic approach?

Richards presents strong concerns when Masterson indicates that Psychoanalysis seems contraindicated for these patients but then fails to make it clear why conflicts relating to separation, loss, autonomy, and individuation cannot be dealt with in psychoanalysis. For Richards, this book lacks an accurate "classification of treatment approaches that are based on clear clinical and theoretical criteria." Richards's impression is that Masterson's program is too unidimensional and biased towards finding a developmental arrest due to separation-individuation conflicts, which stand on insufficient data. He further shows concern that these kinds of one-dimensional programs lend themselves to "a 'cook-book' approach to therapy" and simplify the "bewilderingly complex clinical data."

Still, Richards finds that because of the importance of these clinical issues, the book merits attention.

In Chapter 18, Richards reviews Wallerstein's "Forty-Two Lives in Treatment. A Study of Psychoanalysis and Psychotherapy. This study was conducted in Topeka at the Menninger Foundation and was carried out over a 30-year period (1954–1985). Richards begins by offering some preliminary remarks on the study's population and setting including: sampling methods, exclusion criteria and subject population demographics. In total, these had a potential negative impact on the studies overall findings.[6] Throughout the time of the study the Menninger Foundation achieved international acclaim for its extensive treatment approach that allowed them to analytically engage patients with severe psychopathology. Richards notes that at Menninger's, Stone's (1954) "widening scope" was a "day today reality." The level of functioning in these patients would have excluded them in most psychoanalytic centers and research studies.

Richards goes over Wallerstein's findings carefully to let the Psychotherapy Research Project's (PRP) story unfold for the reader. One of the study's main findings was that even with the Foundation's sophisticated evaluation process, major psychopathology was concealed in over 50% of the cases (24 of the 42 subjects.

After reviewing all the findings, Richards tells us, Wallerstein concludes that "clearly, even with all of the availability of hospitalization within a psychoanalytically oriented sanatorium setting, and all of the historical clinical precedents for this course within this specific Menninger Foundation setting, psychoanalysis on the basis of these 'heroic indications' has been found tragically wanting as a treatment course" (p. 678).

---

6 The study's subject population was inordinately weighted with subjects for whom analysis or analytic therapy would be an "heroic treatment choice."

Richards however has a more optimistic view of the data.

In chapter 19 Richards begins his review of Psychoanalytic Treatment: An Intersubjective Approach by noting that Brandchaft and Stolorow attempt to define the basic theoretical constructs necessary for a psychoanalytic science of human experience.

To this end, the authors offer "two fundamental ideas" as "central guiding principles": an intersubjective field[7] and, concretization.[8] These guiding principles are supported by detailed clinical material presented in chapters 4,5,8,&9. The clinical material is aimed at expanding the implications for psychoanalytic understanding and treatment by adopting a consistently intersubjective perspective.

Richards uses this as a good opportunity to test the central aim and the persistent claim throughout the book of the superiority of this perspective over classical psychoanalysis. Richards frames his test with two relevant questions:

1. Does the case material demonstrate any difficulties in understanding and treatment consequent on the adoption of traditional points of view?
2. Does the theoretical approach suggested by the authors evince a superior understanding and yield more effective therapeutic strategies?

Richards answer to both questions is "no." Here he clarifies that he is not questioning the usefulness of the author's conceptualizations, but

---

7 Richards uses the authors definition (p.ix) as a "system of differently organized, interacting subjective worlds [as] invaluable for comprehending both the vicissitudes of psychoanalytic therapy and the process of human psychological development" (p. ix)

8 defined by Brandchaft & Stolorow as "the encapsulation of organizations of experience by concrete, sensorimotor symbols" (p. 132).

"rather any claim that they constitute a distinct and original clinical theory." Richards goes on to discuss this point more fully.

He also, presents another basic criticism with this line of reasoning. It concerns the insularity of the authors' argument. Although some effort is made to locate the intersubjective viewpoint within the evolution of self psychology, there is consistent failure to consider the history of relevant contributions beyond this tradition. These contributions range from Freud, through the object relations and ego pychological theories to current day contemporary theories on a variety of topics, which includes: the authors' discussion of symptom formation, as well as, the dynamics of, and clinical work with borderline and psychotic pathologies.

Richards summarizes his findings by highlighting the authors "sound clinical approach and often insightful appreciation of treatment interactions" but believes these positive aspects are diminished by the authors' continuous elaboration of the "subjective" and "intersubjective." For Richards, these terms "obfuscate" rather than "illuminate". He suggests replacing, "intersubjective transactions" with "personal interactions," and, "experience" for "subjectivity" or "intersubjectivity."

Richards concludes that *"Psychoanalytic Treatment,"* offers much that is clinically helpful. The authors' case would be strengthen "by tempering their philosophical pretensions and wrestling more open-mindedly with what A. Goldberg has" identified as the persisting *"tension* within psychoanalysis between realism and relativism."

SECTION 5: CONCLUDING VIEW—*POLITICS AND PARADIGMS*

In section 5, Richards presents his Concluding View—Politics and Paradigms. In this Chapter, he asks us to consider. . ."the extent to which the development of psychoanalysis has been affected by organizational and political schisms over the years?" He offers an example from Aron and Bushra (1998) in which, Paul Gray and Harry Stack Sullivan demonstrate an unexpected convergence in their approach to anxiety. He wonders how their theories might have developed had their institutions maintained affiliation.[9] He goes on to illustrate the different paths that Columbia and William Alanson White followed while sharing some important cultural determinants. This highlights how politics and personalities enter our attitudes toward theories.

He concludes with a final example of convergence in the concept of unconsciousness in the analytic situation held by Bach and, separately, by Bromberg. He wonders when there is a paradigm shift (e.g., from drive theory to relational theory) how much of this movement is based on political considerations. Ultimately, he thinks that the theoretical distinctions will become less clear-cut and advanced less insistently as new compromises are put forth. This follow Rangell's impression of how new findings and information gets added to the knowledge base but not detracted.

CONCLUSIONS

Richards in Volume III of his Selected Papers continues to carve out a special place for his contributions from the second generation of Contemporary Conflict Theorists. In these five sections he has provided an organized view of how the mind works and has heard the suggestions from others that Unconscious Fantasy should be included with compromise formations and unconscious conflict in

---

9 The Washington School of Psychiatry and the Baltimore-Washington Institute.

any definition of how the mind works. Likewise, he has shown the beginning integration of a definition of science that is inclusive of both a narrow (Brenner, 2006) and broad (Rangell, 2007) understanding. Finally he has shown us his methodology in being an analyst. He sees patients, supervises, teaches, reads broadly in both psychoanalysis and beyond. When he finds something of interest he usually drafts something about his findings and shares this with colleagues and students and later writes something up for the professional community (e.g., Richards, 2020). This has led him to be incredibly productive, innovative and unusually generative. In this way he epitomizes the Freudian tradition.

REFERENCES

Abend, S.M. (1974). Problems of Identity—Theoretical and Clinical Applications. In: *Contemporary Conflict Theory: The Journey of a Psychoanalyst. The Selected Papers of Sander M. Abend,* MD. New York: IPBooks, 2018.

Aron L. & Bushra, A. (1998). Mutual Regression: Altered States in the Psychoanalytic Situation. *J. of the American Psychoanalytic Association* 46(2):389–412.

Arlow, J.A., (1961). Ego psychology and the study of mythology. *J. Amer. Psychoanal. Assn.* 9:371–393.

——— (1969a). Unconscious fantasy and disturbances of conscious experience. *Psychoanal. Q.* 38:1–27.

——— (1969b). Fantasy, memory, and reality testing. *Psychoanal. Q.* 38:28–51.

——— & Brenner, C. (1964). *Psychoanalytic Concepts and the Structural Theory.* New York: Int. Univ. Press.

——— (1980). Object Concept and object choice. *Psychoanal. Q.* 49:109–133.

——— (1981). Theories of pathogenesis. *Psychoanalysis Psychoanal. Q.* 50:488–514.

Bach, S. (1994). *The Language of Perversion and the Language of Love.* Northvale, NJ, Jason Aronson.

Bachant, J.L., Lynch, A.A., & Richards, A.D. (1995a). Relational models in psychoanalytic theory. *Psychoanalytic Psychology* 12:71–87.

——— (1995b). The Evolution of Drive Theory in Contemporary Psychoanalysis: A Reply to Gill. *Psychoanalytic Psychology,* 12(4):565–573.

Brenner, C. (1982). *The Mind in Conflict.* Madison, CT: Int. Univ. Press.

——— (2006). *Psychoanalysis or Mind and Meaning.* Psychoanalytic Quarterly Press, New York.

Fleck, L. (1935). *Genesis and Development of a Scientific Fact,* Editors: T.J. Trenn & R.K. Merton, transl.: F. Bradley & T.J. Trenn. Chicago: University of Chicago Press, 1970.

Fraiberg, S., E. Adelson, & V. Shapiro. (1975). Ghosts in the Nursery: A Psychoanalytic Approach to the Problem of Impaired Infant-Mother Relationships. *J. Amer. Acad. Child Psychiat.,* 14:387–421.

Freud, S. (1900). Wish-fulfillment. In The Interpretation of Dreams. *Standard Edition* 5:550–572.

Holt, R.R. (1992). Some Problems Created by Freud's Inconsistency *Psychoanal. Psychol.* 9:111–114.

Jacobson, E. (1964). *The Self and the Object World.* New York: Int. Univ. Press.

Kramer, Y. (1988). In the visions of the Night: Perspectives on the work of Jacob A. Arlow. In: *Fantasy, Myth & Reality: Essays in*

Honor of Jacob A. Arlow, M.D., Editors: H.P. Blum, Y. Kramer, A.K. Richards, A.D. Richards. Madison, CT: Int. Universities Press.

Lynch, A.A.; Richards, A.D. & Bachant, J.L. "Afterword." (2013). In *The Rangell Reader*. Editors: B. Kalish & C. Fisher. New York: IPBooks, pp. 243–254.

Rangell, Leo (2007). *The Road to Unity in Psychoanalytic Theory.* New York, Jason Aronson Press,

——— (1967). Psychoanalysis, Affects, and the 'Human Core'—On the Relationship of Psychoanalysis to the Behavioral Sciences. *Psychoanalytic Q.* 36:172–202.

Reisner, S. (1991). Reclaiming the Metapsychology *Psychoanal. Psychol.* 8:439–462.

Richards, A.D. (2015). Psychoanalysis: *Critical Conversations. The selected papers of Arnold D. Richards, M.D.,* Volume I. Editor: A.A. Lynch. New York: IPBooks.

CHAPTER 1

Jacob A. Arlow (1912–2004)

[Richards, A.D., Goodman, S.M. (2004).
Int. J. Psycho-Anal., 85:1513–1518.]

Jacob Arlow

Jacob Arlow, one of the most respected and admired contributors to psychoanalysis, was born in Brooklyn on 3 September 1912. One of three children and a first-generation American, he took pride in his combined modern secular and traditional Jewish education. He often spoke with great fondness of his large and loving extended family.

He spoke, with that uniquely Jack Arlow grin of his, of his mother as 'illiterate' in three languages. She was one of the founders of The Pride of Judea Children's Home. His father, who ran a millinery business, always encouraged his son's intellectual interests. Jacob was an avid reader; as a child the days he had to stay home sick were a pleasure for the scholar-to-be, since they gave him the opportunity to read without interruption.

As he talked with both of us, in a lively banter, about his early life, he was always ready to acknowledge his weaknesses. When he applied at the age of 16 for admission to Columbia College, he included on his application a long list of the books he had devoured, including works by Sigmund Freud and William James. In fact, he had as yet not got to James, but, as his luck would have it, James was the author his interviewer quizzed him on. His application was deferred; he was told to apply again the following year. But Jack decided he could not wait a year to start college, so he enrolled at New York University (NYU). He was proud of the fact that, although he attended what was then considered an 'inferior' school, he still was able to reach the top of his profession and do as well as colleagues who graduated from more prestigious schools. He also had a keen sense of inferiority as a child of immigrants, considering himself a guest who had to work hard to show he deserved this country's hospitality.

He married his wife Alice Diamond in 1936. They met at a training program for young Jewish leaders; Jack caught Alice's attention because he was always the first to raise his hand in class. When he was 18 he told her 'I'm going to marry you', but it took about two years before she came around to seeing things his way. They married six years later, after he completed medical school. Determined not to raise their children in the city, they moved to a small community in a suburb of New York City. Jack commuted daily to his office in Manhattan. As his professional commitments, practice, teaching, and organizational work grew, he spent more time in the city than at home. During his last months he spoke to one of us (SMG) of a regret that he and his wife fell into the then prevailing pattern: 'She took care of the children and I was out in the world of psychoanalysis'. He quoted Lowell: 'He sings to the wide world and she to her nest. In the nice ear of nature which song is best?' He often said, 'One of my major failings was that I could never say no', and added, 'A curriculum vitae is for others, not for oneself'.

After interning at Harlem Hospital, he completed psychiatric and neurological residencies at the United States Public Health Service, Montefiore Hospital, New York State Psychiatric Institute and Kings County Hospital. He earned his diploma in neurology and psychiatry in 1944, graduated from the New York Psychoanalytic Institute (NYPI) in 1947, and held supervising and training positions at NYPI, the Columbia Center and Down State/NYU.

His teaching positions included: Instructor in Neurology and Psychiatry at Columbia University Medical School, Professor at the State University Of New York, Clinical Professor at NYU, Instructor at Hillside Hospital, Visiting Professor at Louisiana State University, Visiting Professor at Albert Einstein, and Visiting Professor at Mount Sinai.

His awards include the International Clinical Essay Prize of the British Psycho-Analytic Society, A.A. Brill Memorial Lecture, Freud Memorial Lecture, Lenox Hill Distinguished Clinicians Award, Lenox Hill Hospital, Heinz Hartmann Award, Journal Prize, American Psychoanalytic Association, Sandor Rado Lecturer at Columbia, Mary S. Sigourney Award, Emmanuel Windholz Memorial Lecture at the San Francisco Institute, Division 39 of American Psychological Association and Freud Lecture of the New Jersey Psychoanalytic Society.

He was a prolific writer. His bibliography includes five books, more than 140 papers and more than 30 book reviews. His work has already been translated into six languages, and his unpublished papers considerably exceed his published contributions. Among his published works are six presentations delivered at International Psychoanalytic Association (IPA) Congresses: Stockholm (Arlow, 1963); Rome, 1969; Jerusalem (Arlow, 1977); and Amsterdam (Arlow, 1993). *The legacy of Sigmund Freud* (Arlow, 1956, unfortunately, currently out of print) is a book put together on the occasion of the Freud centenary celebration that took place in Chicago; in it you may read a delightful, authoritative, and informative synopsis of Freud's life and scientific contributions.

Arlow was Editor-in-Chief of the *Psychoanalytic Quarterly*, 1972–1979. He looked at our sometimes vague and obscure lexicon with a clear eye. Charles Brenner has written eloquently about Jack's achievements as editor in the 50th anniversary issue; how his friend of 50 years, through energy and editorial wisdom, transformed a first rate journal into one of the outstanding psychoanalytic journals in the world. Under Jack's leadership the *Quarterly* became what, before the Holocaust, the *Internationale Zeitschrift für Psychoanalyse* had been, with Freud as its publisher and Abraham, Ferenczi, Bibring and Hartmann as editors (1981, p. 476).

Jack Arlow's organizational and scholarly abilities were fully recognized by the psychoanalytic community. He was elected President of APsaA and Chairman of the Board on Professional Standards, Chairman of the Committee on Psychoanalytic Education, first Secretary, then President of the NYPI, and first Treasurer, then Vice-President, of the IPA. During this part of his career he traveled widely. He spoke with pride about the part he had played in mediating the 'Cleveland dispute'. He said that

in order to learn the lessons that experience teaches, every organized group has an obligation to study and to try to understand its history. Otherwise important lessons and guidelines for the future may be overlooked and missed. Instead there is the temptation for the victors in any struggle to romanticize and mythologize their history by omitting significant facts from the record of the past (Arlow, personal communication, 2004).

Dr Arlow belonged to that transitional time in psychoanalysis, after the death of Freud, which is, by some, called the Hartmann era. This was a time of great optimism in the USA. As a result of the political convulsions in central Europe which began in the 1930s and culminated in World War II (WWII), psychoanalytic institutes in our country, especially NYPI, benefited greatly; European leaders of psychoanalytic thought, including Hartmann himself, Kris Loewenstein, Waelder and Rapaport were welcomed and took up there work here.

During WWII, medical officers in the armed forces treated soldiers suffering from battle fatigue using psychoanalytic principles. This raised the prestige of psychoanalysis in the medical profession, and with the general public as well. At that time any intellectual worth their salt, especially in New York, was expected either to have been in psychoanalysis, or to at least be knowledgeable about psychoanalysis. The power of the dynamic unconscious fascinated the public, and creative artists used psychoanalytic insights in works of literature, on the stage and on the screen. Moss Hart's *Lady of the dark* and Hitchcock's *Spellbound* contributed to the aura surrounding psychoanalysis. Within the medical profession and the wider world of academia, psychoanalysis was welcomed and actively courted. Psychoanalysis could be viewed as a transcendent psychology of conflict and illness and it was accorded status as a general psychology. Hartmann was an exemplar of this protean image of psychoanalysis.

It was against this backdrop that Jack Arlow, David Beres, Charles Brenner, and Martin Wangh formed their study group. They met weekly for over 25 years to share and exchange ideas, revisit the basic texts and explore the new contributions to the field. They invited Hartmann himself to meet with them after they had read all of his work. Fortunately for this illustrious gathering, near the beginning of their study group, the book on neurosis by Fenichel (1946) appeared, and over the next two years they covered every chapter in the book in extraordinary detail. It became a principle not to be broken for them that any theoretical issue that was raised had to be supported with precise clinical data from cases under treatment. In fact, Arlow's paper on anal sensations (1949) owed its origin to a challenge that Beres directed against the idea proposed by Starcke and van Ophuijsen that the paranoid's persecutor represents a projection of the sensations generated by the patient's disturbing fecal mass. This group of four remained close friends throughout the years, maintaining their association as they followed their own individual pursuits.

LEO RANGELL

Leo Rangell who was in residency with Jack should be included in this cohort. For years, Jack and Leo took the train into the city together to see their respective analysts. Rangell was in the middle of his second year of courses at NYPI when the call to serve during WWII interrupted his training, loosened his ties to New York, the city of his birth, and turned his destiny in the direction of Los Angeles. After WWII, Rangell relocated to the West Coast, but the geographical distance did not diminish the closeness of their personal relationship or their sympathetic psychoanalytic outlook.

We find in Arlow's first published contribution (Dunbar and Arlow, 1944) an emphasis on the importance of precision in defining criteria for intervention and finding the best theory to fit the data (in this case, for psychosomatic disorders); scholarly and analytic attitudes which he maintained thoughout his life. His papers on theory, technique, education, and the application of psychoanalysis to the arts all share the clarity and sharpness of that first contribution.

As a person Jack was direct and honest, and immediately genuine. He would not try to impose what for him were self-evident concepts on his students; this was not his way. He posed questions that encouraged his students to find their own answers rather than docilely follow his lead. His aim was to help them achieve a richer understanding of the material and find their own therapeutic voice. He was remarkably intuitive but at the same time stressed the need to gather evidence and look for confirmation. In response to a report on a session he could proceed from the patient's first communication to outline the theme of the entire hour. He had a clear, diamond-hard perception of a patient's universe, unclouded by sentimentality or intellectual prejudice. His comments, despite his brilliance, were always direct, modest, reassuring, respectful and free of condescending superiority.

He was always circumspect and cautious about what could be anticipated therapeutically. He was not one to subscribe to fixed doctrine; every paper, supervisory session or lecture was a conversation with the reader or listener that took on special meaning. He could select from the cacophony of the hour what was central for the patient. He could be there in several times and places at once; zoom in and out between the macro- and microscopic levels of understanding. His observations were always delivered with the freshness and excitement of insight, and through his eyes we were able to see the hour with ignited imaginations.

At the heart of his method was an understanding of the nature of conflict and the patient's use of a developmental hierarchy of unconscious fantasies to integrate their identity and personal mythology. He taught us that, by close study of the immediate effect of the analyst's intervention and the ensuing interaction, we become privy to the nature of the patient's constructed compromise formations. This is a joint endeavor which leads to insight for analyst and analysand. Forces in conflict are realigned but do not disappear (Brenner, 1979). They are replaced by more effective and adaptive formations. The analyst follows the moment-to-moment variations in the sequence of associations that reflect the interplay of forces and imperatives in opposition.

Arlow was attracted to ideas drawn from mythology, Jewish theology, science, language, poetry, and film. Access to this large reservoir of ideas and images allowed him to expand the psychoanalyst's expressive, communicative, and therapeutic reach. This multitude of diverse images provided kindling for the blaze of his imagination and productivity. Due to his education in medicine, neurology, psychiatry, and the social sciences, he could bring rich and unique insights to the interfaces of psychoanalysis with other disciplines—to those problems peculiar to the areas where psychoanalysis and other sciences overlap. His readings in ancient literature [even during his last months he told one of us (SMG), that he had promised himself he would reread all the Greek tragedies and he did!] and modern writing provided him with a rich mosaic of ideas which were in tune with his own sentiments. Metaphor was one of the most important themes in his writings—Arlow (1979) demonstrates the consiliance of psychoanalysis, science, history, and art, one of his favorite and most important papers (Goodman, 2003, personal communication).

Arlow was always interested in the sharp controversies that have been part of psychoanalysis. Arlow believed that most of the contention followed from differences of opinion about pathogenesis and normal development. He judged theories of pathogenesis by their ability to comprehend and parsimoniously fashion the data being observed. Or to use his own words, 'The analyst's understanding of why people fall ill invariably influences the nature of the technique that is employed to help the patient get well' (private communication to SMG, 2003). He firmly believed that the vicissitudes of the drives and of the development of object relations in the course of psychic structuring are inseparable. Any effort to sequester one element as pathogenic on either side of the dynamic equation will inevitably fail to do service to the complex process of pathogenesis. Here he was very much in tune with Freud.

Despite its omissions, even this abbreviated review of Jacob A. Arlow's contributions makes clear how in the field of psychoanalysis he was outstanding as a scholar, a theoretical innovator, a clinician, a teacher, and a master in the art of applying the insights offered by psychoanalysis to our understanding of the manifold activities of man.

Jacob Arlow was a dynamic thinker who in his life harmonized thought, action, and word, using two basic approaches: the aesthetic-intuitive and the scientific-rational. His vision is as much artistic as scientific. He has taught us to listen and speak to our patients without dogma or cant. This is his legacy.

During his last days, and up to the final moments, his company was remarkable and enlightening. Toward the end he spoke with SMG about being prepared for death, his rich life wondrously settled; perhaps we have been less ready for the loss of one of the most valuable teachers and, most importantly, the dear friend we have known.

On 21 May 2004, in Great Neck, New York, USA, at 91 years of age, Jacob Arlow died peacefully in the house he had lived in for 68 years.

REFERENCES

Arlow, J.A, (1949). Anal sensations and feelings of persecution. *Psychoanal. Q.* 18:79–84.

——— (1956). *The legacy of Sigmund Freud*. New York: Int U. Press. 86 p.

(1963). Conflict, regression, and symptom formation. *Int. J. Psycho-Anal.* 44:12–22.

——— (1969). The psychopathology of the psychoses: A proposed revision. *Int. J. Psycho-Anal.* 50:5–14.

——— (1977). Affects and the psychoanalytic situation. *Int. J. Psycho-Anal.* 58: 157–70.

——— (1979). Metaphor and the psychoanalytic situation. *Psychoanal. Q.* 48: 363–85.

——— (1986). Discussion of papers by Dr McDougall and Dr Glasser. Panel on identification in the perversions. *Int. J. Psycho-Anal.* 67:245–50.

——— (1993). Two discussions of 'The mind of the analyst' and a response from Madeleine Baranger. *Int. J. Psycho-Anal.* 74: 1147–55.

Brenner, C. (1979). The components of psychic conflict and its consequences in mental life. *Psychoanal. Q.* 48:547–67.

——— (1981). Jacob A. Arlow: An appreciation. *Psychoanal. Q.* 50:475–8.

Dunbar, F., & Jacob, J.A. (1944). Criteria for therapy in psychosomatic disorders. *Psychosom. Med.* 4:283–6.

Fenichel, O. (1946). *Psychoanalytic theory of the neurosis*. London: Routledge. 714 p.

Hale, N.G., Jr. (1995). *The rise and crisis of psychoanalysis in the United States: Freud and the Americans, 1917–1985*, Vol. 2. Philadelphia: American Philological Association.

CHAPTER 2

Symposium: The Clinical Value of the Concepts of Conflict and Compromise Formation

November 17, 1990, New York
Psychoanalytic Society and Institute

[Richards, A.D., (1994). *Journal of Clinical Psychoanalysis* 3:317–321.]

INTRODUCTION

Psychoanalysis, the science of mind, that grew out of the discoveries of Sigmund Freud, is now a field of rival theories. This trend, which Robert Michels has termed the "theoretical pluralism in psychoanalytic dialogue," shows no sign of abating. We now belong to a discipline consisting of classical analysts, object relational analysts, relational analysts, interpersonal analysts, self psychologists, Kleinian analysts, and Lacanian analysts, to name the proponents of only the most important theories.

This trend toward theoretical pluralism, a fact of our professional lives, is both good and bad. In one sense theoretical ferment as witnessed by lively dialogue at our meetings and in the pages of our journals, is constructive. The vitality of any science is measured by the vigor with which key issues are debated. For a science to be in a stage of growth and development it must meet two conditions: There must be clear-cut diverging points of view and there must be passionate proponents of each of the respective positions. Innumerable examples from the history of science demonstrate the relationship between sharp controversy and scientific advance. Is light understandable in terms of particles or waves? Does an ether exist? Does phlogiston exist? Did the universe get started in a big bang or is it a steady state? In these and many other instances, human knowledge has advanced out of the dialectical clash of competing theories. In each instance one can specify the points at issue and the proponents of rival viewpoints.

But there can be a downside to theoretical pluralism. I refer to the organizational developments that so often accompany the growth of competing theories. Groups tend to form around a new theory and take as their raison d'être its promotion and continued development. Hand in hand with the productive exchanges promoted by emerging theories comes a push toward factionalism. In the case of the current psychoanalytic scene, we see this trend most clearly with self-psychology, which now has its own society, annual conferences, and publications. This tendency toward institutional autonomy by proponents of a particular theoretical point of view frequently promotes isolation and an absence of inter-theoretical dialogue.

Although our symposium today has not been organized to highlight the differences among the proponents of various psychoanalytic theories, it takes place against this backdrop of "theoretical pluralism" that I have just described. The participants in this symposium are not unaware of the controversies in the field. In fact, it is for the very reason that they appreciate and have reflected on the criticism of colleagues who champion different viewpoints that they are taking the opportunity provided by this symposium to explore two of the core concepts associated with the classical model of psychoanalysis: conflict and compromise formation. Despite significant differences among them, the participants share the belief that these two concepts along with the concept of unconscious fantasy provide the basis for a comprehensive science of mind. Moreover, that in this science of mind the psychoanalytic method of investigation can be grounded and the therapeutic action of psychoanalytic treatment can be understood.

How do the following presentations on conflict and compromise formation relate to the current climate of theoretical pluralism? Another negative consequence of pluralism related to the factionalism which I have referred to above, is the tendency of proponents of particular theories to misunderstand and therefore dismiss opposing theories. This seems to be increasingly true of the critics of classical psychoanalysis. Such critics identified with relational psychoanalysis and intersubjectivity theory and self psychology converge in conflating the classical viewpoint with what they term "drive psychology." Stephen Mitchell (1988), for example, in a recent influential book presenting the viewpoint of relational psychoanalysis invokes the metaphor of the "baby as beast" to designate the classical approach. In an earlier book, coauthored with Jay Greenberg (1983), he invoked the equally unsettling image of the seething cauldron to characterize the viewpoints of classical psychoanalysis. Their idea in both cases is that classical psychoanalysis is founded on a hydraulic model in which the explosive energy of instinctual drives is bottled up, always seeking discharge.

And on a similar tack, proponents of psychoanalytic self psychology use a reductionistic view of drive psychology to differentiate a conflict model from a deficit model of psychopathology. Their point is that psychoanalytic theory rooted in Freud's notion of drive can only explain higher level kinds of intrapsychic conflict. More primitive and hence severe grades of psychopathology evolve out of preconflictual psychic deficits and require the explanatory perspective of self psychology. This viewpoint derives from the work of Heinz Kohut (1971), the founder of self psychology. He elaborated as ideal types the notion of "guilty man" and "tragic man," arguing that the oedipal conflicts of the former were amenable to the viewpoint of classical analysis, whereas the more profound existential problems of the latter require the viewpoint of self psychology, with its emphasis on the preoedipal facets of self formation.

The participants in today's symposium will respond to such criticisms, I believe, by arguing for the vitality and explanatory richness of the classical viewpoint as it exists today. An important thrust of their presentations will be to show how this point of view has evolved in the decades following Freud's death, countering the efforts of critics to equate our viewpoints with a drive psychology based on dated energic assumptions. Collectively, I believe, today's participants share the belief that the classical model as enriched by the contributions of ego psychology is far from static. It has evolved significantly in recent decades so that its explanatory reach is adequate to what Leo Stone referred to in 1954 as the widening scope of indications for psychoanalysis. Stone was referring to the clinical reality that many if not most patients who come to contemporary analysts have problems that are qualitatively different and more severe than simple symptom neuroses.

Anna Freud, Heinz Hartmann, Ernst Kris, Rudolph Loewenstein, Edith Jacobson, and Annie Reich, all but the first, members of the New York Psychoanalytic Society, are among those whose ego psychological contributions expanded the reach of the classical model in the 1940s and 1950s. Jacob Arlow's and Charles Brenner's monograph of 1964, *Psychoanalytic Concepts and the Structural Theory*, is another signpost in the development of what I would term the expanded classical model. Arlow's more recent studies on the role of unconscious fantasies in the therapeutic process and Brenner's reformulation of Freud's structural model in his most recent book, *The Mind in Conflict* (1982), represent yet a further evolution of classical theory.

The point I want to emphasize is that the concepts of conflict and compromise formation as we use them today have evolved from Freud's original usage. They include a psychological as opposed to a biological view of drives, a broadened understanding of defensive processes, and a less reified approach to Freud's structural model as a way of understanding the dynamic interactions among various wishes, defenses, and affects. Again, Brenner's *The Mind in Conflict* is an important statement of these latter themes.

It would be wrong to conclude from what I have said so far that there is agreement among all the contributors working within this framework. There is disagreement about the usefulness of Freud's theory of development and the role of developmental issues in different kinds of psychopathology. There is also disagreement about the usefulness of Margaret Mahler's observational research and about the relevance to psychoanalytic adult issues of data derived from infant observation. There are classical analysts who believe that the concepts of conflict and compromise formation are too all-inclusive to be maximally useful in clinical work. Ernest Kafka in a recent contribution ("Is Psychoanalysis A Conflict Theory?" This paper was part of a panel and is unpublished.) argues pointedly that it is inconsistent to view classical theory as a theory of both conflict and compromise formation since the two concepts are conceptual opposites. He would opt for a theory of compromise formation over and against a theory of conflict.

But these differences are to be welcomed. They point to the continuing ability of this model to serve as a framework for controversy, dialogue, and scientific advance. The differences underscore that the classical model as we understand and use it today has evolved far beyond Freud in coping with the theoretical and clinical developments of recent decades.

REFERENCES

Arlow, J.A., & Brenner, C. (1964). *Psychoanalytic Concepts and the Structural Theory.* New York: International Universities Press.

Brenner, C. (1982). *The Mind in Conflict.* New York: International Universities Press.

Greenberg, J., & Mitchell, S.A. (1983). *Object Relations in Psychoanalytic Theory.* Cambridge, MA: Harvard University Press.

Kohut, H. (1971). *The Analysis of the Self.* New York: International Universities Press.

Mitchell, S.A. (1988). *Relational Concepts in Psychoanalysis.* Cambridge, MA: Harvard University Press.

CHAPTER 3

Technical Consequences of
Object Relations Theory

Ernst Ticho, Ph.D. and Arnold D. Richards, M.D.[10]

[(1980). *Journal of the American Psychoanalytic Association*, 28:623–636.]

Ernst Ticho, chairman, set the stage for the panel by defining its focus—an ego psychology object relations theory, based primarily on the work of Jacobson, Mahler, and Kernberg and with some affinity for the works of Winnicott, Balint, and Fairbairn. He characterized this theory as a link between metapsychology and the clinical and experential aspects of psychoanalysis. The theory stresses the influences of early internal archaic fantasy on external object relations and their repersonification in the transference relationship, where they are available for scrutiny by the analyst and the analysand. Countertransference, empathy, and intuition are important tools for the analyst in this work. Ticho related that he has had particular experience with patients who come for second analyses stating that they can understand themselves but cannot apply this knowledge.

---

10 Held at the Fall Meeting of the American Psychoanalytic Association, December, 1978. Panelists: Otto F. Kernberg, Selma Kramer. Discussants: Heinz Lichtenstein, James T. McLaughlin

Ticho believes that this state of affairs results when important early object relations are either not perceived by the analyst or not communicated to the patient.

The first presentation, "Technical Consequences of Object Relations Theory: The Significance and Application of Separation-Individuation Theory," was given by Selma Kramer. In her view, Mahler's symbiosis-separation theory is much more than an object relations theory in that it adds to our understanding of the ego, of the drives, of basic moods, of self and object differentiation, of psychic structuring, and object constancy. Psychoanalytic developmental psychology contributed most significantly to psychoanalysis as a "general psychology," and our widened knowledge of early preverbal and paraverbal communications of infants has added a significant new dimension to psychoanalytic technique in the treatment of children, adolescents, and adults.

In the analytic situation, nonverbal communication includes a wide range of phenomena, including changes of affect and mood, anal or genital sensations, rigidity, fidgeting, flushing, headaches, dizziness, itching, and desires to urinate, defecate, suck, smoke, or leave the couch or office during the analytic session. Certainly many writers before Mahler had stressed the importance of body language, but it was Mahler who showed how these phenomena, as screen sensations analogous to screen memories, could be used to elucidate the nature of early prestructural preoedipal conflicts. Through what Mahler calls "coenesthetic empathy" and the understanding of countertransference, the analyst is able to understand what Loewald called "psychic substructures" and the genesis of ego and superego defects. Empathy is used along with the analyst's alertness to repetitive themes which emerge in the transference. Kramer noted that empathy can be used safely only if one knows where the patient is and where he is going.

Mahler's frame of reference helps the analyst understand the rapprochement subphase conflicts of neurotic patients as well as of more disturbed patients and helps him avoid serious blind spots and countertransference reactions which may impede their reconstruction in the analysis. Mahler's theories alert the analyst to the influence on the transference neurosis of superego precursors arising in the rapprochement subphase. Serious preoedipal conflict affects the postoedipal superego and contributes to masochistic and depressive features of the transference neurosis. Finally, unresolved rapprochement subphase conflicts may result in a transference neurosis in which magical expectations of the analyst's omnipotence are a significant element. The second part of Kramer's paper was devoted to two clinical examples which illustrated the technical contributions of Mahler's theories to the treatment of neurotic patients.

The first example came from her having supervised two analysts on the same adult case. The patient, a depressed, hostile woman with work problems, attempted to conduct with the first analyst what Kramer called a "do-it-myself analysis"; the patient spoke in a monotonous fashion and insisted on doing her own dream interpretation in an attempt to maintain her distance from the analyst and avoid his intrusion. The analyst could not accept Kramer's suggestion that the patient's behavior might be a re-enactment in the transference of rapprochement subphase experiences, preferring to see it as a resistance to getting into the "real" (i.e., oedipal) analysis. Needless to say, the patient left this unempathic analyst and consulted the second analyst who, coincidentally, came to Kramer for supervision. The second analyst connected the patient's need for a "do-it-myself-analysis" with the fear that she might lose her independence. His comment, "So you have to invent the wheel all by yourself," focused on her need to maintain autonomy at any cost, which coexisted with the wish that the analyst "move in." The picture was that of an ambivalent rapprochement-subphase child who had to attract and yet elude the swooping-down and shadowing mother described by Mahler. The continued effort of the analyst to be available but unobtrusive eventually permitted the patient to form a good therapeutic alliance and a transference neurosis.

Kramer's second case illustrated the importance of working through the separation-individuation transference phenomena in the analysis. A homosexual young woman came into treatment because of work inhibitions, severe recurrent depressions, and problems in relating to her female lovers. The patient was the daughter of teenage parents who had to get married. When she was a toddler in the practicing subphase, the father was called into military service and her depressed mother turned to her daughter for comfort; an overweening closeness continued throughout the rapprochement subphase and into her pre- and postoedipal life. Even after the father returned from the service, mother and daughter continued to spend much of their time together. She did not physically separate from her mother until she went off to college, at which time she had her first homosexual relationship. Although she dressed in a mannish fashion in her homosexual relationships, in fantasy she was a little girl seeking the maternal object. However, a fear of fusion and of loss of identity kept her from achieving orgasm and drove her to continually change her homosexual partners.

In her account of the course of the treatment Kramer illustrated how analysis of the transference facilitated the resolution of conflicts from early preoedipal phases as well as positive and negative conflicts. Early in treatment, the patient's need for closeness was typified by her misremembering a popular song as "You've Got Me Under Your Skin." When the patient had to be away on business trips, she became anxious and depressed, repeating with the analyst the difficulties she had with separation from her mother. A dream in which she had a dildo stuck in her at a thirty-degree angle, as in a Greek vase, brought into focus her negative oedipal wishes and the fantasy when she was young that her mother would love her more if she had a penis. As the transference regression in the analysis proceeded, first practicing-subphase activity was awakened and then attitudes reminiscent of the rapprochement phase proper and of a rapprochement like crisis. Working through of this material, characterized by exaggeration, ambivalence, and accusation toward the analyst, was followed by the emergence of oedipal themes and heterosexual dreams and fantasies. There was increased separateness from her mother and decreasing anger at her father, whom she blamed primarily for not interfering with her mother's keeping her too close. At the same time she was able to acknowledge her own positive wishes and fantasies about her young, handsome father.

Kramer concluded by asserting that Mahler's theories, by enriching our understanding of the developmental tasks of the infant and toddler, help us analyze not differently but better, because how these phases are negotiated has a profound effect on latency, adolescence, and adulthood.

The second paper, "Some Implications of Object Relations Theory for Psychoanalytic Technique," was presented by Otto F. Kernberg, who agreed with Ticho's view of object relations theory as intermediary between psychoanalytic metapsychology and direct clinical formulations. Object relations theory is not an additional metapsychological viewpoint but a special approach within the structural viewpoint that links structure more closely with the developmental, genetic, and dynamic aspects of mental functioning. Kernberg's underlying assumption—a view shared with Jacobson and Mahler—is that the earliest internalizing processes have dyadic features, a self-object polarity, even when self-and object representations are not yet differentiated. He conceives of units of self- and object representations, linked by an affect disposition, as the building blocks for later internalized object and self-representations and, later still, for the ego, superego, and id.

Kernberg asserted that in the course of psychoanalysis there is a gradual dissolution of pathogenic superego and ego structures and an activation of internalized object relations in the transference. The patient may re-enact the early self-representation while projecting the object representation onto the analyst or may project his self-representation onto the analyst while identifying with the object representation. The analyst is aided in his understanding by empathy through transitory or trial identification with the patient's self-experience or with his associated or projected self- or object representations. The analyst's empathic understanding is transformed into intuitive formulations and then into more restricted formulations which clarify the nature of the drive derivative activated and defended against in the object relation that predominates the transference.

Kernberg considered four specific applications of ego psychology object relations theory to the psychoanalytic situation. First is the nature of the conflicts to be interpreted. In regressive conditions with severe preoedipal conflicts, there is a pathological development of oedipal conflicts, not an absence of them. Primitive defensive operations centering around splitting, and excessive preoedipal aggression contaminate later object relations with sadistic and masochistic components of genital conflicts but the degree to which preoedipal features have distorted the oedipal constellation. Even in nonanalyzable borderline conditions or in cases of narcissistic personality with severe pathology of object relations, one always finds evidence of crucial oedipal pathology.

Second is the varying relationships between transference, genetic history, and early development. Oedipal conflicts condensed with pathological preoedipal object relations, as well as the predominance of partial, nonintegrated self- and object representations, contribute to creating fantastic (in the literal sense) transferences in patients with early fixation points and marked regressions. In such patients the gap between actual childhood experiences, the intrapsychic elaborations of such experiences, and their structuring in the transference is so great that early childhood experiences can be reconstructed only in advanced stages of treatment: hence the danger of equating primitive transferences with early object relations "in a mechanical, direct way" and the danger of "reconstructing" the earliest intrapsychic development on the basis of primitive transference manifestations. Transference developments in which primitive defensive operations predominate and in which preoedipal and oedipal conflicts are condensed need to be interpreted in an "as if," that is, nongenetic mode. The analyst's interpretations reflect a layering of the patient's "personal myth" and not a hypothesis regarding the actual sequence of childhood developments. Actual regression to modes of functioning that predate object constancy have to be differentiated from the patient's fantasies about such regression. Actual regression to subphases of separation-individuation rarely occurs in the analysis of patients carefully selected for psychoanalytic treatment and requires a long time to develop. Further, a "language of regression" may be artificially induced by an inappropriate introduction of the analyst's theory into the interpretive comments.

Kernberg's third application has to do with regression in the communicative process in the analytic situation. In states of severe regression, wherein part-objects predominate in the transference, the normally subdued influence of the psychoanalytic setting severely distorts the interaction with the psychoanalyst. As a result, the analyst finds it difficult to maintain empathy with the content of the patient's verbal communications. Dramatic acting out may also occur as the patient loses his capacity to listen or interact with the analyst verbally.

In such situations, two major technical tools may prove helpful. First, the analyst attempts to integrate cognitively the patient's confusing behavior and use of language, becoming an auxiliary ego to the patient, yet maintaining a technically neutral position. Second, the analyst assumes what Winnicott calls the "holding function," which includes the analyst's respecting the patient's autonomy, the analyst's "survival" in the face of the patient's aggression, and the analyst's empathic availability at points of significant regression.

Finally was the question of empathy and regression in the transference. Severe distortion of the patient's ego does not require that the analyst abandon his position of technical neutrality; such a requirement entails the view that it is the therapist's empathic presence rather than his interpretation which is really helpful. But empathy is a precondition of interpretive work, not its replacement. An empathic attitude is a necessary precondition in all psychoanalysis, and this attitude should extend not only to the patient's objective experience but also to what the patient has to dissociate or project because he cannot tolerate it in himself.

Before concluding, Kernberg presented an analytic case to illustrate how primitive dissociative or splitting mechanisms in the transference, temporary weakening of reality testing, and regressive shifts from verbal to nonverbal communication could all be resolved analytically in a patient who might otherwise have been considered unanalyzable.

The first discussant was Heinz Lichtenstein, with a prepared presentation entitled "Questions Raised by Object Relations Theory for the Theory and Practice of Psychoanalysis." For Lichtenstein one of the most important issues confronting present-day psychoanalysts has to do with our understanding the nature of being human. Freud showed us that there is a unifying bond which links the normal, the exceptional, and the definitely abnormal individual and links analogous phenomena in the same individual. Object relations theory may help us to understand the nature of this unifying principle of diverse ways of being human. Object relations theory points to the importance—in the control of feelings as well as in determining motivation, conflict, and psychopathology—of direct and indirect, specific role relationships. The interpretation of feeling states which are close to the surface becomes the primary consideration in our technical approach. This implies a need for greater emotional involvement on the part of the analyst and his willingness to provide the patient with a measure of fulfillment of his need for human relationship. The change from neutrality on the part of the analyst implies great risks, but these risks are required by the new human predicaments we find in our patients, particularly the danger of the loss of the potentiality for being human. According to Mahler, the earliest awareness of being is not of who I am but that I am. Lichtenstein cited the work of Mahler, as well as that of Winnicott and André Green, to support his assertion that the individual is not able to achieve an awareness of being without having had the experience of being reflected by the mother before separation is achieved. Some patients who manifest markedly contradictory aspects of their personality can be understood as responding to a strong urge to repair a damage to their earliest awareness of being. Such a patient was a 30-year-old scientist who was successful in his career and also successful as a novelist, publishing under a pseudonym. Although married and a devoted father, he at the same time maintained an underground love life with women colleagues. He also was an avid gambler and his involvement in a circle of horse-playing friends constituted "another life." Lichtenstein believes that through reconstruction of this patient's childhood he was able to define the unifying principle by which these contradictions could be understood. His earliest awareness of being, during the second year of life, was disturbed because during that year the patient's father left him and his mother alone in Nazi Germany as he went off to make preparations for a new life for his family. His mother during that year, alone in Hitler's Germany, must have been anxious and depressed. As a result, the patient must have had a sense of his mother's being dead in Winnicott's sense, for she was unavailable. His sense of being must have been severely damaged and hence the subsequent constant search for reaffirmation through instant contact and stimulation.

James McLaughlin, the next discussant, pointed out that Freud as early as 1895, writing in "The Project," was aware of the essential nature of the human dyad and of the importance of internalizing of object relations in the maturation of each of us from our earliest beginnings. McLaughlin applauded both Kramer and Kernberg for emphasizing structural, genetic, and dynamic viewpoints over economic considerations, which are often overly abstract and impersonal.

In presenting some of his own ideas about the importance of object relations theory for increasing our understanding of neurotic patients and especially in enlarging and shaping our perspective on the nonverbal communication of out patients, McLaughlin found it useful to recall the three modes of mental processing which psychoanalysis has identified in human thought: (1) the enactive mode—the proprioceptive, kinesthetic elements by which the earliest experiences of the infant are mediated and remembered; (2) the imagic mode—the visual, olfactory, aural, and tactile perceptions, which together with the enactive mode comprise primary-process thinking; and (3) the verbal-lexical mode by which reality-dictated categorizing of the world is attained. Although the verbal-lexical mode is the chief carrier of our psychoanalytic dialogue, the enactive and imagic modes are also always present, even in a neurotic patient, and take on fresh perspective and meaning when viewed in object relations terms. McLaughlin focused particularly on one example of enactive mode phenomena, namely, the patient's hand-arm kinesics on the couch. He cited Felix Deutsch's work on posturegrams of analytic patients, which showed in particular the enduring consistency, cross-culturally, of the meanings of right and left: right standing for father, good, strength, heterosexual, etc., left for mother, bad, weak, homosexual, etc. McLaughlin has been gathering data on hand-arm kinesics from analytic patients. He cited the case of one patient who, in recounting key early traumatic memories, gestured to her left with her left hand [accompanying gesticulation] and gestured to her right with her right hand when she felt more comfortable and put together. McLaughlin presented in some detail the consonance of the patient's kinesic phenomena with the configuration and valence of the conflicts as they unfolded in the analysis.

In regard to the verbal-lexical mode phenomena, McLaughlin cited material from Kramer's clinical presentations to show the way in which patients use their words in "thing fashion" to titrate the distance between themselves and the analyst, re-enacting the quality and spatial components of the relevant mother-child relationship. Kramer's patient and other patients with separation-individuation problems showed a change in verbal usage from passive to active modes as the analysis progressed.

McLaughlin concluded with some comments concerning the potential liabilities to the analyst's technique of the point of view the panel focused on. He cited the hazard of straight-line extrapolation in the analytic situation of the dynamics of the early months and years of separation-individuation, and the mistaken notion that these early events are truly remembered or enacted as such. He also cited as a potential liability the wish on the part of the analyst to remedy the defects and make up for the deficiencies stemming from the patient's early experience. McLaughlin strongly supported Kernberg's ideas about the use of an "as if" approach to avoid the coercion of certainty.

The discussion was opened by Arnold Richards, who saw a basic agreement between Kramer and Kernberg regarding the major clinical and theoretical issues raised by the topic of the panel. Both Kernberg's point of view and Mahler's point of view as presented by Kramer were readily integrated within the overall psychoanalytic theoretical framework, which included the tripartite model. Neither Kernberg nor Mahler is presenting a new clinical theory and both would disagree, Richards thought, with those theoretical pluralists— Cooper, Gedo and Goldberg, and Kohut—who believe that new and different clinical theories are needed and suitable for different kinds of psychopathology. Kernberg and Kramer agree about the relationship between preoedipal and oedipal conflicts, about the importance of preverbal communication, and about the role of empathy in the analytic process (namely, that it is important but must be cognitively informed). Both assert that ego deficit neither precludes conflict nor requires us to abandon an analytic stance. If one is to find a possible disagreement, it could be with regard to the issue of the relation between the transference, genetic history, and early development in the analytic situation. Kernberg believes that reconstruction of earliest intrapsychic development is difficult to achieve in the analytic situation, yet separation-individuation-phase issues and inferences provide the architectonics of the unfolding analytic material of Kramer's patient. Richards then presented material from the analysis of a man with severe hypochondriacal concerns. A fantastic (Kernberg's adjective) transference attitude early in the analysis could be viewed only in an "as if" mode, but later in the analysis the transference attitude served to point the way to the elucidation and successful resolution or the pathologic object representations determining the patient's pathology. Citing Abram's classification of the genetic point of view as relating to both genetic antecedents and developmental transformation, Richards noted the particular relevance of object relations theory for this broadened concept of the genetic point of view.

Kramer, in response to McLaughlin, wished to stress that she does not believe that early preoedipal events are truly remembered but rather that certain feelings from this period, the sense of relationship of closeness or distance, for example, are reenacted in the transference. In her patient, preoedipal material appeared and was handled early, but she does not believe that this is always the case. One analyzes material as it appears, although her training as a child analyst may help her to deal with primitive material earlier than an adult analyst would do.

Kernberg agreed with Lichtenstein that the lack of integration and sense of self is of central importance, but it seems to him that Lichtenstein was drawing from contradictory frames of reference—Mahler, Lacan, Winnicott, and Green. Kernberg also thought that in his case presentation Lichtenstein seemed to be limited to the patient's conscious information, which showed enormous contradiction. In stressing the fact that the patient was born in Nazi Germany under terrible circumstances, Lichtenstein may have been overemphasizing external reality as against intrapsychic reality. Kernberg has seen patients born under similar circumstances who do not demonstrate such pathology; indeed, patients raised under very sheltered conditions may show severe borderline or narcissistic pathology. Finally, Kernberg believed that Lichtenstein's emphasis on the emotional availability of the analyst is in reaction to an exaggeration of Freud's concept of the analyst as a screen.

Kernberg agreed with McLaughlin's stress on the importance of nonverbal communication and its classification into the enactive, imagic, and verbal-lexical modes. He felt in particular agreement with McLaughlin's emphasis on the importance of the analyst's "holding" the various channels of communication—fantasy, conscious content, etc. for the patient.

Kernberg found important and germane to the object relations point of view Richard's demonstration of the way in which the meaning of a hypochondriacal concern changes in time and shifts during different stages of the analysis—that the symptom could not be simply and definitely traced to an element of the past. Kernberg viewed the course of analysis as strictly nonsequential. You topple primitive transferences, and, at a point of resistance, primitive transferences reappear. Rather than moving in a sequence of developmental stages, you move back and forth in the context of regression.

Finally, Merton Gill, speaking from the floor, expressed his appreciation of the panel, which he felt was conducted at a very high level. In regard to the relationship between object relations theory and metapsychology, Gill does not view object relations theory as intermediary between clinical theory and metapsychology, but rather takes the position that object relations theory offers us the possibility of developing a clinical theory unencumbered by the natural science assumptions of metapsychological theory.

Technically, he felt that the central point that emerged from the panel was a reaffirmation of the centrality of the analysis of the transference. The emphasis on the transference should not be misunderstood as a rejection of drives, intrapsychic structure, or intrapsychic conflict. The concept of transference is concerned with the manifestations of conflict in the analytic situation without any necessary commitment to a particular etiology of conflict. Gill found Richard's remarks generally cogent, although he would give priority to transference interpretation in the here-and-now in the conduct of an analysis rather than to genetic interpretation. Gill questioned Kernberg's use of the term "as if." He would prefer that Kernberg refer to what was taking place currently in the transference, for that is what gives us our cue to what is affectively meaningful to the patient and what can be presented to the patient as a plausible interpretation.

Gill thought McLaughlin's presentation was especially useful because it told us about the several different avenues of cues which we have available to indicate what is going on in the present in the transference.

CHAPTER 4

Afterword from *The Rangell Reader*

by Arthur A. Lynch, Arnold D. Richards, and Janet L. Bachant

[(2013). *The Rangell Reader: Commentaries on and Selected Papers by Leo Rangell, M.D.* Astoria, New York: IPBooks.]

JULY 10, 2013

A book is often a metaphor for how one has lived life. Here the students and friends of Leo Rangell have gathered together once more to commemorate the countless contributions from a man who had a life well lived. We, the authors of this afterword, have worked with Leo Rangell separately and together for many years. His work has touched our lives in an enduring way and we are grateful to make this small contribution to a very significant work.

Leo Rangell was interested in all things human. Throughout his career Leo Rangell was a major contributor to the psychoanalytic literature. He was a devoted advocate for the unification of psychoanalytic theory. He was a man on a mission—the development of what he called—the total composite psychoanalytic theory. In this pursuit he stood at the crossroads that defined some of the greatest shifts in psychoanalysis, for the past 60 years. He had witnessed and contributed to the great debates of our time and added significantly to our understanding of clinical and theoretical issues, as well as providing sensible input on complex group, organizational, and political dilemmas.

As you have seen, his contributions were prolific. His works include: 9 books; 438 professional publications; 25 reprints in other languages; 23 written, delivered but as yet unpublished articles; and of the three projects under his supervision that were in progress; the current book is the first to reach completion. Rangell's insights, in these works, have remained a cut above the rest. This may be due to his commitment to remain in a dialogue with the pertinent issues of the day. Or, it may be due to his meticulous efforts to adequately fit the originality of his contributions solidly within the body of psychoanalytic theory.[11] Or, it may simply be due to the wisdom of his life experience informed by six decades of clinical work, and by his leadership experience as: twice as President of the International Psychoanalytic Association; twice as President of the American Psychoanalytic Association, and thrice as President of his local Psychoanalytic Institute; all eventuating in the unparalleled distinction of Honorary President to both the International and American Psychoanalytic Associations.[12]

THE MAN

Who was Leo Rangell? He was the oldest of four children of Russian and Polish immigrants. Born on Oct. 1, 1913 he was raised and educated in Sheepshead Bay, Brooklyn, N.Y. He earned a scholarship

---

11 Rangell was grounded in the works of Freud and his successors, chief among them were: Otto Fenichel, Heinz Hartmann, David Rapaport, Anna Freud, Annie Reich, Edith Jacobson, Margaret Mahler and the structural theorists Charles Brenner, Jacob Arlow, Martin Wangh, David Beres to name a few.

12 An honor first bestowed to him.

to Columbia University when the country was in the grips of a depression and after graduating with honors studied medicine at the University of Chicago, graduating in 1937. He married Anita Buchwald in 1939 and they had four children.

With a deep interest in neurology and the hopes of becoming a neurosurgeon Rangell moved his family back to New York and did a neurology residency at Montefiore Hospital. There he met and became quick friends with Jacob Arlow and Victor Rosen and his interests in psychiatry and psychoanalysis began to grow as his interests in neurosurgery faded, mainly from the barriers to further training prompted by Anti-Semitism.

Rangell entered a psychiatry residency program that began at Grasslands Hospital in Valhalla, N.Y. and ended at the New York State Psychiatric Institute at Columbia University. This residency stimulated Rangell to begin his formal training at the New York Psychoanalytic Institute. Rangell recalled that he and Arlow began their personal analyses on the same day, February 1, 1941, and followed the same routine for a year. Each day they would meet at the hospital and take the Broadway #1 line down to Columbus Circle to their respective analysts. After they would return together. The discussions on these rides were about the world of psychoanalysis. Rangell believed that this may have qualified as the first psychoanalytic study group. This was a time for Rangell and psychoanalysis that was full of excitement and possibility. With the advent of World War II Rangell joined the U.S. Army Air Forces and left New York. After the war, he moved to Santa Monica, Calif., and studied at the Los Angeles Psychoanalytic Institute.[13] Rangell opened a practice in Beverly Hills, but later moved his office into his home in the Brentwood neighbourhood of

---

13 In his final thesis—of a man suffering from a doll phobia, we see the beginning of a lifelong theme—the Total Composite Psychoanalytic Theory.

Los Angeles. There he practiced his craft for 60 years and raised his family. The editors and authors have told the rest of his history in the previous chapters.

THE HUMAN CORE

Rangell began his efforts to unify psychoanalytic theory by looking at the problem of anxiety and then considered four additional concepts. He placed unconscious intrapsychic conflicts at the center of what he identified as the human core. In subsequent papers, he elaborated on this concept demonstrating the interconnected and contiguous nature of psychic phenomena, which consists of: anxiety, the intrapsychic process, a new ego function of unconscious decision making, the syndrome of the compromise of integrity, and the exercise of free will as an aspect of ego autonomy.

Rangell began his unifying efforts by addressing Freud's problem of anxiety. Freud had two separate theories of anxiety. Anxiety was: 1. Viewed somatically as the painful transformation of libido due to repression, and 2. Understood in a psychological formulation as a signal of danger. Rangell asserted that a broader view was necessary to account for the phenomena of early traumatic anxiety and proposed integrating the two theories. This effort resulted in the "Unitary Theory of Anxiety", (Rangell, 1955) and took into account not only the signal function of anxiety but also the overwhelming state of anxiety in trauma. This latter concept had been illustrated repeatedly in the literature. It was in this broader "complemental series" that the earlier states of helplessness were identified or tagged as elements that would herald a future state of impending helplessness or danger. Clinical applications of this theory are found in many of his papers, most notably: "The Psychology of Poise" (*RR* 9), "Beyond and Between the No and the Yes" (*RR* 55), and "Castration" (*RR* 67).

From Intrapsychic Conflict to Intrapsychic Process

Rangell defined the domain of psychoanalysis as the area of unconscious intrapsychic conflict (1967). He began this line of inquiry earlier by spelling out the scope (1963a) and structural problems (1963b) of unconscious conflict and followed it up later (1990) by charting 12 sequential steps of the microscopic view, which advanced from the initiation of the precipitating stimulus to some final psychic outcome. This project was later expanded to include the broader and more comprehensive sequences of intrapsychic process (1969a).

To summarize this sequence, the ego initially tests for the signal of anxiety by initiating a series of trial actions. The ego then appraises the reactions from the superego and the external world to determine if either the signal of anxiety or of safety appears. If there is an anxiety signal, conflict has ensued. If there is not an anxiety signal, the ego indicates safety in movement toward the intended acts. This sequence mapping project by Rangell continued well into the 1980s. The sequence he outlined moved from dilemma / choice conflicts to oppositional conflicts and back again to dilemma / choice types with choices and compromise formation outcomes at different stages. His microscopic view is contrasted with the macroscopic view of the clinical material, seen in the therapeutic situation, where the manifest surface reflects derivatives of the underlying intrapsychic process. His paper on "The Intrapsychic Process and its Analysis" (1969, *RR* 97) and the preceding commentary captured the complex nuances of this process.

The Unconscious Decision-Making Function

As Rangell (1969b, 1971) continued to explore the unconscious process, he turned his attention to the final common pathway for the expression of action: the unconscious decision-making function of the ego. Rangell clearly saw that making choices and carrying out decisions among competitive alternatives was a key and essential unconscious function found in both conflict and nonconflict spheres. This function chooses whether or not to institute defense to minimize danger or, in times of safety, the decision leads to an outcome: resolution of conflict, choice between alternatives, or compromise formations, which includes choice of compromise, autonomous acts, or adaptive responses. The individual's personal history of previous internal solutions determines the facilitating pathways that guide future alternatives so that these choices seem, at times, to be automatic or seamless. Over time choices are incorporated into durable character traits and fixed expectations from the individual. Rangell emphasized that unconscious choice and the function of decision making are not always automatically followed by compromise formations, even though this may be a major psychic outcome. This point was highlighted in greater depth in the commentaries of this volume. Other possible outcomes may involve choice between alternatives (for example, the choice of one arm of a conflict over another), or instinctual discharge, or denial. Whether behavior is pathological or not, outcome choice is made during the intrapsychic event sequence. Symptoms, for Rangell, are as much an unconscious choice as non-symptomatic behavioral outcomes.

The Compromise of Integrity

Addressing the matter of mental functioning in social and political life, Rangell introduced the syndrome of the compromise of integrity (1974, 1976). Integrity, Rangell observed, relied upon a necessary willingness to live by superego values. The compromise of integrity is ubiquitous: it ranges from being ego syntonic to ego alien and falls on a continuum of psychopathology from mild to severe. While neuroses arise from conflicts between the ego and the id, the syndrome of the compromise of integrity is the outcome of conflicts between the ego and the superego. Unbridled narcissism, Rangell thought, "is the enemy of integrity" (1974, p. 8). These moral and ethical conflicts, like the subclinical neuroses, are built into ordinary human conduct and play a part in the psychopathology of everyday life. Rangell points out that ambition, power, and opportunism in the service of the ego are desired qualities sought after in our culture. These traits can become excessive in direct proportion to the reward wished for or expected, and any of these traits may be a prodrome for the pathological syndrome of integrity. Clinically, we see these excesses in greed, jealousy, and envy. Therapeutically, one addresses these conflicts as any other conflict, through analysis, where the analytic aim is to turn out an honest person, as free from the compromise of integrity as from neurosis. This aim is never met completely. These demands play out in the continuous pull from the interaction of the analytic relationship. This is not a cold, sterile engagement void of any genuine relationship. Instead, it is a fusion of empathy with objectivity.

Free Will

This brings up the question of free-will (1986b, 1989a). Rangell differentiated free-will from both the instinctual wish and from a superego demand or requirement. Free will, also an ego faculty, is a directing capacity that takes into account motivations from the id, superego, external reality, and the goals and intentions of the ego itself. For Rangell, the extent of the presence of freedom of the will is a measure of the degree to which there is ego autonomy. Free-will is not absolute but is on a spectrum that paired against psychic determinism. Psychic determinism is derived from the instinctual wish; free-will is the result of the active, directing, executive function of the unconscious ego that shapes intention and purpose and creates action. The operation of relatively-free-will is firmly rooted in unconscious intrapsychic activity He stated: "Life is a combination of what has to be, and what we make of that" (2004, p. 314).

As we end this section on the mind, we recall another stunning paper "The Nature of Conversion" (1959). This paper and its commentary address the relationship between the psychic and the physical realms.

THE PSYCHOANALYTIC PROCESS

Rangell was a practical clinician and believed that the final test of any idea was in the clinical realm. When assessing the range of Rangell's clinical contributions one can see two distinct types of contributions: those 'essential elements' of technique—the psychoanalytic core, and other contributions written about specific clinical problem in the applications of technique.

A Psychoanalytic Core

Contributions made to the psychoanalytic core concentrate on the essential technical procedure. Rangell believed that psychoanalytic change comes from strengthening the ego's control over anxiety, defense, trauma, and symptom formation. Rangell (1954, 1981) focused on defining the borders of psychoanalysis, as well as, how to extend these borders to establish a wider province without losing the center. Early in his contributions, he had asserted sharp demarcations between psychoanalysis and dynamic psychotherapy by clarifying what was essential in psychoanalysis and what was not. By the midpoint of his career he was more comfortable with the "essential" aspects of treatments. He was less concerned with formal and logistic considerations—the number of times per week and the posture of the patient—than with the words and attitudes of the analyst. He had become more technically flexible noting that inner processes, not external ones, determined treatment.

Rangell challenged the trend advanced by transference purists. He maintained that transference was the most difficult and subtle part of analysis. He highlighted that excessive dependence or the absence of working through can result in the same poor outcome. Countertransference can lead equally in either direction. Rangell offered three additional thoughts about the inherent limitations in transference and its relationship to other critical elements of the clinical method. The transference was not sufficient to capture the complex development of a neurosis; transference was more likely to demonstrate issues of separation anxiety than castration anxiety or negative oedipal phenomena; and transference was not the best vehicle to reveal the patient's aggression.

In summary, Rangell rejected privileging of any technical aspect of the psychoanalytic process until it was clinically called for. He viewed the unfolding of the psychoanalytic process as immersing oneself in an understanding of the analysand's life. This process is facilitated technically by working with material closest to consciousness, with an understanding of its multidetermined derivatives and functions. What distinguishes psychoanalysis from psychodynamic psychotherapy, for Rangell, was the process that goes on between analyst and analysand. Where there is not a psychoanalytic process, there is not analysis. The condition of seeing a patient four times a week on the couch might facilitate the process but cannot define it.

In his plenary address to the International Psychoanalytic Congress in Rome, Rangell (1969, *RR* 97) showed how the intrapsychic process moves from the core to the periphery and back. Clinically, Rangell noted, "one is confronted by a composite mass, an aggregate consisting of diverse elements" (1990, p. 518). Technically, the task is to deconstruct, to "... analyze, break up the agglutinated whole into its component parts, and set the latter into...their logical syntactical relationships, according to cause and effect" (ibid). Hence the therapeutic alliance, which was popular at the time, he thought, is between "the analyzing function of the analyst and the observing, critical and judging functions of the ego of the patient, i.e., between the analyst and the healthy part of the patient's ego" (1990, p. 523). The core of this process is a self-analysis that outlives the analysis in the post-analytic phase. Perhaps one of the most demonstrative papers regarding the process of treatment is From Insight to Change (1981, *RR* 223–227). This paper and its commentary have been finely detailed.

Applications

Specific clinical issues in the applications of technique include the components at the core of psychoanalytic treatment, in the process of change. Here Rangell returns from the more abstract and moves closer to the experience-near. In 'On Defense and Resistance' Rangell (1983) looked at the present status of these subjects fifty years after Anna Freud's classic book on the topic. In 'On Understanding and Treating Anxiety,' Rangell (1978) followed anxiety from its theoretical centrality to its role throughout the clinical treatment situation. Other papers examine the nature of structural change (1989a, 1989b), the core of the treatment process (1987), the phases of insight and after insight (1980/81), and the termination phase (1966, 1982).

In these papers, he has elaborated the developed body of Freudian thought in a way that highlighted its long-standing attention to both wholes and parts. While he rejected any easy dichotomy that would identify a psychology of the whole as humanistic and a psychology of the parts as mechanistic, he insisted that "the self, and the object, as whole entities, have always had a firm place in central unified psychoanalytic theory" (1990, p. 6). That theory is not ego psychology but a total composite psychoanalytic theory, embracing id, ego, and superego, as well as the external world. Pluralism is not an option for Rangell. Borrowing from Fenichel's axiom, Rangell believed, "There are many ways to treat neuroses but there is only one way to understand them" (quoted in Rangell, 2004, p. 52). Resisting the widespread tendency to characterize the classical position narrowly as drive theory or ego psychology or structural theory, Rangell presented an approach whose aim was to render unnecessary a plurality of competing theories. For Rangell's concise take on treatment read 'The Analytic in Psychoanalytic Treatment, How Analysis Works'(1996, RR___) and its commentary. Another commentary and chapter—'The Creative Thrust: A Psychoanalytic Theory' (1978, *RR* 223–227) offers an application of psychoanalytic theory to the topic of creativity.

MODELS OF THEORY

Rangell believed that the main problem for psychoanalysis today is the current state of theoretical pluralism. He repeatedly outlined his view of how pluralism had cumulatively been the most erosive force to psychoanalysis leaving it fragmented and deadlocked. Ultimately the problem of pluralism shakes the confidence of the psychoanalytic consumer and inspires doubt and insecurity.

Rangell (2004, 2007) showed how the various stages in the emergence of pluralism were fostered by four basic fallacies. The first fallacy is the replacement of a pre-existing set of observations or parts of explanatory theory by another when both new and old are valid. The second fallacy is the pathogenic fallacy—"pars pro toto"—a selection of a part and its replacement for the whole. Parallel to this is the simple discarding of necessary elements within the whole. The third illogical position is when knowledge and insight gained in one sphere are not aptly applied to related relevant situations. Finally, the fourth logical flaw is the failure to follow up one's thought or actions with the consequences that could be expected from new discoveries or insights. This haphazard management of theory construction has led to a drifting of the theory with no real efforts at "retention of consistency or intellectual unity" (Rangell 2007a, p.99). Instead, we have the current state of theoretical pluralism and its consequential fragmentation.

His countermeasure for this disarray was the proposal of a single Total Composite Psychoanalytic Theory, (1988, 2000) a theory that is cohesive and cumulative, aiming at "completeness with parsimony" (2007a, p. 116): *total*—containing all nonexpendable elements; *composite*—a blend of all valid discoveries; and *psychoanalytic*—fulfilling the criteria of psychoanalysis. The total composite psychoanalytic theory continues to develop alongside of the alternative partial theories growing as new clinical evidence is established. This first emerged with Freud's five metapsychological points of view: topographic, economic, dynamic, genetic, and structural. This morphed into a second phase encompassing all that is under the condensed title of Ego Psychology, including: the original metapsychology, the adaptive point of view, defense analysis; the advances in the genetic perspective. Currently, we are in the third wave of such a total composite theory. What is accepted into the theory is decided at both the collective and the individual level. Contributions converge from many directions and all follow the principle of the complemental series: attachment and separation, conflict and adaptation, neutrality and empathy, drive and object, tragic and guilty man, historical and narrative truth.

How then does pluralism affect technique? Rangell answered this question by observing that small innovations in technique have become exaggerated into major dimensions of treatment. This is both an example of pars pro toto and, often, the result of a transference to theory. Rangell reviewed the leading themes interaction, including: self-disclosure, enactment, and intersubjectivity and concluded that "these [are] irrational incursions into the analytic instrument itself, and through that into the analytic process, which need to be recognized and corrected.... It is as though laxity and lapses, which may be unavoidable, are regarded instead as flexibility, which is desirable" (2007a, pg. 83). To correct this view, Rangell follows Fenichel's adage that 'treatment occurs with a rational ego' and that technique "must be arranged according to rational criteria" (Fenichel, 1941, p. 13; quoted in Rangell, 2007a, p. 83). This does not imply technical rigidity, but highlights the aim of explaining the irrational by the rational. Technical variations in clinical psychoanalysis, Rangell thought, are as diverse as people are. In his journey to become a "developed Freudian," (Lynch & Richards, 2010, p. 361) Rangell made an enormous contribution to the literature and to the field. His close friend Jacob Arlow (1988) summed this up best, in his appreciation to Rangell: He "has made an indelible mark on the development of psychoanalysis in our time, not only in the United States but in the rest of the world as well" (p. 297). Whether you agree with Rangell or not, the breadth and depth of his work reminds us just how complex our work is and how difficult it is to live a life well. To these ends he has succeeded brilliantly.

REFERENCES

Arlow, J.A., (1988). Leo Rangell an Appreciation. *Psychoanalytic Quarterly.*57:297-301.

Lynch, AA & Richards, AD. (2010). Leo Rangell: The Journey Of A Developed Freudian. *The Psychoanalytic Review,* Vol 97, Iss. 3. p. 361–391.

Rangell, L. (1954). Similarities and Differences between psychoanalysis and dynamic psychotherapy. *Journal of the American Psychoanalytic Association,* 2:734–44.

——— (1955). On the Psychoanalytic Theory of Anxiety—A Statement of a Unitary Theory. *Journal of the American Psychoanalytic Association,* 3:389–414.

——— (1959). The nature of conversion. *Journal of the American Psychoanalytic Association,* 7:632–662.

——— (1963a). The Scope of Intrapsychic Conflict—Microscopic and Macroscopic Considerations. *Psychoanalytic Study of the Child* 18:75–102.

——— (1963b). Structural Problems in Intrapsychic Conflict. *Psychoanalytic Study of the Child,* 18:103–138.

——— (1966). An overview of the ending of an analysis. In: *Psychoanalysis in the Americas*, ed. R.E. Litman. New York: International Universities Press, pp. 141–165.

——— (1967). Psychoanalysis, Affects, and the 'Human Core'—On the Relationship of Psychoanalysis to the Behavioral Sciences. *Psychoanalytic Quarterly,* 36:172–202.

——— (1969a). The Intrapsychic Process and its Analysis—A Recent Line of Thought and its Current Implications. *International Journal of Psychoanalysis,* 50:65–77.

——— (1969b). Choice-Conflict and the Decision-Making Function of the Ego: A Psychoanalytic Contribution to Decision Theory. *International Journal of Psychoanalysis,* 50:599–602.

——— (1971). The Decision-Making Process—A Contribution from Psychoanalysis. *Psychoanalytic Study of the Child,* 26:425–452.

_____(1974). A Psychoanalytic Perspective Leading Currently to the Syndrome of the Compromise of Integrity. *International Journal of Psychoanalysis*, 55:3–12.

——— (1976). Lessons from Watergate a Derivative for Psychoanalysis. *Psychoanalytic Quarterly,* 45:37–61.

——— (1978). On Understanding and Treating Anxiety and its Derivatives. *International Journal of Psychoanalysis*, 59:229–236.

——— (1980–81). Some notes on the post analytic phase. *International Journal of Psychoanalytic Psychotherapy,* 8:165–170.

——— (1981). Psychoanalysis and Dynamic Psychotherapy—Similarities and Differences Twenty-Five Years Later. *Psychoanalytic Quarterly* 50:665–693.

——— (1982). Some thoughts on termination. *Psychoanalytic Inquiry,* 2:367–392.

——— (1983). Defense and Resistance in Psychoanalysis and Life. *Journal of the American Psychoanalytic Association,* 31:147–174.

——— (1985). On the theory of theory in psychoanalysis and the relationship
of theory to psychoanalytic therapy. *Journal of the American Psychoanalytic Association*, 33:167–185.

——— (1987). A core process in psychoanalytic treatment. *Psychoanalytic Quarterly*, 56:222–249.

——— (1989a). Action Theory Within the Structural View. *International Journal of Psycho-Analysis* 70:189–203.

——— (1989b). Rapprochement and Other Crises—The Specific and Nonspecific in Analytic Reconstruction. *Psychoanalytic Study of the Child,*. 44:19–39.

——— (1990). *The Human Core: The Intrapsychic Base of Behavior. Vol. 1, Action within the structural view. Vol. 2, From Anxiety to Integrity.* Madison, CT: Int. Univ. Press.

——— (1996). The "Analytic" in Psychoanalytic Treatment: How Analysis Works. *Psychoanalytic Inquiry* 16:(2) 140–166.

——— (1997). Into the second psychoanalytic century: One psychoanalysis or many? The unitary theory of Leo Rangell, MD. *Journal of Clinical Psychoanalysis* 6(4): 451–612.

——— (2000). Psychoanalysis at the Millennium: A Unitary Theory. *Psychoanalytic Psychology,* 17(3):451–466.

——— (2004). *My life in theory.* New York: Other Press.

_____(2006). An Analysis of the Course of Psychoanalysis: The Case for a Unitary Theory. *Psychoanalytic Psychology,* Vol. 23, No. 2, 217–238.

——— (2007). *The road to unity in psychoanalytic theory.* New York: Jason Aronson.

CHAPTER 5

The Narcissistic Patient

(with Arlene Kramer Richards, Ed.D.)

[(1995) *Psychodynamic Concepts in General Ps ychology*, edited by H.J. Schwartz, E. Bleiberg, & S.H. Weissman, Washington, DC: American Psychiatric Association Publishing.]

CURRENT PSYCHODYNAMIC PERSPECTIVES

Narcissistic personality disorder was listed as a diagnostic category in neither the DSM-I (American Psychiatric Association 1952) nor the DSM-II (American Psychiatric Association 1968). It first appeared in DSM-III (American Psychiatric Association 1980) and was retained in DSM-III-R (American Psychiatric Association 1987). In both of these, the diagnostic description drew heavily on the contributions of two psychoanalysts, Otto Kernberg and Heinz Kohut, who in the early 1970s became the first to write about this condition. In the DSM-IV (American Psychiatric Association 1994), narcissistic personality disorder continues to be listed as a diagnostic category (301.81) with diagnostic features similar to those in DSM-III and DSM-III-R.

At the level of clinical description, narcissistic personality disorder is characterized by an unrealistically inflated sense of self-importance. Such patients feel they are special or unique and can be understood only by other special people. Preoccupied by "fantasies of unlimited success... and... an exhibitionistic need for constant attention and admiration," they tend to feel entitled to admiration "even without appropriate achievement" (American Psychiatric Association 1987, p. 350). Their exaggerated self-esteem is fragile, however, and grandiose feelings of superiority alternate with feelings of unworthiness and despair: "For example, a student who ordinarily expects an A and receives a grade of A—may, at that moment, express the view that he or she is thus revealed to all as a failure" (American Psychiatric Association 1980. pp. 349-350). "The person may be preoccupied with how well he or she is doing and how well he or she is regarded by others. This often takes the form of an almost exhibitionistic need for constant attention and admiration. The person may constantly fish for compliments, often with great charm. In response to criticism, he or she may react with rage, shame, or humiliation, but mask these feelings with an aura of cool indifference" (American Psychiatric Association 1987, p. 350).

Bach (1994, pp. 29–30) captured this two-sidedness of the narcissistic personality structure—grandiosity, intense ambition, and feelings of entitlement countered by insecurity, hypersensitivity, and feelings of inadequacy—by invoking the notions of "overinflated narcissistic type" and "depleted narcissistic type." Both sets of feelings are present in these patients, whose constant need for admiration renders them all but blind to the needs of others; others' assertions of their needs are, in fact, often experienced by the narcissistic individual as a personal affront. As a result of this extreme preoccupation with the self and its validation from without, feelings of empathy are either atrophied or altogether absent.

In their understanding of narcissistic personality disorder, Kohut and Kernberg differ significantly: their views on the disorder's etiology, pathogenesis, development, and treatment are often sharply at odds.

76

For Kohut, the disorder reflects a psychological deficit due to faulty development—the result of parental failure to provide the proper interest and emotional support in the child's early years. The parents draw the child into their own concerns, repeatedly disappointing the child's need for affirmation. Repeated disappointments by the parents interfere with the child's ability to internalize appropriate feelings of self-regard or to develop self-control. The deprived child thus remains an emotional primitive, never developing a healthy sense of self.

Where Kohut sees a lack, Kernberg (1975) sees rampant, inappropriate feelings of rage and hatred (aggression) brought on by the child's internalization of disturbed relationships with others (pathological object relations). Kernberg views the narcissistic patient as the victim of exploitative and frustrating parents toward whom the child responds with rage, which in turn provokes further aggression. This is followed by projection and paranoid constellations, which are defended against by what Kernberg refers to as faulty, grandiose, and controlling behavior.

Historical Review

Although the literature on narcissism as a psychoanalytic concept is considerable and dates back to the beginning of the Freudian era, the use of *narcissistic* to indicate a category of patients is relatively recent. (Freud used the term *narcissistic neurosis* in contradistinction to *transference neurosis,* usually in the context of broad generalizations regarding analyzability; he did not in general consider it a specific diagnostic category but did refer to melancholia as a *narcissistic psychoneurosis* [Freud 1924/1961].)

It should come as no surprise that there are problematic features to the category of narcissistic personality disorder, given that the concept of narcissism from which it is derived has long suffered from ambiguity as regards both its meaning and its proper application. Freud first used the term *narcissism* in 1910 (in a footnote he added to "Three Essays on the Theory of Sexuality"), in order to account for object choice in homosexual persons, who "take themselves as their sexual objects—that is to say, they proceed from a narcissistic basis and look for a young man who resembles themselves and whom *they* may love as their mother loved *them*" (Freud 1905/1953, pp. 144–145). In the Schreber case, Freud (1911/1958) posited a stage in sexual development between autoeroticism and object love in which the subject "begins by taking himself, his own body, as his love object" (p. 60) and so unifies the sexual instincts.

By the time Freud wrote "On Narcissism: An Introduction" (1914/1957), he had been discussing the concept for some time. (He borrowed the term from Havelock Ellis. Paul Nacke had coined the term in 1899, but it was Ellis who first related it to the concept of perversion.) In this paper, Freud focused on the relation between self-love and object love (or, in the energic terminology he then favored, between libido cathecting the ego and libido cathecting objects). He postulated an initial libidinal cathexis of the ego that "fundamentally persists and is related to the object cathexis, much as the body of an amoeba is related to the pseudopodia which it puts out" (p. 75). Freud assumed a tense balance between self-love and object love: "The more the one is employed, the more the other becomes depleted" (p. 76). Thus, the ego was considered "a great reservoir of libido, from which libido is sent down to objects and which is always ready to absorb libido flowing back from objects" (p. 75). Narcissism was for Freud, as for his disciple Karl Abraham, a state of excessive self-love at the expense of object love. This imbalance is seen in its most extreme form in patients with *dementia praecox,* a dynamic state related developmental^ to the infantile phase known as autoeroticism.

Although the concept of narcissism was presented initially as an extension of libido theory, it has since been lifted from this limiting framework. As Moore (1975) noted, "The concept... played a pivotal role in the development of the structural theory. Narcissism was a seed which germinated into ego psychology" (p. 243). Unfortunately, as he also noted, the term is often overused, for the very reason that it appears useful in describing such a variety of phenomena. It "may refer descriptively to a type of libido or its objects, to a stage of development, to a type or mode of object choice, to an attitude, to psychic systems and processes, or to a personality type which may be relatively normal to pathological, neurotic, psychotic, or borderline" (p. 244).

The problem that arises from this conceptual looseness is that theory in this area does not at present afford the therapist any clear guides in diagnosing and treating patients. This state of affairs stands in contrast to the useful diagnostic role played by such concepts as anxiety and depressive affect. But perhaps this judgment should be placed in the past tense. The classic view of narcissism, as presented first by Freud and then by his successors—including Abraham, Ferenczi, and later Hartmann, Jacobson, and Waelder—indeed did not provide a clear basis upon which to understand psychopathology. But this theoretical failing has been arguably corrected by Kohut and Kernberg; even though their theories are to some extent incompatible, each is coherent within its set of assumptions and hence may serve as a foundation for clinical theory. Freud's concept of narcissism suffered from an ambiguity regarding the relation between self and ego in his 1925 structural model, a failing Hartmann (1950/1964) tried to remedy, if not entirely with success. Kernberg himself has outlined some of the difficulties. Referring to Freud's (1931/1961) article on libidinal types, he criticized as too restrictive the attempt to classify the narcissistic character as another such type (Kernberg 1975).

Kernberg noted that Fenichel (1945), one of Freud's most important systematizers, had objected to Freud's description of libidinal types, finding all such categorizations unsatisfactory: "Psychoanalysis is essentially a dynamic discipline. It evaluates given phenomena as a result of conflict. It has never considered the characteristics in terms of the actual strength of the forces operative but rather with respect to the functional relation of these forces to one another. A categorization of id person, ego person, and superego person is not a dynamic concept" (Fenichel 1945, pp. 525–526). Psychoanalytic formulations that rely primarily on the dispositions of psychic energies are, according to Fenichel, of limited clinical use.

DIFFERENTIAL DYNAMIC DIAGNOSIS

Although clinicians seem generally to agree about the kind of presenting picture they are inclined to call narcissistic, this consensus regarding phenomenology does not extend to psychodynamics. Because the two most developed and widely accepted formulations— those of Kernberg and Kohut—are either incompatible or must be taken to apply to very different patient populations, the status of narcissistic personality disorder as a clinical entity remains in doubt. It may well turn out that narcissism is encountered as a prominent feature in a variety of disorders, and that as each treatment progresses, the lineaments of the patient's specific disorder are revealed as typical of one or another of the more firmly established diagnostic categories. Whether a residue of patients would then remain for whom narcissistic personality disorder—however defined—would be the appropriate diagnosis is a question that cannot yet be answered with any certainty.

As regards treatment, Kernberg has recommended interpreting the narcissistic patient's striving for omnipotence and his or her need to idealize and denigrate the analyst. Rather than allowing these patients to project upon the analyst their feelings of exalted self-worth—or, conversely, of worthlessness—Kernberg believes that interpreting the patient's narcissistic, infantile strivings will bring to the fore the hidden rage and paranoia that lie beneath the surface of, for example, the patient's need to idealize the analyst. In such instances, the patient needs to be shown that his or her strong desire to cooperate with the analyst is a defense against deep and uncontrolled anger and a fear of being harmed. According to Kernberg (1975), the patient tries to control and devalue the analyst, to treat the analyst like an appendage and to render the analyst impotent. The task of the analyst is to interpret the patient's need to make the analyst feel deflated. If the analyst interprets this need continually, the patient will begin to express his or her rage and to reveal fears that are part of a paranoid stratum of his or her personality. Kernberg has identified the following factors as suggestive of a favorable prognosis: a capacity for depression and mourning; a transference potential for guilt in contrast to a tilt toward paranoid rage; a capacity to sublimate; an emphasis by the analyst on interpretation of the superego; and an absence of life situations granting unusual narcissistic gratifications. Keeping these factors in mind helps the therapist decide which narcissistic patients can more readily be worked with.

Despite their differing views of etiology and divergent treatment strategies, Kohut and Kernberg agree that patients with narcissistic personality disorder are extremely difficult to treat. The problem is that these patients tend to experience their symptoms as ego-syntonic—that is, as compatible with their wishes and acceptable to their egos. They fail to recognize that their need for constant reassurance and praise is extreme, and that their inability to empathize with others is a psychological deficiency. Only when the world fails to provide them with narcissistic supplies in the form of special recognition do they experience fright and despair. Whereas their presenting symptoms are often vague, their diffuse feelings of shame and unworthiness on the one hand, and of grandiose entitlement and narcissistic rage on the other, may run deep over the course of treatment.

Through much of treatment, such patients tend to persist in a persona of extreme self-sufficiency. They seem not to need other people, the analyst included, and they have great difficulty even perceiving others as separate individuals. Often, the patient exploits the therapist as a foil in order to overcome disturbances of self-constancy and self-regulation, or to shore up flagging self-esteem. For instance, the patient may achieve a temporary sense of self-sufficiency by devaluing the analyst, thereby fending off feelings not only of weakness and failure but also of rage, the latter feeling betokening the patient's inability to actualize grandiose fantasies in the real world.

Kohut, in developing his diagnostic formulations and treatment approach, introduced the term *selfobject* to capture the fact that the narcissistic patient relates to another person as if that person were functionally a part of him- or herself. According to Kohut, these patients use other people to regulate their tension states and to bolster their self-esteem; they are largely unable to relate to others in any other way or for any other purpose. Kernberg (1975) described a similar phenomenon from his own theoretical perspective, noting that narcissistic patients experience "an unusual degree of self-reference in their interactions with other people, a great need to be loved and admired by others, and a curious apparent contradiction between a very inflated concept of themselves and an inordinate need for tribute from others. Their emotional life is shallow. They experience little empathy for the feelings of others. They obtain very little enjoyment from life other than from the tributes they receive from others or from their own grandiose fantasies... they envy others... their relationships with other people are clearly exploitative and sometimes parasitic" (p. 228).

Because the narcissistically disturbed patient relates to the therapist only insofar as the latter sustains the patient's sense of self-worth, the therapist is in the paradoxical position of having to accept the patient's need for mirroring and affirmation while simultaneously attempting to help the patient to recognize that others exist in their own right, not just as selfobjects. Kohut has labeled the therapeutic solution to this paradox the "transmuting internalization." According to him, when treatment is successful, the patient is able to use the relationship with the therapist to develop a sense of self. In this context, "self" signifies a permanent psychic structure that neither dissolves nor expands unrealistically with every mood swing or minor loss.

The treatment of narcissistic patients is very difficult owing to their extreme need to control the therapist and to use the therapist to provide them with a sense of self-esteem. In particular, they will fend off efforts to help them perceive and accept the therapist as an autonomous being with feelings, wishes, and needs. Likewise, these patients will resist efforts to interpret their sense of grandiose entitlement as a defense against profound feelings of inadequacy and worthlessness. As Kohut observes, "The patient who experiences again... the helplessness and loss of power he felt as a child tries to regain a feeling of bliss and power by projecting onto the analyst these treasured feelings. The patient vacillates between total idealizing of the analyst and a cold rejection of him or her" (Kohut 1971, p. 67). In treatment, the patient may swing wildly between seeing the therapist as an omnipotent being whose power will energize the patient—in Kohut's terminology, an "idealized parental image"—and seeing the therapist as the ineffectual, powerless being onto whom the patient has projected a despairing sense of worthlessness.

Alternatively, the patient may adopt an attitude of superiority while simultaneously revealing inordinate self-consciousness, shame, and hypochondriacal preoccupations.

Bach (1994) underscores the essential two-sidedness of the clinical phenomenology by pointing to the countertransference issues that further complicate treatment: "Many clinicians agree that the countertransference provides the major stumbling block in treating narcissistic patients, either because we cannot tolerate the consistent disregard shown for our human rights and our very existence by the overinflated, entitled narcissist, or because we cannot tolerate the idealizations projected onto us by the insecure and depleted narcissistic patient. It may help us to remember that behind the latter's experienced inadequacy lie deeper feelings of grandiose entitlement" (p. 39). Bach adds that successful treatment, with its analysis of the patient's defenses, brings together the complementary sides of narcissistic disturbance, so that "ultimately the presenting distinctions between the two types should dissolve as a more complete human being emerges" (p. 9).

As for transference, the difficulty in establishing it with narcissistic patients was noted first by Freud, who (as has been mentioned) distinguished the "narcissistic" from the "transference" neurosis. The former was characterized by the withdrawal of interest from the outside world in favor of the self, and the latter by the patient's ability to invest real or imaginary objects, including the analyst, with libidinal and aggressive interest. Kohut's conceptualization of the "narcissistic transference" (1971), later designated the "selfobject transference" (1977), was intended to denote a mode of relatedness according to which patients with narcissistic neuroses, in Freud's sense, could develop a special kind of transference that rendered them treatable by psychoanalytic methods. In his earlier writings, Kohut (1971) stressed that in successful treatment, the narcissistic transference was followed by the engagement and working through of an "object-libidinal transference," so that narcissistic pathology ultimately gave way to the libidinal and aggressive conflicts associated with neurotic pathology, with the analyst serving now as a transference object proper.

Kohut's concept of selfobject transference requires the therapist, for at least a major portion of the treatment, to comply with the patient's childhood wishes by providing heretofore unmet needs: for mirroring, for affirmation, for an alter ego, and for a selfobject to idealize. Only through these empathic provisions can the patient's archaic narcissistic structures (e.g., the primitive grandiose self) evolve into mature narcissistic structures capable of sustaining a healthy, reality-tested sense of self-worth. Commensurate with this treatment orientation is the need to refrain from interpretations that might prematurely rupture the patient's narcissistic defenses. As noted by Bach (1994), "premature confrontations often lead to narcissistic rage reactions in the overinflated patients and a pseudo acquiescence in the depleted patients, but not to structural growth. Effective interpretation of libidinal and aggressive conflicts become possible only when the patient begins to really understand that *the same reality can be viewed in different ways by different people and that his point of view and the therapist's point of view can both have reality and legitimacy.* Before that time, such interpretations are often counterproductive and, indeed, may spring more from the therapist's countertransference than from the patient's needs" (p. 9, *emphasis added*).

As might be gathered, the narcissistic patient presents in many ways the greatest challenge for the psychodynamically oriented psychotherapist. Patients with severe anxiety, phobias, depression, or obsessive or compulsive systems readily acknowledge their suffering and need for treatment. The adverse impact of their symptoms on their functioning is clear both to themselves and to their therapists;

these symptoms can readily be connected with both developmental history and current life stresses, and psychopharmacological agents are available that can reduce their severity and facilitate psychodynamic treatment. By contrast, narcissistic patients present with neither clear-cut symptoms nor clearly identifiable dysfunctional behavior. Some patients sense that there is something wrong with them but don't know what it is; often, these patients' family members and friends are largely unaware of their psychopathology. In other cases, however, these others are far more aware of the disturbed functioning and relationships than are the patients themselves. Although this state of affairs—in particular, the tendency to ego-syntonicity and the lack of clear-cut symptoms or dysfunction—is to some extent shared with other patients who fall into the broad diagnostic category of personality disorders, certain aspects of the pathology of narcissistic patients—in particular, the tendency to self-absorption and grandiosity—significantly impair their ability to engage in psychotherapy, thereby diminishing the possibility of a favorable outcome. It is generally agreed that psychopharmacological agents are of limited use in the treatment of such patients. Some authorities consider psychoanalysis the treatment of choice, because often these patients can benefit only from intensive, long-term treatment. However, because psychoanalysis is often not feasible and, in any event, is not offered by most psychotherapists in private practice, the treatment possibilities for narcissistic patients are, in point of fact, severely limited.

CASE EXAMPLE

History

Ms. V, the patient, was a well-groomed, brisk woman of 45. Married with no children, this aspiring actress had held several low-level clerical jobs, had had roles in a few amateur theatrical productions, and was currently engaged in an extramarital affair.

Brought up in a small southern town by her mother in the home of her maternal grandparents, Ms. V reported that she was never told anything about her father, although he and his family lived in the same town. She learned about him only when he died and a high-school friend advised her to attend the funeral. She believed her mother had intimated then that he had deserted them when the patient was 2 years old. Her mother had held a light manufacturing job throughout the patient's childhood and was an important source of income to the family. The patient recalled her as cold, distant, and suspicious, as well as being angry and contemptuous toward men. By contrast, Ms. V always had many friendships, several quite close and of long duration. She described herself as even-tempered; she never cried, and maintained a humorous, story-telling, wisecracking attitude with friends. She believed that they, like her husband, found her attractively tough.

Ms. V's narcissistic personality disorder met the DSM-III criteria. She had an exaggerated sense of self-importance, believing herself to be a great actress on the basis of a few roles in semi-amateur companies and expecting a career as a star when none of her performances had even been mentioned in reviews in the local newspapers. Her need for attention and the fragility of her self-esteem were apparent in her constant wisecracking and her catastrophic reaction to having to wait for her husband to pick her up. A lack of empathy was evident in her relationships with her husband and mother, as will be seen in the specimen session below. The vacillation between idealizing and devaluing objects was shown most clearly in her conviction that she was worthwhile only when her husband was around, which alternated with a conviction that he was worthless because he treated her so badly.

The psychotherapy sessions were all about Ms. V's husband; they were attempts to understand *him* in order to save her marriage. All of her concerns were interpersonal. She talked about her therapy sessions with friends, using their opinions to define her reality. She described having similarly used her friends to "check out" her mother's perceptions and explanations when she was growing up. She connected waiting for her husband when he was on a business trip or when he was late for a date with her with waiting for the father who never came when she was a child.

Themes of abandonment pervaded Ms. V's life narrative. Struggles emerged between a fear of being abandoned—repetition of the trauma—and attempts at reversal by abandoning others. At the end of a year of psychotherapy, she declared herself much better and began to talk of ending treatment within a few sessions. Interpretations of her need to repeat the abandonment were to no avail. She referred to the feared separation from her husband as "his going away, his leaving me" and, later, as "when he left." Ms. V left the therapist and then provoked her husband to leave her. She was away from treatment for 6 months. When finally she returned, it was for help in coping with the breakup of her marriage.

Her therapy had resulted in an impasse. Ms. V's persistent lack of insight convinced the therapist that she could not be helped by psychotherapy precisely because of the narcissistic disorder that had driven her to treatment. In these extreme circumstances, it seemed that if anything could work, it would be analysis. It was with the hope that her narcissism was analyzable that this recommendation was made. After a brief consultation, analysis was initiated on a four-times-per-week schedule, on the couch, which was maintained for 6 years. The legal process for a divorce was initiated several months after the analysis was begun.

Course of Analysis

Ms. V alternated transference attitudes from the very beginning of her analysis. Some weeks she would present herself as misunderstood, a helpless victim, beginning each session with a demand for help. In other sessions, her attitude and manner of speech were imperious in an infantile, omnipotent way. These distinct attitudes never overlapped in the same session and initially were extremely impenetrable, lasting from session to session and from week to week. Imperious, mirroring sessions would begin with such opening lines as "I *have* to tell my mother to go to Florida to live" or "I *know* why I don't get along with my husband. It is the birth order factor." Desperate, idealizing sessions would open with such lines as "I had a terrible dream" or "I had a traumatic phone call." A feature of the idealizing sessions was that she would call the analyst "my wizard." The quality of the session was predictable from the opening statement or question.

In the imperious mood, with the mirroring transference, Ms. V reported that when her husband came home from work an hour late, saying, "You be nice to me and I'll be nice to you," she screamed at him. She was surprised to hear that the analyst considered this response an expression of rage at her husband. In this mood, her manifest complaints dealt always with the other person, never with her own feelings. The way she dressed in the imperious mood was stylish but severe. Her posture, gestures, and tone of voice were definite, dramatic—and severe.

In her beseeching, idealizing mood Ms. V would speak of her fears. One session she began by saying that if her husband left her, her mother would move in and take over her life. She implored the analyst to protect her; she painted such a frightening picture of a cold, demanding mother that the listener could only tremble for her. One especially dramatic scene was reported after a weekend visit from her mother; the patient woke up in the middle of the night to see her mother standing at the foot of the bed, staring at her. Terrified, she sat bolt upright on the couch as she had on the bed. The analyst behind the couch became as powerful a figure as the mother at the foot of the bed. If the analyst helped her, she would be great; if not, she was nothing. When she manifested the idealizing attitude, the patient presented herself as an innocent requiring rescue from the intrusive, demanding mother. She dressed in printed silk little-girl dresses with bobby socks and running shoes over her stockings. Her posture was flaccid, her voice high-pitched.

Following is an example of a complete session from the first months of the analysis, in which Ms. V took an imperious, angry, isolated position, manifesting a mirroring transference.

Ms. V began by saying, in a defiant tone, "I didn't call my mother on Mother's Day. And I didn't like her calling me and saying she was afraid I was sick." She then described her mother's conciliatory attitude, to which she had nonetheless responded with rejection. Although she complained that her mother was cold and indifferent, she herself was not at all that way. Refusing to talk to her mother made her feel better. She felt less left out, less isolated, when she didn't have to talk to her mother.

Ms. V then spoke about her husband. He was being difficult, refusing to discuss the young woman who was his new assistant at work. She wanted him to explain himself, to tell her why he had to work late so many evenings, to promise her that he wasn't having an affair with this young woman. She wanted also to tell him that she was jealous of a client of his she had read about in a promotional piece he had done for the client. In this account, the client was a superwoman. Although Ms. V realized that it was necessary for her husband to present his client in the best possible light, she resented the fact that he'd done his job so well. She was sure that her husband admired this "perfect" woman more than he admired her.

Ms. V complained that the analyst would misunderstand and think that she was just feeling in need of bolstering up because she felt guilty about the affair she was having, and that neither her mother nor her husband understood how much she needed to be admired. The analyst intervened—for the only time in the session—to connect the idea of guilt with the need to be admired for doing something she thought was wrong. Scornfully admitting that this was correct, Ms. V pointed out that she had provoked her mother by not calling her on Mother's Day and had also provoked her husband, by accusing him, with no evidence at all, of having an affair with his assistant. She ended the session by describing how nice she really was to her husband: she had allowed him to eat his lunch an hour late on Saturday when he was working at home, not interrupting him as she usually did.

In this session, the patient's defiant tone of voice was the first indication of her transference attitude, and her statement that she had not called her mother on Mother's Day clearly challenged a social norm she believed the analyst accepted. So she went on to describe her mother's conciliatory attitude. Her next statement, however, that her mother was the cold and indifferent one, contradicted her description of their roles in this incident. Clearly, she was challenging the analyst either to accept her self-contradictory view or to challenge her. She then repeated this self-contradictory narrative twice over, each time with a new set of characters: first her husband and his assistant, and then her husband and his superwoman client. Each time she gave evidence that she had wronged someone; each time she accused the victim of what she herself had done. This evoked in the analyst a mounting countertransferential wish to protest, to set her straight, to show her that she was contradicting herself. The patient's expectation that these contradictions would go unchallenged left the analyst feeling gulled and humiliated. That Ms. V wanted simply to be mirrored rather than responded to seemed evident; any response at all would have produced a confrontation that would be used to preclude her understanding the self-accusation she was defending herself against. Her aggressive stance seemed to afford her sufficient pleasure to keep her functioning well. When the patient projected the idea that she felt guilty about the love affair onto the analyst and then saw this as an accusation, the interpretation aimed to elucidate the defense. The scornful exhibitionism and challenging unreasonableness of her characterization of the events she narrated were revealed to the patient as a cover for her guilt, as an invitation to the analyst to punish her for it, and as a discharge of aggression. Interpretation of the transference attitude at this point would have been premature, affording the patient just the nugget of reality that would convince her that she had to fight this out not with her superego but with the analyst. Nonetheless, some interpretation connecting the exhibitionism or mirroring transference attitude with the guilt was necessary so that her need to maintain that attitude might be diminished.

This session began with a defiant account of her controlling and punitive behavior toward her mother. At the same time, she was controlling and punishing the analyst; her description of her mother as cold and rejecting was a warning to the analyst of how any intervention at that point would be received. The session's only intervention was indeed met with scorn. The attempt to connect her need for approval with her guilt was a beginning at revealing to her the superego aspects of the conflict that undermined her self-esteem. She finished the session with an anecdote in which she again described her angry control of a love object; this time, however, she was able to allow a small concession—a late lunch—which only served to accentuate the degree of control she had been exercising.

Thus, in this session she manifested coldness, superiority, and the tendency toward self-consciousness and shame that Kohut considered diagnostic indicators of the grandiose mirroring transference. Yet the analyst's interpretation of her defensive use of this posture, linking it to guilt over a sexual transgression, had the effect of softening her attitude. Extreme grandiosity thus appears to be an artifact of the treatment, as does its eventual toning down.

Another early session began with an account of a mortally ill woman who doesn't dare ask for help. The patient was low-key in her manner, evoking a countertransferential wish to help, even to rescue. She described herself as pitiable. Again, only one interpretation was made in the session—that she experienced the analyst as bound to her by pity. This time, the interpretation was received in a helpless way, not at all rejected and possibly even confirmed by the production of a relevant memory. Again, the session ended with a slight modification of her stance; instead of merely accepting, she was actively confirming. Just as she had been unaware of being angry at her husband even as she was delivering tirades against him, so she was only dimly aware of how much her helpless, needy feelings directed her behavior and how her behavior evoked specific responses from others.

Although this alternation of attitudes continued right up to the end of treatment. the attitudes themselves became less extremely divergent. In the first year of the analysis, this modulation first became apparent in a session she opened by announcing, "I'm glad I don't have tantrums any more." During that session, she explored her sexual jealousy of her husband and was able to grasp the unconscious meaning of her suspicion that he was having affairs: she was envious of his ability to have sex with a woman, envious indeed of his penis. She began to complain that he kept his closets too organized, that he scheduled his appointments too closely, and that he was excessively conscientious in attending to the administrative details of a fraternity to which he belonged. She noted, however, that as he became more organized, he advanced in his career. She was able to realize that she preferred her lover, who suffered from premature ejaculation, because he didn't make her feel as envious as did her virile and efficient husband.

By the next session, though, she had returned to the complaints, expressing them now with a penitent "I see what's wrong now." Her mood had shifted back to the infantile, dependent state. Now, instead of being the imperious, envious, and spiteful one, she was the victim. She listed all the complaints her husband might have about her. She described in detail how 1) her field was not as prestigious as that of her husband, 2) her position in her field was not as advanced as her husband's in his, 3) her salary could never compare with his professional fees, and 4) although he said he didn't want the encumbrances of a house or family, she was the one he could blame for their childless state as well as for their failure to invest in a house. Her despair over these complaints—which her husband had never actually made—was total. She could not believe that if she was this bad, she could have any redeeming features whatever. When these pronouncements were interpreted as fantasy, she bitterly accused the analyst of believing that her self-reproaches were only cover-ups for the reproach that she had not been faithful to her husband. She had the fantasy that her sexual transgressions would be repeated in the analysis, as analyst and husband were equated. This fantasy was then traced back to a fantasy that her father would accuse her of sexual activity with her mother. She recovered a memory of sleeping in the same bed with her mother until adolescence.

Later on, she began to challenge the analyst by missing appointments and by arranging her schedule and finances so that she couldn't help leaving treatment. She left a job that provided insurance that allowed her to pay a full fee for one providing no insurance at all. When the analyst agreed to accept a reduced fee so that she could accept a job with more responsibility but without health insurance, she became suspicious. She feared that she would have to reciprocate, as she would if a friend lent her money or invited her to stay with her. A decision about whether to leave the analysis engendered a transference crisis. A new phase of treatment was ushered in by her understanding of the offer as a seduction similar to her fantasied seduction by her mother. She was then in the third year of treatment, the second of analysis. As she became aware of her sexual yearnings toward the analyst, her fear of them, and her need for a man in her life to protect her from the fulfillment or even awareness of these wishes, her negative oedipal desires came into focus. The helpless stance or idealizing transference was a wish to be loved; the imperious or mirroring transference was the wish to be the active lover.

A session after the transference crisis, in which the idealizing, dependent stance was modified by her emerging capacity to see complex compromises between good and evil, power and weakness, in the analyst as well as in other people in her life, began this way:

I want to talk about Bill—with him I can really see what you said last time. I *do* demand more and reject him for not giving me more than he really owes me!

A significant shift in her understanding of her interpersonal difficulties appeared later in the same session:

Janet can't understand me—she has acquaintances, friends, and a best friend—me. She can't understand why I put people into only two categories—in and out. She thinks it's okay to see people every couple of weeks for a drink, enjoy it, and not want more from them. Not *all* her relationships are that way, but she can enjoy the ones that are!

Later yet, a modulated form of the mirroring transference appeared in a session that began this way:

Funny how I think—can't really understand it. First 1 get so angry at things, then when I think about it, I'm not really angry at all.

She drew comparisons between her attitudes toward the analyst and her attitudes toward other people in her life:

It's just like asking about my father. I knew it was so painful not to know—but I was afraid I'd learn something unbearable if 1 asked. I couldn't stand asking. But I'd have been so much better off! I really put myself through a lot of pain unnecessarily because I couldn't ask! Like asking you about my vacation sessions. I thought you'd hate me because I was going away at the wrong time. And tell me I was bad—and you didn't. I was so relieved! I should have done it before!

Later in the analysis, idealizing sessions began with such statements as "1 have to tell you. I really believe *one* thing you said now," or her remark about Bill: "With him I can really see what you said last time." Such statements are restricted. No longer the all-knowing wizard, the analyst is now given credit for knowing *one* thing or saying something that applies to *one* of the patient's relationships. Thus, she began to see that her former way of characterizing the analyst as either all-good, all-giving, and all-knowing or as all-bad, depriving, and destructive was not the only way to relate to her. The same applied to other people. She could see that she had experienced her husband, and now her lover, as simply not there when she was angry because disappointed by them.

She persisted in characterizing her own affects by contrasting them with her mother's attitudes, but now by modulation rather than through simple reversal. She was able to see her splitting of affects as unusual; it was beginning to be dystonic to her that she could not tolerate the ambivalence of human relationships by maintaining an intermediate distance between herself and other people—neither being overly demanding nor shutting them out, neither idealizing nor scorning.

Ms. V's depressive affect was expressed mostly in complaints about her inability to work, a craving for drinks in the afternoon, and a conviction that her rival would get promoted before she would, thus forcing her to quit a job she enjoyed because of the humiliation of being passed over. This paranoid attitude was modified sufficiently for her to see that her rival was not omnipotent and to give up the conviction that she would be passed over for promotion because of what she considered the invincible self-esteem of the rival. Now she was able to bear the interpretation of her projection as well as the inference that she was in charge of the powers that would decide her fate. By the end of the analysis, she was neither imperious nor imploring. She was more indulgent toward her own feelings. She neither had to project so rigidly nor required the sharp division of her world into all good and all bad. She became capable of more empathic understanding of others as well as able to expect more from them. The latter capacity allowed her to ask for such things as vacations rather than taking as reality her fantasy that her requests would be denied.

SUMMARY

Ms. V's analysis was conducted using a classic psychoanalytic technique. The l-year psychotherapy that preceded the analysis was an analytic psychotherapy in that the patient was encouraged to explore her ideas and feelings. She never received any advice or special help. She was never the recipient of any special empathy. No educative attempts were made. Transference interpretations were balanced by interpretations that clarified affect, linked affect to the gratification of instinctual wishes, and explicated superego fears. It was the patient's gradual shifting and remodelling of her views of the world and her own experience in it that resulted in her change of behavior.

The transference developed from a set of rigid postures in which the analyst was either the all-powerful, idealized parent or the scorned, impotent one. While various figures of the patient's childhood were experienced in both guises, the attitudes themselves softened. At times the all-powerful, idealized figure represented the mother, at other times the grandfather, and at still other times the father. The most dramatic change resulting from treatment was a drastic revision of the patient's early history. Able to ask her mother about her early life in short conversations over a period lasting from the second through the fourth years of treatment, she discovered that her father had, in fact, been present; he had visited frequently in the home she and her mother shared with her grandparents. She eventually came to recall sitting on his lap while he read her the funnies. Indeed, her humor was traced to an identification with this powerful figure doing the reading.

The transference deepened and was enriched by the many threads of transferences from all the objects of the patient's early life. A major feature was the development of an ability to experience anger and disappointment toward the analyst despite the fear of losing that beloved figure, whom she might psychically kill off as she had her father. The reorganization of her inner life came about through a gradual removal and replacement of warped strands with new ones in the fabric of her understanding. Thus, this patient uncovered, disconnected, and reconnected her affects, wishes, and fears, and her memories and fantasies, to form a more viable mental tapestry.

For Further Study

Bursten, B. (1973).Some narcissistic personality types. *International Journal of Psychoanalysis* 54:287–300.

Freidman, J. A. (1988). The idea of narcissism in Freud's psychoanalysis. *International Review of Psycho-Analysis* 15:499–514.

Glassman, M. (1988). Kernberg and Kohut: a test of competing psychoanalytic models of narcissism. *J Am Psychoanal Assoc* 36:597–626.

Meissner, W.W (1985). A case of phallic narcissistic personality. *J Am Psychoanal Assoc* 33:437–469,

Robbins, M. (1982). Narcissistic personality: a symbiotic character disorder. *Int J Psycho-Anal* 63:457–173.

Rothstein. A: (1979).An exploration of the diagnostic term narcissistic personality disorder. *J Am Psychoanal Assoc* 27:893-912.

Schwartz, L. (1974). Narcissistic personality: a clinical discussion. *J Am Psychoanal Assoc* 22:292–306.

Spruiell, V. (1974). Theories of the treatment of narcissistic personality. *J Am Psychoanal Assoc* 22:268–278,

REFERENCES

American Psychiatric Association (1952). *Diagnostic and Statistical Manual: Mental Disorders.* Washington, DC, American Psychiatric Association,

——— (1968). *Diagnostic and Statistical Manual of Mental Disorders, 2nd Edition.* Washington, DC, American Psychiatric Association.

——— (1980). *Diagnostic and Statistical Manual of Mental Disorders, 3rd Edition.* Washington, DC, American Psychiatric Association.

——— (1987). *Diagnostic and Statistical Manual of Mental Disorders, 3rd Edition,* Revised. Washington. DC, American Psychiatric Association.

(1994). *Diagnostic and Statistical Manual of Mental Disorders, 4th Edition.* Washington, DC, American Psychiatric Association.

Bach, S. (1994). *The Language of Perversion and the Language of Love.* Northvale, NJ, Jason Aronson.

Fenichel, O. (1945). *The Psychoanalytic Theory of Neurosis.* New York, WW Norton.

Freud, S. (1905). Three essays on the theory of sexuality, I: the sexual aberrations in *Standard Edition* 7:135–172, 1953.

——— (1911). Psycho-analytic notes on an autobiographical account of a case of paranoia *(dementia paranoides*in Standard Edition 12:3–96,

——— (1914). On narcissism: an introduction in Standard Edition 14:67–102,

——— (1924), Neurosis and psychosis *Standard Edition* 19:148–153.

——— (1931). Libidinal types *Standard Edition* 21:215–220.

Glassman, M. (1988). Kernberg and Kohut: a test of competing psychoanalytic models of narcissism. *J Am Psychoanal Assoc* 36:597–626.

Hartmann H. (1964). Comments on the psychoanalytic theory of the ego. In *Essays on Ego Psychology.* New York, International Universities Press, pp 13–141, 1950.

Kernberg, O. (1975). *Borderline Conditions and Pathological Narcissism.* New York, Jason Aronson.

Kohut, H. (1971).*The Analysis of the Self.* New York, International Universities Press.

——— (1977). *The Restoration of the Self. New York,* International Universities Press.

Moore, B. (1975). Toward a clarification of the concept of narcissism. *Psychoanal Study Child* 30:243–278.

CHAPTER 6

The Replacement Child: Variations on a Theme in History and Psychoanalysis

(with Leon Anisfeld, DSW)

[(2000). Psychoanalytic Study of the Child 55:301–318.]

The Theme of Survivor GuilExperience on the Couch Inheres in the Very Origins of Psychoanalysis. In his letter to Wilhelm Fliess on October 3, 1897, Freud declares that he greeted the birth of his brother Julius "with adverse wishes and genuine childhood jealousy," and that Julius's death, when he himself was less than two years of age, left the "germ of reproaches" in him. He adds that his relationships to Julius and to his half-nephew John, who was his elder by a year, "have determined what is neurotic, but also what is intense, in all my friendships" (Masson, 1985, p. 268).

As every student of psychoanalysis knows, this letter comes at the turning point in Freud's self-analysis. It immediately follows the letter in which he repudiates the seduction theory and precedes that in which he first ventures his interpretations of *Oedipus Rex* and *Hamlet*. It is likewise generally known that in the *"Non vixit"* dream in *The Interpretation of Dreams,* Freud restates his insight from the letter to Fliess, but omits any mention of Julius. As he writes, "My emotional life has always insisted that I should have an intimate friend and a hated enemy," and "all my friends have in a certain sense been re-incarnations of John" (1900, p. 483).

We sound these familiar refrains because they introduce the theme of the replacement child that is the focus of this paper. Although even in psychoanalytic writing it is relatively rare for authors to acknowledge the subjective motivations that inform their work, we cannot avoid doing so here. For one of us (L.A.) is a replacement child, born in 1948 in a D.P. camp outside Berlin to parents who had both been previously married to other spouses, with whom they had had children. His sister, Ina, was born two years later in Munich, where his parents had gone to search for their families of origin. All had been murdered by the Nazis—his parents' parents and fourteen of their children, seven in each family.

In Munich his parents also looked for the families of their first marriages. His mother' s first husband, a gentile, was taken away and killed by the Nazis. Their eleven-month-old daughter died of starvation as his mother fled across the Polish countryside. His father' s first wife died in a concentration camp, as did their two daughters, both approximately six years of age. Anisfeld is not certain of their ages because, as so often happens with Holocaust survivors, the matter was not discussed as he was growing up in New Jersey. What is more, his father was fifty years old when he was born while his mother was thirty.[14] The author' s father died of a coronary when the author was eleven, in large measure, he believes, because of the horrors of the war and the losses his father suffered during the Holocaust.

Thus, he is a replacement child, and both of us, like Jews everywhere, have struggled to come to terms with the legacy of the defining traumatic event of the twentieth century. In this spirit, we

---

14 This age disparity intriguingly parallels that between Freud' s parents; the forty-year-old Jacob Freud was twenty years older than his wife, Amalie, when Freud was born.

offer this paper as a contribution to a collective act of self-reflection, in the hope that it will inspire readers to bring their own subjectivity to bear as one or another aspect of our discussion resonates with their experience.

In the narrowest sense, a replacement child is a child born to parents who have experienced the death of a child and then conceived a second child in order to fill the void left by the loss of the first. Other situations may show a similar configuration, as when one sibling dies at an early age and another must fulfill the expectations the parents had previously invested in their deceased offspring. Or a couple unable to conceive may adopt a child, who then has to take the place of the biological child who never was, with all the parents' attendant fantasies. In yet another permutation, a child has a severe mental or physical handicap; and whether he or she is reared in the family or institutionalized, the other siblings will inevitably be affected by the demands of their "special" brother or sister. As Bergmann and Wolfe (1971) observe, "Just as the sick child wondered 'why did it happen to me?', many of the healthy children wondered 'why did it not happen to me?', or even, 'can it happen to me?'" (p. 146). Parental anxiety typically takes one of two forms, both of which inflict damaging consequences: "The parents are either preoccupied with the sick child and in this way arouse in the healthy child depressing feelings of being neglected and slighted, or they concentrate on the healthy child, pushing him to succeed and forcing him to strive for achievements, so that he might compensate for the inability of the sick child and so alleviate the parents' feeling of failure and defeat." (p. 146)

As Wolfe and Bergmann make clear, even when a child does not literally die, the healthy sibling may have to cope with survivor guilt and thus be a replacement child. The psychological dynamics of parents who have themselves survived the trauma of the real or symbolic death of a child mediate between the sick or deceased child and the sibling who is his or her surrogate. In the most far-reaching extension of the concept, Jacob Arlow (1972) has proposed that even an only child experiences sibling rivalry and survivor guilt because "the only child blames himself for the fact that there were no other children" (p. 533). As Arlow contends, "What is striking about the 'survivor guilt' of only children is that it appears whether or not there has actually been a sibling who died before or after the birth of the only child" (p. 514).[15] From this standpoint, there is no great difference between being an only child and a replacement child since the only child regularly entertains the fantasy that "while he was in his mother' s womb, he eliminated his rivals by devouring them in one way or another" (p. 516). The only child thus holds himself responsible for his status and comes to believe that "the power of his wishes has denied life to an unspecified number of potential children" (p. 516), from whom he then, by the law of talion, fears retribution. In Arlow' s words, "The specific fear was the danger of retaliation from the embryos that had been destroyed. What the only child unconsciously fears is an encounter with these adversaries in the claustrum and being devoured from within by the rivals whom he had devoured and incorporated" (p. 533).

As this series of examples suggests, the replacement child in a narrow sense forms part of a continuum in which the extreme case metamorphoses into one that is normal and even universal. As Arlow remarks, every first child was for a time an only child, and many youngest children—especially if widely separated in age from their predecessors—may entertain a similar fantasy: "The early attitudes of the oldest child, formed during the period when he was an only child, are overlaid with the subsequent conflict connected with the birth of a

---

15 Irving Leon (1996) remarks that of the four clinical examples in Arlow' s paper, three "described patients who were not 'only' after all, having had siblings who either died, sometimes at birth, or were institutionalized due to severe difficulties" (p. 164).

younger sibling" (p. 513). This insight is relevant to Freud, who, after a fleeting period as his mother' s only child, was succeeded first by Julius and then by Anna, whose arrival caused the temporary disappearance of his mother (on the heels of the arrest of his nurse), which Freud symbolized in his half-brother Philipp' s joking expression that his mother had been "boxed up." In this extended sense, *every* child (not just an only child) is metaphorically a replacement child, the first-born in that he is replaced by a successor, and the later-born in that he takes the place formerly occupied by someone else.

In the Ashkenazi tradition, it is customary to name a child after a deceased person, thus making him or her a replacement not only of another sibling but of the ancestor whose name has been bestowed as well.[16] One of us (L.A.) is named after his mother' s beloved younger brother, while his sister was named after their mother' s mother, who was regarded more ambivalently. Each of these names carried its own emotional freight and had a great deal to do with how the two of them were treated in childhood. But a child born to Holocaust survivors replaces not simply a specific dead child or ancestor but all those who have perished. As Bergmann and Jucovy (1982) remind us, on Israel' s annual day of commemoration, "the children participate in the mourning ritual and replace for their parents the generation that perished" (p. 24). Such collective rituals of mourning hold out hope for the future for the Jewish people, but they likewise underscore the incalculable magnitude of the loss. It might be said that the state of Israel itself is a replacement child for the entire civilization that was destroyed in the Holocaust.

---

16 Interestingly, whereas Freud departed from tradition in naming his own children, his father gave him the name of Schlomo in memory of his own father, who died three months before Freud was born (Gay 1990). On the place of memory in Jewish history and Jewish experience, see Yerushalmi (1982).

Leon Berman adduces "Those Wrecked by Success" and "Criminals from a Sense of Guilt," two of "Some Character Types Met with in Psycho-Analytic Work" (Freud, 1916), as points of reference for the issues he treats in his paper "Sibling Loss as an Organizer of Unconscious Guilt" (1978). He cites Freud's account in *Beyond the Pleasure Principle* (1920g) of those individuals whose repetition compulsion shows them to be in the grip of a "fate neurosis": "The impression they give is of being pursued by a malignant fate or possessed by some 'daemonic' power; but psychoanalysis has always taken the view that their fate is for the most part arranged by themselves and determined by early infantile influences" (p. 21). Berman's patient, a depressed middle-aged physician for whom the death of a baby sister he never saw when he was three years of age was the central trauma of his life, exhibited such a fate neurosis (exemplified by his twice marrying women who had a son and daughter from a previous marriage). His unconscious sense of guilt thwarted Berman's efforts, leading to a negative therapeutic reaction and an abrupt termination of his analysis. Berman quotes Freud's remarks added in 1914 to *The Interpretation of Dreams* (1900) on children's jealousy toward new siblings and the far-reaching effects if their death wishes should be fulfilled: "Deaths that are experienced in this way in childhood may be quickly forgotten in the family, but psychoanalytic research shows that they have a very important influence on subsequent neuroses" (p. 252).

All the texts Berman cites have an autobiographical dimension, which becomes evident once one reflects on the fact that Freud had a younger sibling who died in infancy. In his biography of Freud, Ernest Jones (1955, p. 146) drew on "Some Character Types..." to propose that Freud was himself "wrecked by success" when fate fulfilled his death wishes against Julius. Extending this line of argument, Max Schur (1972, pp. 153–71) stressed the importance of the *"Non vixit"* dream as evidence that Freud was plagued by a recurring experience of "guilt of the survivor," which likewise had its earliest roots in Julius's death.

It is clearly no coincidence that the same texts that bear on the topics of survivor guilt and the replacement child should have what Freud, in the preface to the 1908 edition of *The Interpretation of Dreams,* called "a further subjective significance" (p. xxvi), although this is often overlooked by commentators concerned with the theoretical import of Freud's ideas. If one returns to the 1914 footnote to *The Interpretation of Dreams* on the experience of deaths in childhood, one reads in the first edition:

Children at that time of life [less than three] are capable of jealousy of any degree of intensity and obviousness. Again, if it should happen that the baby sister does in fact disappear after a short while, the elder child will find the whole affection of the household once more concentrated upon himself. If after that the stork should bring yet another baby, it seems only logical that the little favorite should nourish a wish that his new competitor may meet with the same fate as the earlier one, so that he himself may be as happy as he was originally and during the interval (1900, pp. 251–52).

Apart from the reference to a "baby sister" instead of a brother, this passage describes Freud's own experience as an "elder child" whose reign as the "little favorite" was interrupted by the arrival of Julius, whose disappearance "after a short while" caused "the whole affection of the household" to be "once more concentrated upon himself." But when the stork inconveniently brought "yet another baby"—in this case, Freud's sister Anna—he "nourish[ed] a wish that his new competitor may meet with the same fate as the earlier one," so that he might once again be the adored only child.

The type of reading we have offered of this passage from *The Interpretation of Dreams* can be profitably employed at many points in Freud' s writings. In "The Psychoanalytic Literature on Siblings," Colonna and Newman (1983) aptly note that Freud "placed particular emphasis upon the feelings of the older child toward the new sibling" (p. 286). They quite the *Introductory Lectures on Psycho-Analysis:* "A child who has been put into second place by the birth of a brother or sister and who is now for the first time almost isolated from his mother, does not easily forgive her this loss of place; feelings which in an adult would be described as greatly embittered arise in him and are often the basis of a permanent estrangement" (1916–17, p. 334). Freud concentrates on the displaced child' s animosity toward his mother rather than on his feelings of sibling rivalry, but his observations are relevant to his own case. Like Berman, however, Colonna and Newman overlook the subjective dimension of Freud' s remarks and assert: that "since so many of Freud' s discoveries derived from his clinical observations of patients, it is not surprising that the emphasis on the role of siblings in the formation of neurosis seems to predominate" (p. 292). But if Freud highlighted sibling rivalry as a factor in neurosis and saw the situation mainly from the standpoint of the older child, it is because he experienced its effects in his own childhood long before he made any clinical observations.

As a final instance of our autobiographical mode of reading, we turn to *Beyond the Pleasure Principle,* a pivotal text for the study of the Holocaust because it introduces the concept of the death instinct.[17] Berman, as we have seen, quotes Freud' s account of the workings of a "fate neurosis" exhibited by "normal people." Freud offers a series of illustrative vignettes:

---

17 For a profound meditation on trauma and the Holocaust using the concept of the death instinct, see Laub (1998).

Thus we have come across people all of whose human relationships have the same outcome: such as the benefactor who is abandoned in anger after a time by each of his *protégés,* however much they may otherwise differ from each other, and who thus seems doomed to taste all the bitterness of ingratitude; or the man whose friendships all end in betrayal by his friend; or the man who time after time in the course of his life raises someone else into a position of great power or public authority and then, after a certain interval, himself upsets that authority and replaces him by a new one (1920g, p. 22).

By now it should not be surprising that each of these ostensibly fictional sketches is a disguised confession—indeed, three versions of the same story. It is Freud himself who is in the grip of the repetition compulsion, which causes him to taste the "bitterness of ingratitude" when he is betrayed or abandoned because "all of [his] human relationships have the same outcome."

But if Freud' s texts that bear on the death of a sibling and survivor guilt are tacitly autobiographical, it remains to ask why this "further subjective significance" should be latent rather than manifest in the text. In part this may be due to Freud' s reluctance to bare more of his soul in public than necessary. Beyond this deliberate aspect of Freud' s self-concealment, however, there is a sense in which the autobiographical component of his theoretical writing remains veiled and unconscious by virtue of the nature of trauma itself. As literary critic Cathy Caruth has argued, citing Freud' s comparison in *Moses and Monotheism* between the deferred effects of a traumatic neurosis in an accident and that experienced by the Jewish people following their murder of Moses, it is crucial to Freud' s concept of trauma that there be "an inherent latency within the experience itself.

The historical power of the trauma is not just that the experience is repeated after its forgetting, but that it is only in and through its inherent forgetting that it is first experienced at all" (Caruth, 1996, p. 17). Just as trauma can be experienced only through its forgetting, which is figured temporally as a period of latency, so it can be remembered only through a later retelling in which the most important aspects are repressed. It is therefore Freud' s own exemplary status as a traumatized subject that we can discern by excavating the buried autobiographical layers of his theoretical texts, though these must in large measure remain unconscious to Freud himself, no less than to any other writer.

Our investigation has proceeded along three converging paths: (1) a reflection on Freud' s life and work as inexhaustible sources of psychoanalytic knowledge; (2) an examination of the theme of the replacement child as it occurs in more or less typical contexts; and (3) a meditation on the Holocaust as a collective tragedy that defies comprehension, against the backdrop of which the issues of survival and replacement take on their most urgent meaning. What we continually find is that an insight that confronts us in any one of these three contexts also lies in wait in each of the other two, and it is this cumulative convergence of perspectives that affords us the closest approximation to understanding.

Freud claims in his letter to Fliess that the death of Julius left the "germ of reproaches" in him. But how can he be said to have remembered an occurrence that took place when he was still an infant? It seems probable that the impact of Julius' s death was transmitted to Freud indirectly through its effects on his mother and his subsequent elaboration of it in fantasy, rather than as an unmediated experience. As Samuel Slipp (1988) suggests, Freud' s response to Julius' s death may have been complicated by the fact that it was preceded only a month earlier by the death of his mother' s brother, also named Julius, though he nowhere mentions this circumstance. If Amalie Freud was in mourning for both her son and her brother at the same time that she was pregnant with Anna, it is unlikely that she would have had much energy left to devote to her first-born; and it may be for the effects of his mother' s depression as much as for the death of Julius per se that Freud continues to harbor a lifelong sense of self-reproach.

In a clinical paper dealing with the fantasies of children who take the place of deceased siblings, Vamik Volkan (1997) introduces the concept of deposit representations, a form of Klein' s projective identification. In Volkan' s words, "This concept refers to a type of intergenerational transmission where a parent or other important individual deposits into a child' s developing self-representation a preformed self-or object-representation that comes from the older individual' s mind" (p. 89). A precondition for the development of the intrapsychic structures characteristic of the replacement child, according to Volkan, is "the permeability between the psychic boundaries of the very young child and his mother, which allows the 'various psychic contents' to pass from one to the other' s self-representation" (p. 92).

Volkan' s formulation provides a theoretical framework for the observations of Wolfe and Bergmann about how the psychological dynamics of parents intervene between an incapacitated or deceased child and the sibling who is the latter' s surrogate. Masud Khan (1963) has elucidated the mother' s function as a protective shield against trauma for the infant. Because a depressed mother is often unable to perform this task successfully, this leads to what Khan calls a "cumulative trauma" in the child. Some such "intergenerational transmission" presumably took place between Amalie and Sigmund Freud, the effects of which can be traced in Freud' s preoccupation with survivor guilt and his sense of himself as "wrecked by success" owing to the death of Julius.

In the Holocaust context, the way the deceased child functions as an intermediary between the parent and the replacement child is illustrated by the experience of Anisfeld, who as a child was reminded of his father's lost children, not because they were ever spoken about, but because of his father's periodic "absences" or dream-like escapes from the present into the past. These fugue states of his father became Anisfeld's psychic reality. That his half-sisters were never spoken about left more room for him to fantasize about his father's relationship to these daughters. But rather than reducing the pressure to live up to the memory of these idealized first children—which is bad enough even in non-Holocaust families with replacement children, where the dead child is often talked about continuously—this intensified it, since Anisfeld and his sister felt as though they were saving an entire generation of people who were dead. Although his mother initially did not speak about her baby daughter who had starved to death, she eventually recounted this story. In contrast to his father, whom Anisfeld imagines gazing into the void and waiting to rejoin the children who were still present to his mind's eye, his mother loved all the people she had lost—the brother and mother after whom she named Leon and Ina, as well as her daughter, first husband, father, and other siblings—but also succeeded in loving her new children for who they were in their own right. How she managed not simply to survive but to bring Anisfeld and his sister into the world and make it possible for them to live remains for him a mystery as incomprehensible as the tragedy of the Holocaust.

Along with "Those Wrecked by Success" and "Criminals from a Sense of Guilt," the third paper comprising "Some Character Types Met with in Psycho-Analytic Work" is "The 'Exceptions.'" In this paper, Freud cites Shakespeare's crippled villain Richard III as a literary paradigm of those patients whose "neuroses were connected with some experience or suffering to which they had been subjected in their earliest childhood, one in respect of which they knew themselves to be guiltless, and which they could look upon as an unjust disadvantage imposed upon them" (1916, p. 313).[18] From one point of view, the claim to exceptional treatment on the part of those who have suffered unjustly in childhood may be regarded as the antithesis of the situation of replacement children, whose fate is to have been permitted to live where someone else has died. But these two cases are mirror images of one another. For if to be a replacement child involves a sense of not having being chosen, it also involves a sense of burden. This dialectic is a version of the pattern of the "oedipal victor," the son or daughter growing up in sole possession of the opposite-sex parent (most commonly after a divorce), whose triumph is purchased at the expense of a feeling of guilt for having psychically murdered the parent whose place he or she has assumed. But more than oedipal dynamics are involved in the case of the children of Holocaust survivors, for, as Bergmann and Jucovy have shown, the fantasy is transmitted across the generations that "the child has a special mission: his or her life goals are to be directed at restoring family pride by personal achievement, in order to heal past injuries" (1982, p. 288).

A key factor contributing to the ambivalent feelings of specialness in replacement children is the overprotectiveness often displayed by their parents, who hold themselves responsible for the deaths of their previous offspring. Bergmann and Jucovy report that the replacement children of Holocaust survivors "were often passionately protected; and when they became ill or were even mildly injured, the response of the parent was often more intense than in an average family or even in one where a child had died from illness or accident" (p. 12). This

---

18 Freud's example of Richard III has a heightened poignance for Anisfeld, whose struggle to accept the unalterable realities of the world entered a new phase when he contracted multiple sclerosis as a graduate student in his twenties.

either leads to spoiling the replacement child or makes him or her vulnerable and dependent, or both.

The consequences of extreme overprotectiveness can, of course, also be pathological in replacement children of parents who have nothing to do with the Holocaust. In one of the first and still most illuminating papers on this topic, Albert and Barbara Cain (1964) remark that "the mother' s normal or, in some cases, initially abnormal phobic concerns over illness and accidents were much magnified. She carried the constant panic-laden fantasy of this child, too, dying" (p. 447). In four of the six cases of "substitute children" they studied, Cain and Cain found that "the child had been very closely tied to the mother—the world was much too dangerous a place for the child to move freely and explore. He must stay nearby, lest 'something' happen." Not surprisingly, the results of such an upbringing were "infantile, immature, home-bound children, with strong passive-dependent elements and widespread ego restrictions" (p. 449).

Valuable support for the Cains' conclusions is provided by the Hungarian analyst Terez Virag (1984). Although Virag' s concern is with the transgenerational transmission of trauma among Holocaust survivors, her material bears on the replacement child syndrome.[19] In the case of Paul, a phobic boy brought to treatment by his mother because he resisted going to kindergarten, Virag reports that on one occasion he received an electric shock from a lamp, following which his mother grabbed him and dashed from the room. The salient feature in the family' s history is that the mother, born in 1948, sought to keep secret from Paul the fact of her Jewish origin and that her own mother had been deported with her parents to Auschwitz, where the latter had been gassed. Paul' s mother, who had several accidents involving

---

19 Although written before she was able to read *Generations of the Holocaust*, Virag' s paper draws on the work of Judith Kestenberg on the children of survivors, which is included in that volume.

gas poisoning and explosion in her life, was acutely sensitive to the danger of death from electricity, as she knew that the fence around the concentration camp was electrically charged. Thus, in this case of a grandchild of the Holocaust, as well as in others studies by Virag, "unconscious identification with the persecuted or exterminated members of the family was clearly observable—the more strikingly when the parents never talked about their Jewish origins with their children." She continues: "The symptoms, the play activity, the dreams, and fantasies of the children made it very clear that they knew about the family 'secrets'" (p. 58).

Virag' s narrative exemplifies Volkan's concept of deposit representations, though it must remain an open question whether the boy knew of his mother' s anxieties about electricity before the incident in which he received the shock or whether it took on its cathexis (Strachey' s translation of *Besetzung,* one definition of which is an electrical charge) of trauma only after witnessing his mother' s horrified reaction. In any event, Virag's vignette bears out Cain and Cain' s emphasis on the tendency even of non-Holocaust parents to magnify "phobic concerns over illness and accidents" that seem to threaten their replacement children. What is more, the mothers' proclivity to inhibit their children' s natural desire to explore the world lest disaster strike is exemplified in Virag' s report by the fact that the grandmother had "tied the daughter to herself in an extreme manner, insisting, for instance, that they take baths in the same tub even after the daughter had passed adolescence" (p. 52). As she elaborates, "the mother becomes unable to detach her child from herself as gently as she should for she knows that the external world is more likely to destroy than to nurture the child" (p. 57). Little Paul's kindergarten phobia thus becomes comprehensible as the third-generational outcome of a dynamic in the family system, in which his inhibition symbolizes the anxiety transmitted from his grandmother, the Auschwitz survivor, to his mother, for whom, tragically, this legacy was a shameful secret.

The behavior of Paul' s mother, although contaminated by the factor of Jewish self-hatred, raises the question of the attitude of the children of Holocaust survivors toward their parents. Such a child—whether or not literally a replacement—inevitably has an image of parents who were weak or humiliated, although this may be counterbalanced by a view of them as heroes for having survived the concentration-camo ordeal. In its negative aspect, the need for a child of Holocaust survivors to come to terms with the realization that his or her parents—far from being omnipotent—were actually powerless can be regarded as the cultural culmination of the famous incident, reported by Freud in *The Interpretation of Dreams,* in which his father told him how, in his youth, an anti-Semite had knocked his cap off his head and ordered him to get off the pavement. Upon learning that his father had meekly picked up his cap, Freud was fired with indignation at his "unheroic" conduct and consolidated his own identification (bound up with his inhibitions about traveling to Rome) with the vengeful Hannibal.

In his own childhood, Anisfeld looked upon his parents as heroes for what they had been through and upon his half-siblings as martyrs. At the same time, he recalls an anecdote that strikingly parallels that in the life of Freud. As a boy of seven years old, he began attending a primarily non-Jewish—indeed, anti-Jewish—school in southern New Jersey, where his recently immigrated parents had bought a chicken farm. During one of his first days at this new school, another child jumped on Anisfeld, bit a chunk out of his back, and called him a "dirty Jew."

In retaliation, he knocked out the attacker' s two front teeth. When he came home, he told his parents what had happened; the next day his father accompanied him to the school and confronted

118

the principal. The principal tried to make light of the incident, but his father would not let him do so. Anisfeld felt proud of him, but at a deeper level it wasn't enough. He wished that his father too had beaten up whoever was responsible for what happened—the principal, the child' s father, anyone! Like Freud' s father, Anisfeld' s father—who as a Holocaust survivor knew what anti-Semitism really meant— behaved with irreproachable dignity under the circumstances; but the boy, in the grip of his own inner world of fantasy, experienced a bitter feeling of disillusionment.

The last set of issues to be explored can be classified under the dual heading of incomplete mourning and identity disturbance. Since a replacement child in the strict sense is one who has been conceived in order to take the place of another child who has died, the first child has not been properly mourned—or even thought of as genuinely existing at all. Rather, in the parents' fantasy, he or she has been magically restored to life by the birth of the second. As C. Legg and I. Sherik (1976) point out, the premature replacement of a dead child by a new one may interrupt, distort, and delay the mourning process but cannot resolve it even though the expectations once held for the dead child are now transferred to a new one. They caution that in order for such a child to have a possibility of becoming a person in his own right, there should be an appropriate lapse of time between the death and either conception or the start of adoption proceedings for a new child. Along the same lines, Cain and Cain conclude that parents of replacement children exhibit a "distortion of the mourning process, a *pseudo resolution* of mourning" (1964, p. 452), beginning with the failure to accept the reality of their initial object loss. If there has been only a "pseudo resolution of mourning," the child who has been put in the place of someone else will necessarily have only a "pseudo identity." Cain and Cain observe that the parents of replacement children "compelled them to be like their dead siblings, to be identical with them, yet made it clear that they would never be accepted as 'the same,' and could never be really as good" (1964, p. 451).

The luxury of having time to wait was not available to Holocaust survivors. Having just emerged from a shattered and depopulated world, Jews both as individuals and as a group felt a great urgency to marry and have children as soon as possible. Each new child born in the D.P. camps was viewed as a phoenix rising from the ashes and celebrated as a "victory over Hitler." At the same time, the impossibility of adequately mourning everyone and everything that had been lost frequently gave rise to identity disturbances in the children of the postwar generation. Anisfeld idealized his parents as heroes and his perished half-siblings as martyrs, but what were he and his sister? He could not escape the thought that they were opportunists. He could never be certain that he was loved for who he was or for the genuineness of his achievements. When he performed an action from which he reaped a reward at someone else' s expense, he was convinced that he had initiated it; if his deeds were in any way altruistic, he doubted their sincerity. He believed that he should have been able to do the impossible and save the lives of his half-sisters even though he had not yet been born. This grandiose fantasy paradoxically made him scorn his actual accomplishments as worthless and even led him to be taken advantage of by others for their own glorification. Being unable to save the lives of his half-sisters led him, he believes, to treat his sister, Ina, in a manner that would not reveal to his murdered half-siblings that he loved Ina but not them. "I am sure" says Anisfeld, "that writing this paper is motivated in large part by my need to apologize to my sister Ina."

The literary and clinical dimensions of the replacement-child phenomenon have been probed in a richly suggestive paper by Andrea Sabbadini (1988). For Sabbadini, the key issue is that of dissociative ego processes, or what Freud (1919h) described as the uncanny. As

Sabbadini observes, the replacement or substitute child "is treated more as the embodiment of a memory than as a person in its own right" (p. 530). His primary clinical example, Jill, a woman in her early thirties who suffered from attacks of acute depressive anxiety, was born exactly nine months after the death of a nine-month-old sister, Angela. Sabbadini notes that if Jill was conceived on or near the day that her sister died, "in fantasy this could mean that the sexual intercourse responsible for Jill' s birth had taken place at the same time as Angela' s death" (p. 532).

Jill' s fantasy corresponds to a motif regularly found in replacement children and those afflicted with survivor guilt. It is summed up in the title of Maurice Apprey's 1987 paper, "When One Dies Another One Lives." This is, of course, the law of talion that is so often revealed in the unconscious thoughts and fantasies of those whose very survival was and continues to this day to be ruled by an unconscious sense of guilt. If someone else had to die so that I could live, I must have caused that person' s death, and I will then be haunted by the ghost of the rival I have slain, who becomes my double. As in the case of the oedipal victor, triumph and guilt are inextricably fused. Indeed, this is precisely what it means to be a survivor—to be forced to wonder why fate took someone else' s life instead of one' s own. As Magda Schoenfeld, born in Hungary after World War II to a mother who had lost all her family in the camps, told Anisfeld in an interview, her mother never ceased to lament: "Why did she have to live when the others had died? Why couldn't she die too? Why did she have to go on? Why did she have to live to carry on their memory?"

It is a striking coincidence that Angela should have died at nine months while Jill was born nine months after her sister' s death. Such symmetries and repetitions are regular features of the replacement-child syndrome. A truly uncanny example is provided by Vincent van Gogh (Nagera 1967). His brother, Vincent Willem van Gogh, was a still-born baby; one year later to the day, the artist was born and given exactly the same name (including Willem) as his brother. What is more, he was inscribed in the parish register under the same number as his brother had been a year earlier—that is, 29—and he later committed suicide on July 29, a few months after the birth of yet another Vincent, his brother Theo's child.

In a series of influential papers, George Pollock (1970) has studied the dynamics of mourning and anniversary reactions. In his view, "anniversary reactions result from unfinished or abnormal mourning, usually from childhood. With the resumption and resolution of mourning in the therapeutic situation, anniversary phenomena disappear permanently, leaving memories devoid of conflict" (p. 480). If anniversary reactions are the symptoms of incomplete mourning, what appears to be coincidence in the suicide of van Gogh can be seen as a psychologically motivated expression of emotional conflicts dating back to before his birth.

What is more, according to Pollock, in the case of replacement children "the dead sibling usually remains remembered at the age he was at the time of his death, and hence there is some arrest of the image in the minds of the survivors" (p. 478). That the image of the dead sibling—or anyone who is incompletely mourned—tends to be introjected at the age he or she was at the time of death is pertinent to Sabbadini's case of Jill, where the symbolic interval of nine months functions to consolidate her identification with her deceased sister, Angela. In addition to being the term of pregnancy, at nine months Angela had become a toddler and entered the individuation phase. Her sister's "lethally dangerous step toward independence" (Sabbadini 1988, p. 537) from the mother was reenacted when Jill experienced an overwhelming fear of death in the weeks preceding her menarche. Pollock has coined the term "double coincidence" to describe how the "temporal triggers" of anniversary reactions can reinforce each other (p. 347), as when a man arrives at the age that his father was at death while the man' s son is now the age that he was at that time. Pollock contrasts replacement with succession: "In succession we have progression, differentiation, and further development; in replacement we have the wish to keep time and events as they are or once were" (p. 353). Unfortunately, even when the analyst possesses theoretical understanding and seemingly inexhaustible patience, the wounds of trauma may be too deep for this transformation to be possible.

At the conclusion of his chapter "World Beyond Metaphor" in *Generations of the Holocaust,* James Herzog writes:

Elie Wiesel has repeatedly stated that survivors of the Holocaust live in a nightmare world that can never be understood. Although his opinion has its stark and bitter truth, we believe that the nightmare can be dispelled; that, through words, analysis can penetrate the shadowy inner world of the patient, which operates in metaphor, and, by illuminating it, diminish pain, and heal. Furthermore, analysis can demonstrate how the tragedy of one generation may be transmitted to the next, and then break the chain of suffering. Then survivors, children of survivors, and their children can remember, but not relive, and concentrate on the difficult task of being (1982, p. 119).

This passage eloquently expresses the dilemma with which we have struggled in this paper—the conflict between despair stemming from our participation in the legacy of the Holocaust and hope engendered by our belief in the curative powers of analysis. Wiesel' s pessimistic attitude is echoed even more insistently by Claude Lanzmann, whose eleven years devoted to the making of *Shoah* were guided by the conviction that, in his words, "there is an absolute obscenity in the very project of understanding" the Holocaust (1991, p. 478). Much as we admire Lanzmann' s achievement as an artist, however, we share with Herzog a faith that this cannot be the last word. As Harold Bloom (1991) has put it, "Freud' s peculiar strength was to say what could not be said, or at least to attempt to say it, thus refusing to be silent in the face of the unsayable" (p. 135). As adherents of analysis, we refuse to be silent in the face of the unsayable, even when that unsayable thing is the horror of the Holocaust.

Whether or not one is literally a replacement child, there will always be what Selma Fraiberg and her colleagues have called "ghosts in the nursery" (1975) whenever there is a personal or collective history of suffering. But unless the agonizing experiences that called these ghosts of the past into being can be recalled, and at least imperfectly communicated through the resources of language and art, they will remain unsaid forever.

REFERENCES

Anisfeld, L. (1998). "The Education of the Psychotherapist," in J. Reppen, ed., *Why I Became I Became a Psychotherapist.* New York: Jason Aronson, 1998.

Apprey, M. (1987). "When One Dies Another One Lives": The Invariant Unconscious Fantasy in Response to a Destructive Maternal Projective Identification. *Journal of the Melanie Klein Society* vol. 5, no. 2:18–52.

Arlow, J. A. (1972). The Only Child. *Psychoanal Q.* 41:507–536.

Bergmann, M. S., & M. E. Jucovy, eds. (1982). *Generations of the Holocaust.* New York: Basic Books.

Bergmann, T. & S. Wolfe. (1971). Observations of the Reactions of Healthy Children to Their Chronically-Ill Siblings. *Bull. Phila. Assn. Psychoanal.*, 21:145–61.

Berman, L. E. (1978). Sibling Loss as an Organizer of Unconscious Guilt: A Case Study. *Psychoanal Q.* 47:568–587.

Bloom, H. (1991). Freud: Frontier Concepts, Jewishness, and Interpretation. *Am. Imago*, 48:135–52.

Cain, A. C. & B. S. Cain. (1964). On Replacing a Child. *J. Amer. Acad. Child Psychiat.*, 3:443–56.

Caruth, C. (1996). *Unclaimed Experience: Trauma, Narrative, and History.* Baltimore: Johns Hopkins Univ. Press.

Colonna, A. B. and Newman, L. M. (1983). The Psychoanalytic Literature on Siblings. *Psychoanal. Study Child* 38:285–309.

Fraiberg, S., E. Adelson, & V. Shapiro. (1975). Ghosts in the Nursery: A Psychoanalytic Approach to the Problem of Impaired Infant-Mother Relationships. *J. Amer. Acad. Child Psychiat.*, 14:387–421.

Freud, S. (1900). The Interpretation of Dreams. *Standard Edition* 4 & 5.

——— (1916) Some Character-Types Met with in Psycho-Analytic Work. *Standard Edition* 14:311–33.

——— (1916–17). Introductory Lectures on Psycho-analysis. *Standard Edition* 15 & 16.

——— (1919h). The "Uncanny." *Standard Edition* 17:219–56.

——— (1920g). Beyond the Pleasure Principle. *Standard Edition* 18:7–64.

Gay, P. (1990). *Six Names in Search of an Interpretation. In Reading Freud: Explorations and Entertainments.* New Haven: Yale Univ. Press, pp. 54–73.

Herzog, J. (1982). World Beyond Metaphor: Thoughts on the Transmission of Trauma. In *Bergmann, M.S. and Jucovy, M.E., eds.*

Generations of the Holocaust. New York: Basic Books. 1982, pp. 103–19.

Jones, E. (1955). *The Life and Work of Sigmund Freud,* 2 vols. New York: Basic Books.

Khan, M. R. (1963). The Concept of Cumulative Trauma. *Psychoanal. Study Child* 18:286–306.

Lanzmann, C. (1991). The Obscenity of Understanding: An Evening with Claude Lanzmann. *Am. Imago,* 48:473–95.

Laub, D. (1998). Thanatos and Massive Psychic Trauma: A Psychoanalytic Theory of Remembering and Forgetting. *PsaElectronic Librarian* 16 pp.

Legg, C. & I. Sherik. (1976). The Replacement Child—A developmental tragedy: Some preliminary comments. *Child Psychiatry & Hum Development* 7:79–97.

Leon, I. G. (1996). Revising Psychoanalytic Understandings of Perinatal Loss *Psychoanal. Psychol.* 13:161–176.

Masson, J. M., ed. (1985). *The Complete Letters of Sigmund Freud to Wilhelm Fliess, 1887–1904.* Trans. J. M. Masson. Cambridge: Harvard Univ. Press.

Morrison, T. (1987). *Beloved.* New York: Knopf.

Nagera, H. (1967). *Vincent van Gogh: A Psychological Study.* London: Allen and Unwin.

Pollock, G.H. (1970). Anniversary Reactions, Trauma, and Mourning. *Psychoanal Q.* 39:347–371.

Pollock, G. (1972). Bertha Pappenheim's Pathological Mourning: Possible Effects of Childhood Sibling Loss *J. Amer. Psychoanal. Assn.* 20:478–93.

Sabbadini, A. (1988). The Replacement Child. *Contemp. Psychoanal.* 24:528–547.

Schur, M. (1972). Freud: Living and Dying. New York: Int. Univ. Press.

Slipp, S. (1988). Freud's Mother, Ferenczi, and the Seduction Theory. *J. Am. Acad. Psychoanal. Dyn. Psychiatr.*, 16:155–65.

Yerushalmi, Y. H. (1982). *Zakhor: Jewish History and Jewish Memory.* Seattle: Univ. of Washington Press.

Virag, T. (1984). Children of the Holocaust and Their Children' s Children: Working Through Current Trauma in the Psychotherapeutic Process. *Dynam. Psychother.*, 2-1:47–60.

Volkan, V. & Ast, G. (1997). *Siblings in the Unconscious and Psychopathology.* Madison, Conn.: IUP.

CHAPTER 7

Isakower-Like Experience on the Couch: A Contribution to the Psychoanalytic Understanding of Regressive Ego Phenomena

[(1985). Psychoanalytic Quarterly 54:415–434.]

ABSTRACT: Since Isakower's original contribution of 1938, Isakower phenomena have been viewed as primitive experiences involving maternal breast, womb, and face imagery. This clinical report harks back to the less well-known hypothesis with which Isakower concluded his paper: he suggested that these perceptual experiences are related to childhood oedipal masturbatory fantasies at the time of going to sleep. In this paper four Isakower-like phenomena experienced by a patient on the couch are reported in the dynamic context in which they occurred. It is argued that these phenomena constitute a type of regressive ego experience that defends against oedipal conflict.

Since Isakower's classic paper of 1938, the "Isakower phenomenon," along with related hypnagogic, dream, and hypnopompic experiences, has been subject to continuing scrutiny in the psychoanalytic literature. Isakower, it will be recalled, described a hypnagogic phenomenon with visual, sensory, and auditory components. On falling asleep, individuals beheld a shadowy, undifferentiated, and usually round object, which got nearer and nearer, and then smaller and farther off. This hallucination included vague sensations of something crumpled and dry in the mouth and on the skin, along with feelings of floating, sinking, or giddiness. Some individuals undergoing these visual and sensory experiences heard vague noises (see Fink [1967] for a more comprehensive summary of the features of the Isakower phenomenon).

Virtually without exception, literature on the Isakower phenomenon has presented the experience as a type of primitive perceptual memory. For Isakower (1938), the phenomenon suggested a "hypercathexis of the oral zone" that took the form of "mental images of sucking at the mother's breast and of falling asleep there when satisfied" (p. 341). Lewin (1946), (1948), (1953) and Rycroft (1951), in extending Isakower's phenomenological description to the "dream screen" and a category of "blank dreams," retained his belief that such phenomena have the significance of early memories. As Lewin (1953) observed, "Genetically, Isakower phenomena, dream screen, and blank dreams are in essence the same thing; they reproduce some of the impressions that the smallest baby has at the breast" (p. 198). Following these pioneering contributions, several theorists sought to expand the range of early experience implicated in the Isakower phenomenon. Spitz (1955) believed that the visualized mass approaching the subject was not only the breast but, perhaps more primarily, the mother's face. Sperling (1957) connected such "hypnagogic hallucinations" to toddler-age experiences of thumb sucking, whereas Almansi (1958), citing Spitz, again traced them to the mother's face and voice as well as to her breast. These conjectures, be it noted, were based on extra-analytic data, especially the hypnagogic reports of persons in treatment.

Isakower (1938) concluded his original presentation with a speculative hypothesis about the onset and meaning of the reported phenomena. He submitted that the phenomena were not normally associated with the act of falling asleep, but instead "indicate[d] a disturbance in the process, occurring at a stage when it [i.e., the process of falling asleep] has already been at work for some time" (p. 343). This disturbance, he believed, emanated from "infantile masturbation, practised while the child is going to sleep, [which] is accompanied by incestuous phantasies which the super-ego repudiates" (p. 344). Isakower phenomena occurred by way of preventing the mobilization of a conflict which would interfere with the process of falling asleep. As a substitute for a "disturbing genital and instinctual wish directed towards the incestuous subject... there appears the situation of the infant at the breast or in the womb, either situation innocent and not subject to any prohibition" (p. 344). In this way, the incipient conflict is mastered, "so that the process of going to sleep may be carried through" (p. 345). Lewin (1948) and Rycroft (1951) posited a comparable dynamic to account for the "rolling away" of the dream screen and the experience of the "blank dream," respectively, but they departed from Isakower in construing these phenomena as successful defenses against early oral conflicts and frustrations (see Stern, 1961).

Neither Isakower nor Lewin nor Rycroft offered analytic data to support their dynamic formulations. Nor, for that matter, have more recent contributors who, following Isakower's lead, have stressed the analytic recovery of primal scene memories and attendant anxiety as catalysts for the defensive mobilization of Isakower-like breast and face imagery (Little, 1970); (Pacella, 1975); (Stern, 1961).

In the clinical material to follow, I will offer analytic data that shed new light on these dynamic considerations. Specifically, I will present a case in which Isakower-like phenomena occurred on the couch, rather than in bed on falling asleep or awakening. I believe this report represents one of the only accounts of such phenomena actually occurring in analysis, a possibility mentioned by Stern (1961) but, to date, borne out only in the clinical data of Fink (1967) and Glenn (1970).[20]

CASE REPORT

Mr. C., now in his fourth year of analysis, is forty-two years old, three times married and three times divorced. He currently lives alone and works as a middle-level executive for a large corporation. His presenting symptoms, which prompted treatment when he was assigned to an overseas branch of his company and his second wife was preparing to leave him, included intermittent severe anxiety attacks with shortness of breath and palpitations, depression, severe insomnia, and intrusive sexual (primarily homosexual), aggressive, and suicidal thoughts. He received psychotherapy, tranquilizers, and a brief period of analysis before being transferred back to the United States and referred to me.

Mr. C. is the third child of a European immigrant couple; his father was fifty-three years old and his mother thirty-six at the time of his birth. The father, a pastry chef, worked long hours six days a week

---

20 Easson (1973) described an Isakower-like experience in a psychotherapy patient who was sitting up. Finn (1955) also reported on a recurrent, waking Isakower-like phenomenon in a psychotherapy patient without making clear whether or not the phenomenon was actually experienced during a therapy session. Isakower, in his original paper (1938), referred to one patient who "fell into the state in question one day during an analytic hour, just as she was speaking of having masturbated during the previous night" (p. 332).

and was inaccessible to the children on his day off. Taciturn and aloof in bearing, but authoritarian in his expectations, he demanded and received absolute obedience from his wife and children. The mother, for her part, was similarly strict and unyielding, although she did spend considerable time with the patient. Mr. C. described her as disapproving and unaffectionate, as "never giving in." From childhood, he had felt much anger and resentment toward both parents, but had always been too fearful to express these feelings.

Mr. C.'s inability to establish satisfying, long-term relationships with women became the main focus of analytic work, particularly during the past two years as his presenting symptoms abated. We initially focused on his choice of attractive but dependent women whose need to be taken care of paralleled his own neediness vis-à-vis his mother and, now, his analyst. More recent work has dealt with the role of oedipal fear and guilt in his continuing inability to achieve a mutually satisfying relationship with a woman.

Mr. C. is my first patient each day, and we occasionally ride up together in the elevator. Over the course of the several months preceding the sessions to be reported, he admitted with great reluctance and embarrassment that he had been having intrusive sexual thoughts during these elevator rides to the office. Specifically, he found himself wanting to stare at my back and buttocks, to reach out and touch me and kiss me. These thoughts often continued after he lay down on the couch, when he wanted to reach back, touch me, and hold on to my penis. In the analysis these intrusive thoughts were traced back to childhood wishes toward his father, re-experienced transferentially and in his present maladaptive behavior as well. The latter included intrusive sexual and aggressive thoughts at work, anxiety at meetings with his superiors, and the pattern of finding all the women with whom he established relationships, with the notable exception of his second wife, ultimately disappointing.

The onrush of oedipal material in recent months, particularly as it pertains to the devaluation of his father, has been accompanied by a series of primitive perceptual sensations on the couch. On one occasion, he reported feeling very small, as if he were scrunched up toward his chest and head; this was accompanied by a sense of floating, which was followed by a feeling of weight, of heaviness on his chest. Following this experience, he associated to a dream that revolved around his perception of his father as "a lot less noble" than he would have liked to picture him, i.e., as physically unimpressive, self-centered, and even effeminate. He recalled his wearing an apron to prepare his chocolate sauce. On another occasion, the patient's disparaging remarks about entering the parental bedroom—"it was no great shakes, so what?"—led him to feel blank and giddy; he felt as if a large hole were opening up in front of him, a whirlpool that was expanding in his mouth and into which he was subsequently falling. In a later session, his adoption of a position of authority with respect to his older sister, who had appealed to him for financial guidance earlier in the day, led me to remark that her request had put him "in his father's shoes." With this interpretation, he began to feel dizzy: "The room is spinning, tipping like a ship does in water, like a rocking cradle. I feel very unstable. All of a sudden my supports are falling. I am out of balance." In all these instances, we see perceptual distortion as a regressive defense against revived oedipal fantasies and conflicts.

I now wish to report four sessions in which Mr. C.'s regressive perceptual experiences had a distinctly Isakower-like cast.

Session I

In this session, Mr. C. announced his feeling that he had entered the final stage of treatment. After ruminating about how this wish corresponded to his wish to stop discussing the homosexual fantasies with which we had recently been preoccupied, he associated to S., the wife of M., one of his best friends. S. had come up several times in the past, in dreams and associations, and invariably represented his mother, another married woman who had been inaccessible to him. Mr. C. reported that he had had sexual fantasies about S. while getting dressed that morning. From his thoughts about S., he went on to recall that as he had taken off his jacket in the waiting room prior to his session, he had seen me in the doorway and experienced an impulse to kiss me. He surmised that he had perhaps been thinking about S. in order to push his homosexual thoughts out of his mind. I replied that this might be the case, but added that perhaps his homosexual thoughts were being used to deny his heterosexual designs on inaccessible women. I added that in the past S. had stood both for his mother and for my own wife.

Mr. C. immediately indicated how very difficult it was for him to talk about my wife; it was a subject that was "off limits." He experienced the fear that, if he related his fantasies about my wife, I would throw him out of the office. When I reminded him that his greatest childhood fear had been making his father angry and being thrown out of the house, he became aware of a wish to avoid the entire topic. At this moment he had an image of large bubbles or balloons, perhaps three feet wide, coming toward him from the left at about the level of his mid-section. The bubbles or balloons pressed in on him.

He said:

Your wife's office is next door. That is the direction the bulges are coming from. The bulge is pushing the wall as if the wall is made of some soft material. Then there is a different bulge which is coming more from the right. The first bulge is round and spherical; the other one is longer and cylindrical. It is

135

further away; it is like a giant penis. It feels threatening, destructive, as if it is saying, "Here I am, all this is mine, don't get any ideas."

Mr. C. proceeded to associate to his father's penis, which was "large and noticeable; it made its presence known." When I injected that "it's as if Daddy's penis is saying, 'Mommy is mine,'" the patient became anxious and said:

> I wish we could talk about something else. I would rather talk about homosexuality than this. I feel like kissing you. I don't want to talk about your wife. It still seems off limits to me; it feels off limits, and it's even hard to accept rationally that it is something you want to talk about. I know you tell me that I can talk about it but I feel you're only doing it because you have to, because that's the way it is in the rules, but you're doing it in a half-hearted way. I don't want to pursue it. It's hard for me even to think about it. You're telling me I should talk about it because of all your training, something you would do because you had to but nevertheless you don't want to.

I believe Mr. C.'s imagic experience during this hour involved a vivid Isakower-like phenomenon, although it probably had a perceptual referent beyond that of the mother's breast. To be sure, the round balloon or bulge may well have represented the breast, but it may also have represented a protuberant abdomen. His sense of smallness in relation to the large approaching object certainly suggests that the experience was linked to memories from infancy or early childhood. Sensations of something pressing down on him, which he experienced during this and several sessions, may point to the experience of an adult pressing down on a small child.

136

This analytic event is relevant to the meaning of Isakower-like phenomena by virtue of the dynamic context in which it occurred. It will be recalled that it followed my attempt to point out a resistance and overcome a defense via an interpretation. Mr. C. had been discussing homosexual fantasies directed toward his father and, in the transference, toward the analyst. Although he had already overcome considerable resistance to confronting this anxiety-provoking issue, I decided to explore the possibility that he had overcome one type of resistance in order to defend against a still more threatening topic. My intervention, based on various associations, the material of preceding sessions, and my overall knowledge of the patient, pointed to the possibility that the homosexual fantasies with which we had been wrestling defended against an oedipal fantasy. In effect, Mr. C. had been saying, "Don't worry about me, I'm not a rival for your wife, I am a homosexual. I'm not going to steal mommy-wife; I'm only going to kiss you." This defensive posture had helped him ward off the potentially threatening, powerful analyst.

Session 2

Following oedipal associations to his older sister and, via displacement, to a younger niece, Mr. C. reported a meeting of the preceding day with his supervisor at work. The supervisor, an older man with whom Mr. C. had good rapport, had confided in him about his own marital problems, recounting his first divorce, subsequent remarriage, and preparations for a second divorce. he revealed his loneliness and concerns about meeting people. Mr. C. had felt great anxiety during this conversation; he was shocked that his respected superior could confide in him about his personal life. As he recounted the incident in analysis, the anxiety returned. He experienced a tightness in the center of his chest and reported this Isakower-like phenomenon: I have an image of something moving away from me; it is a large white cloud. It has a stem and a ball at the end. It is like a mushroom cloud. Now it looks like something else.

The "something else" in question was the logo for the Ladd Company that Mr. C. had noticed at the beginning of a movie he had recently seen. The logo was a computer representation which changes into a green tree that then fades into the distance. In his associations to the logo, Mr. C. observed that the Ladd Company is owned by David Ladd, the extremely successful son of the actor, Alan Ladd. He expressed his admiration for the logo, which he saw as an attractive emblem of the outdoors; the tree was green, growing and alive. Then, overcoming considerable resistance, he associated from the logo to the idea of a son surpassing his father, proving himself more talented and successful than his father. This led him to recall again how shocked he had been when his supervisor had turned to him for support and advice. He then associated to a dream in which the manifest content was the large house of his aunt and uncle in which he had spent many happy summers in his youth; the house was a comforting place in which he had always felt safe and protected. He recalled his childhood feelings in that house, contrasting his smallness and dependency with the "adult" role forced on him by his supervisor the previous day.

This Isakower-like phenomenon again assumes a regressive significance in the context of a prospective oedipal victory. The image of the mushroom cloud conveys danger and also has a more regressive, presumably oral significance (see Almansi, 1961).[21] In this

---

21 Note that I am only imputing oral significance to the image of the mushroom cloud; I am not suggesting that this manifest image connotes oral conflict. To the contrary, I am arguing that an oedipal conflict can assume the guise of manifestly oral imagery, be it the "mushroom cloud" reported in this session, or the images of the "cow's udder" and the "white stretcher with the dark center" that emerged in the session described below. To this extent, the clinical data reported here exemplify

way the Isakower-like phenomenon gratifies a preoedipal wish in the context of defending against an oedipal wish. The visual image of the Ladd tree which followed the Isakower-like mushroom cloud seems to represent a step up the developmental ladder. It is transparently related to the overcoming of oedipal anxieties; Mr. C. perceived David Ladd as a son who had surpassed his father and achieved prominence in his own right.

I should point out that the oedipal theme of sons surpassing fathers was very active in the transference at this juncture. At the beginning of the session Mr. C. had complained to me that the door to my office had not been fixed very well, implying that he could do a better job himself. The preoccupation with being stronger, healthier, and more successful than the father continued into the next session. Mr. C. began by telling me how "thin and frail" I looked, then associated to the fact that his supervisor, who had recently appealed to him for support and understanding, was not only saddled with personal problems, but had recently undergone by-pass surgery. He could no longer be counted strong on that score either.

Session 3

Two sessions after the one in which Mr. C. experienced the image of the mushroom cloud, he experienced a different Isakower-like phenomenon. He continued to be preoccupied with "strong" and "weak" fathers, partially displaced onto M., the close friend, to whose wife, S., he was strongly attracted. In this session he reported a dream set in his childhood home. In the dream M. and S. were going out

---

Arlow's (1955) caveat that oral imagery cannot invariably be correlated with oral conflict.

somewhere while Mr. C. was "getting ready" in the bedroom. He was making elaborate preparations, trying to keep safe something of value. His preparations concerned a large, black plastic container which resembled a garbage bag; it also looked like a condom. S. was not being cordial in the dream; she was a background figure. M., on the other hand, got ready fast, donning only a sweater. In the dream, Mr. C. was struck by the fact that M.'s sweater was not very masculine; it was a light-colored, button-up sweater that somehow seemed feminine.

Mr. C. associated from M. to his father, who had also dressed very quickly and worn cardigan sweaters like the one M. wore in the dream. His associations to the garbage bag-condom went back to his sense of oedipal inferiority; he was not able to fill the condom. His small penis was the penis of a child, but it was valuable nonetheless. His father's penis, on the other hand, was big and flabby. In addition to a flabby penis, his father had had rheumatism, false teeth, a bald head, and skinny legs. Mr. C. next associated to the meeting several days ago with his supervisor; he reflected that he alone knew of the latter's impending divorce from his second wife. As the session ended, he had an image of a man in the kitchen wearing an apron, standing next to a large, powerful machine. From the machine, he associated to images of his father in the kitchen during his childhood. His father had a grinding machine—a kind of slicer or mixer—that was dangerous. As Mr. C. went back and forth from the threatening (i.e., castrating) father of his childhood and this same father as sick, weak, and effeminate (i.e., the father who had worn an apron and cardigan sweaters), he had the following Isakower-like experience: a large white mass came toward him and moved away. It looked to him like a cow's udder, a large bag with a long protuberance. He observed that the protuberance simultaneously resembled a nipple and a penis, and then associated once more to his father's flabby penis, an image that had followed his thoughts about M., the cardigan sweater, M.'s high blood pressure, and his father's terminal illness.

I believe this Isakower-like phenomenon can be seen as a regressive reaction to the castration anxiety that had been mobilized just prior to its appearance. Immediately after the association to the supervisor who had called on him for support and reassurance, thereby providing him an "oedipal victory," Mr. C. associated to the menacing oedipal father of his youth. The image of his father in the kitchen with his grinding machine able to inflict injury was a castrating image par excellence. The Isakower-like image of the moving cow's udder thereupon acquired a twofold regressive significance. As a symbol of the nurturant nipple of infancy, it signaled a retreat to primitive oral satisfactions. At the same time, as a symbol of the father's "flabby" penis, it pointed to the devalued father whose poor health, weakness, and effeminate appearance belied his status as a threatening oedipal castrator. In the following session, Mr. C. returned to the Isakower-like image of the moving cow's udder, associating again to his father's penis as droopy and ill-defined, as neither potent nor virile nor formidable.

Session 4

Mr. C. began the session by reporting a dream of the preceding night in which he had a part in a production of Macbeth, but could not remember his lines. In the dream, the play was called off at the last minute, at which point Mr. C. woke up. He immediately associated to the movie, The Dresser, in which another actor had forgotten his lines. He then associated to Macbeth as a play that "didn't seem to come out too well because of Lady Macbeth." From Lady Macbeth he associated to me: just as she had whispered in Macbeth's ear that he

141

should kill the king, so I had been whispering in his ear, telling him to get rid of his father. Mr. C. then recounted that as he had walked to the office that morning, he had noticed a newspaper headline, "Woman Kills Shrink." It made him angry toward me. He recalled the dream in which his lines had not made any sense and then a scene from The Dresser in which Albert Finney attempted to seduce a young girl in the dressing room. This attempted seduction of a "young" woman by an "old" man had strong parental reference, given the age difference between his parents. The character in the movie was "like the young woman I would like but don't have. Somehow the old man is in the way." I reminded him that in his dream he had been unable to "play the part"; he added that the play had been canceled, i.e., he again felt safe, the show was over, he could go home. At this juncture I made an interpretation that brought together the interrelated themes of this and recent sessions. I am referring to Mr. C.'s simultaneous wish to have my support and to kill me (patient kills shrink), the transferential analogue of his childhood conflict toward his father. The transference conflict pertained to Mr. C.'s realization that to be rid of me would be to forgo the support he had come to expect from me, i.e., the support he had expected but never received from his father. I suggested that he wished to be rid of me so that he could go into my wife's adjacent office just as he had wished to dispose of his father so that he could enter his parent's bedroom. The patient was affected by this interpretation, paused, and then experienced the following Isakower-like phenomenon. An image was coming closer and receding into the distance. It was a white hospital bed which, as he described it, seemed more like a stretcher with a dark blanket covering the bed portion of the rolling stretcher. The bed or stretcher was being rolled into an ambulance. The ambulance, too, was white.

Mr. C. observed that the stretcher seemed to be moving on a street with row houses with white sheets hanging out on the lines. He associated this image with the street of his childhood, the locale of his father's several medical emergencies. The images of the ambulance and the hospital bed led back to his father's hospitalization when Mr. C. was between six and ten years old. He recalled being brought to the hospital by his mother and told to look up to the window to see his father; he recollected that he "couldn't give a shit. All I wanted was my mother. I didn't want her to worry about my father so she would be less available to me." From here, he associated to the time of his father's terminal illness. Mr. C. was then twenty-six. He had been summoned home by his mother and recalled going into his parents' bedroom and seeing his deceased father, a veritable skeleton, lying on the bed. But this central memory again pertained to his indifference at the time; he had not even attended his father's funeral. I offered the reconstruction that shortly after he had viewed his father's body, an ambulance had come and taken the body to the morgue for an autopsy. He had remembered that despite his mother's opposition, an autopsy had indeed been performed in view of the fact that his father had died at home.

What can we make of the Isakower-like phenomenon experienced in this session? I believe the visual image of the white stretcher with the dark center moving toward the white ambulance is connected to the repressed memory of his father's body being taken to the morgue in an ambulance; he "sees" the ambulance in the context of confronting his death wishes toward his father which were revived in the transference. The regression to this primitive perceptual mode defended against his conflicted, hostile feelings toward his father. We see this defense at work in the representational "whiteness" of the imagery: the stretcher, the ambulance, and the sheets on the clotheslines (cf., Freud's [1918b, p. 43, n.] remarks on the white color of wolves in the dream of the Wolf Man). On the other hand, the bed-ambulance image, with its dark center, was a moving gestalt which may have represented the approaching and receding bottle with its dark nipple or the breast with its central aureola and nipple.

This moving image, I believe, ties into Mr. C.'s associations to his early fear of losing his mother when his father became ill and required her ministrations. These feelings coalesced in his childhood feelings outside the hospital, where he held on to his mother's hand while looking up at his father, who looked down on him from his window. In this memory, we see the gratification of an oedipal wish (he and his mother are together while his father is away) but also the guilt that is the sequel to this gratification (his father is hospitalized because of his aggression toward him) and the anxiety to which this guilt gives rise (he will lose his mother's support if his father dies). It is this fear of losing his mother's support and affection which underlies his more superficial "adult" concern about losing paternal support by "killing" the analyst; this fear is regressively revived and overcome in the image of the ambulance-breast approaching him. In fact, the instinctual wish is gratified in two ways. With the approach of the ambulance-breast he gratifies his libidinal oedipal wishes; with the moving away of the ambulance-breast, he gratifies the aggressive component of the oedipal fantasy, i.e., his dead father is taken away by ambulance. The complex relationship between the positive oedipal wishes and the anxiety-inducing superego component which jointly account for Mr. C.'s infantile neurosis can thereupon be delineated.

DISCUSSION

I believe the analytic data presented here enlarge our understanding of Isakower-like phenomena in clinically fruitful ways. By attending to the dynamic context in which Isakower-like phenomena occur, I believe I have demonstrated that, clinically speaking, these phenomena must be situated within the larger "universe" of regressive ego phenomena we routinely encounter. This conclusion, which is consistent with findings reported by the Kris Study Group two decades ago (Joseph, 1965), runs counter to the dramatically singular quality that has been imputed to Isakower phenomena over the years. Following the Kris Study Group, I submit that Isakower-like phenomena are but one category of regressive ego phenomena; other categories include distortions of the body image, disturbances of perception in the sense of time, depersonalization, and drowsiness on the couch. With all these phenomena, regression follows "the presence of anxiety and the need of the ego to deal with an anxiety-provoking situation" (Joseph, 1965, p. 93). The Kris Study Group's dynamic explanation of regressive ego phenomena, it should be noted, parallels Arlow's (1959) perspective on a broad range of déjà vu experiences. Pacella (1975) has persuasively demonstrated the similarity between some déjà vu experiences and Isakower-like phenomena. The four sessions summarized here suggest that Isakower-like phenomena, like other regressive ego phenomena occurring within analysis, achieve dynamic significance within the context of those issues of conflict, preoedipal and oedipal, which provoke anxiety in treatment.

Beyond demonstrating that Isakower-like phenomena are regressive ego phenomena that must be explored analytically at the time they occur, I believe the four instances described above contribute to our understanding of the phenomenology of specifically Isakower-like experiences in a number of ways:

1. In contrast to the various speculative attempts to tie Isakower-like phenomena genetically to primitive oral antecedents, my clinical data point to the catalytic importance of oedipal issues in instigating these regressive episodes. This finding, perhaps ironically, harks back to Isakower's own hypotheses about the meaning of the phenomena he

145

reported. While equating these phenomena with a "hypercathexis of the oral zone," he imputed their generation to "infantile masturbation, practised while the child is going to sleep," which is "accompanied by incestuous phantasies which the super-ego repudiates." The data drawn from my case point to the preeminent role of castration anxiety in mobilizing Isakower-like phenomena. This finding is consistent with the Kris Study Group's conclusion that castration anxiety was the most frequent "danger situation" accounting for regressive ego phenomena in general.[22]

2. Within the context of oedipal considerations, my clinical data highlight the frequently defensive function of Isakower-like phenomena which occur in analysis (Fink, 1967); (Glenn, 1970); (Pacella, 1975). In the case of Mr. C., these phenomena defended against (a) consciousness of the oedipal wishes, especially as experienced within the transference (session 1); (b) the oedipal devaluation of the father and the father's penis with respect to his own father (session 3) and in the transference as well (session 2); (c) the anxiety and guilt consequent to the realization of the oedipal fantasies and the adoption of a "fatherly" role, i.e., the anxiety and guilt of sons who surpass their fathers (sessions 2 and 3); and (d) the anxiety that accompanied his realization that, vanquishing his father,

---

22 The analytic findings reported here dovetail with a case reported by Glenn (1970). Glenn's patient experienced an Isakower-like phenomenon in analysis after describing a childhood masturbation fantasy: "Her mouth became dry, she felt as if her tongue, the roof of her mouth, and her body in general were swollen. Her eyes, especially the fingers that touched the couch, felt enlarged. It reminded her of 'swollen breasts and vagina'" (p. 276). Associations subsequent to this perceptual experience revolved around the fact that the patient's clitoris was her only body part that did not feel swollen. Analysis then established that the patient was denying her (oedipal) sexual excitement by having her body swell rather than her clitoris. Glenn thereupon proposed that the case illustrated a "regression from oedipal excitement to a preoedipal oral level of satisfaction and the associated ego state" (p. 276). With respect to a second case as well, Glenn reported that "sexual excitement resulted in a regression to a preoedipal state, evidenced by the experience of the Isakower phenomenon" (p. 279).

he would forgo the support and affection of the mother (and more superficially the "good" analyst-father).

3. The precise nature of the early fixations that gave an oral cast to Mr. C.'s oedipal defenses is an issue that has not been addressed in this communication. Although I do not have a fully satisfactory answer to this question, I can offer a developmental hypothesis consistent with my analytic work with the patient. I believe that Mr. C.'s seeming hypercathexis of the oral zone masked a hypercathexis of the visual sphere. His childhood had been characterized by a paucity of verbal communication with both father and mother. The latter frequently responded to his misbehavior with periods of silence. It was in the context of such episodes that Mr. C. probably tended to make up for verbal silence with visual imagery. I further suspect a primal scene constituent to his early "visualizing" propensities. His bedroom was separated from his parents' bedroom only by French doors covered by transparent curtains. The fact that Mr. C. lay at night facing the wall away from the French doors may have provided additional impetus for the development of a heightened visual imagination.

4. My clinical data support Fink (1967) in assigning an important place to primal scene experiences in the generation of Isakower-like phenomena, though they fall short of supporting her claim that such experiences represent the "one constant psychological situation . . . that is of major etiological significance in the production of the Isakower phenomenon in the analytic situation" (p. 281). In session 1, in particular, primal scene material, while not overt, was seemingly embodied in Mr. C.'s concern with what was happening in the next room, my wife's office. This concern seemed to correspond to his childhood situation when his room had been adjacent to the parents' bedroom.

5. Isakower's original report stipulated as the visual component of the phenomenon a shadowy and undifferentiated round object which

got nearer and nearer, then smaller and farther off. My clinical data suggest that certain Isakower-like phenomena may be differentiated and discrete, while still presenting the quality of getting nearer and larger and then smaller and farther off. With Mr. C., it was this latter characteristic which was a persistent feature of all his regressive perceptual experiences.

6. The frequent "whiteness" of Mr. C.'s visual experiences (especially in sessions 2, 3, and 4) suggest that isolation of affect is a significant feature of Isakower-like phenomena. This feature was most prominent in relation to the memory and perception of the white ambulance in session 4. This finding is consistent with the Kris Study Group's conclusion that with respect to regressive ego phenomena in general, "the regression was in the service of reinforcing the isolation of the affective responses to the provoking situation" (Joseph, 1965, p. 99). Such isolation is one prominent aspect of the defensive function of such regressive phenomena.

In conclusion, I would like to invite colleagues to relate their clinical experience of Isakower-like phenomena, along with the dynamic context in which such phenomena occurred. An infusion of fresh analytic data holds the prospect of providing new insight into this fascinating, if conceivably perplexing, phenomenon.

SUMMARY

Since Isakower's pioneering contribution of 1938, Isakower phenomena have been viewed as primitive perceptual experiences involving maternal breast, womb, and face imagery. Isakower himself understood this imagery in terms of a "hypercathexis of the oral zone."

The clinical data presented here hark back to the less well-known hypothesis with which Isakower concluded his report. He surmised that these perceptual experiences were sequelae to incestuous oedipal fantasies precipitated by infantile masturbation at the time the child was going to sleep. The imagic situation of the infant at the breast or in the womb was a regressive substitute for the "disturbing genital and instinctual wish directed towards the incestuous object." My data underscore the dynamic meaning of Isakower-like experiences as regressive ego phenomena that defend against reactivated oedipal conflicts. This verdict parallels the findings of the Kris Study Group with respect to regressive ego phenomena in general; in fact, I have argued that the dramatic quality of Isakower-like productions recedes once we locate them, dynamically speaking, within the larger universe of regressive ego phenomena.

REFERENCES

Almansi, R.J. (1958), A hypnagogic phenomenon. *Psychoanalytic Q.* 7:539–546.

——— (1961), Cloud fantasies. *Journal of Hillside Hospital* 10:143–153.

Arlow, J.A. (1955), Notes on oral symbolism. *Psychoanalytic Q.* 24:63–74.

——— (1959), The structure of the déjà vu experience. *Journal of the American Psychoanalytic Association* 7:611–631.

Easson, W.M. (1973). The earliest ego development, primitive memory traces, and the Isakower phenomena. *Psychoanal. Q.* 42:60–72.

Fink, G. (1967). Analysis of the Isakower phenomenon. *J. Am. Psychoanal. Assoc.* 15:281–293.

Finn, M.H.P. (1955). A note on a waking "blank stage" analogous to Isakower's phenomena, the dream screen, and blank dreams. *Psychoanal. Rev.* 42 99–103.

Freud, S. (1918b). From the history of an infantile neurosis *Standard Edition* 17.

Glenn, J. (1970). Regression and displacement in the development of the bodyphallus equation. In *The Unconscious Today: Essays in Honor of Max Schur* ed. M. Kanzer. New York: Int. Univ. Press, pp. 274–287.

Isakower, O. (1938). A contribution to the patho-psychology of phenomena associated with falling asleep. *Int. J. Psychoanal.* 19:331–345.

Joseph, E.D., Editor (1965). *Beating Fantasies and Regressive Ego Phenomena in Psychoanalysis. Kris Study Group of the New York Psychoanalytic Society, Monogr. 1* New York: Int. Univ. Press.

Lewin, B.D. (1946). Sleep, the mouth, and the dream screen Psychoanal. Q. 15:419–434 Reprinted *in Selected Writings of Bertram D. Lewin* ed. J.A. Arlow. New York: *Psychoanal. Q.,* 1973 pp. 87–100.

――― (1948). Inferences from the dream screen *Int. J. Psychoanal.* 29:224–231 Reprinted in *Selected Writings of Bertram D. Lewin,* ed. J.A. Arlow. New York: Psychoanal. Q. Inc, 1973 pp. 101–114.

――― (1953). Reconsideration of the dream screen *Psychoanal. Q.* 22:174–199.

Little, R.B. (1970). Behind the dream screen. *Psychoanal. Rev.* 57 137–142.

Pacella, B.L. (1975). Early ego development and the déjà vu. *J. Am. Psychoanal. Assoc.* 23:300–318.

Rycroft, G. (1951). A contribution to the study of the dream screen. *Int. J. Psychoanal.* 32:178–184.

Sperling, O.E. (1957). A psychoanalytic study of hypnagogic hallucinations. *J. Am. Psychoanal. Assoc.* 5:115–123.

Spitz, R.A. (1955). The primal cavity. A contribution to the genesis of perception and its role for psychoanalytic theory. *Psychoanal. Study Child* 10:215–240.

Stern, M.M. (1961). Blank hallucinations: remarks about trauma and perceptual disturbances *Int. J. Psychoanal.* 42:205–215.

CHAPTER 8

Self-Mutilation and Father-Daughter Incest: A Psychoanalytic Case Report

[(1988). *Unconscious Fantasy and Reality: Essays in Honor of Jacob A. Arlow,* Madison,Edited by H.P. Blum, Y. Kramer, Richards, A.K., & Richards, A.D. CT: International Universities Press.]

Self-mutilation by cutting, burning, or other means is a dramatic and troubling symptom encountered in clinical practice, particularly in the treatment of adolescent or postadolescent females. An extensive psychiatric literature on this phenomenon (see Simpson, 1975) draws primarily but not exclusively on hospitalized patients, most of whom are diagnosed as schizophrenic. Reports on patients treated outside the hospital setting are not as common, and case reports of nonpsychotic patients treated psychoanalytically are rare indeed. Two exceptions are several patients included in the report of Friedman, (1972). and a patient of Kafka's (1969) who in a hospital setting began a psychoanalytic treatment of almost five years duration. It is not clear from Kafka's report whether the entire analysis was conducted in the hospital or whether the patient was discharged at some point in her treatment and then analyzed in an office setting.

Despite the paucity of analytic data on self-mutilating patients, clinicians who have encountered such symptomatology have frequently drawn on psychoanalytic concepts to explain the psychology involved. Thus, self-mutilating behavior has been conceptualized in terms of alterego states (Pao, 1969). phallic conflicts involving castration (Novotny, 1972). and compromise formations involving incestuous fantasies (Simonopoulos, 1974). Within their group of self-mutilating and suicidal adolescent analysands, Friedman et al. stressed ambivalent ties to the mother and the wish to destroy the body (or body part) perceived as the source of instinctual urges. The inadequate maternal handling and lack of physical stimulation to which self-mutilating patients are subject in infancy (Graf and Malin, 1967; Pao, 1969; Simonopoulos, 1974). along with a related vulnerability to separation anxiety (Pao, 1969; Asch, 1971; Kwawer, 1980) are threads that run through the literature.

In a recent study of twenty young hospitalized self-mutilators Simpson and Porter (1981) elicited a history of sexual abuse in nine of their subjects, including sexual relationships between the self-mutilating girls and their fathers, sexual fondling during preschool years, and intercourse or rape during adolescence. This recorded incidence of sexual abuse was based on information that surfaced in therapeutic interviews during the patients' hospitalization; the authors believe the actual incidence may have been even greater. This study is a significant emendation of the literature.

Earlier studies of self-mutilating did not specifically link such behavior to sexual abuse or incest, though Green (1967) has linked self-mutilative behavior to parental abuse and the reports of Crabtree (1967) and Kwawer (1980) invite the inference of specifically sexual parental abuse. It is striking, then, that the relationship between incest and self-mutilation demonstrated by Simpson and Porter should be borne out in the present psychoanalytic case.

A CASE REPORT

Fran, a married graduate student, was twenty-two years old at the time she was referred for analysis. The referral came from a hospital psychiatrist who had seen her for approximately a year in psychotherapy, first while she was hospitalized, then as a hospital day patient, and finally as an outpatient working and living with a foster family. Her hospitalization at a private psychiatric facility had been precipitated by a pregnancy that occurred at the end of her freshman year at college. She gave birth to a baby girl while hospitalized, and the infant was given out for adoption immediately thereafter. The patient had no further contact with her daughter.

During the course of her three-year hospitalization Fran engaged in both self-destructive and mutilative behavior: she once set her nightgown on fire and on several other occasions inflicted burns on her breasts and genitals. These behaviors abated when a divorced man almost thirty years her senior became interested in her. she improved to the point of discharge, went to live with him in his home, and subsequently married him. Two years after hospitalization she contacted her former hospital psychiatrist in New York (where she had since become a graduate student) because she was again pregnant and did not want to have the baby. Her distress was compounded by the fact that her marriage was now in trouble. She had become involved with another older man and was thinking of leaving her husband. She was concerned that her husband might not be the father of her child. Fran's anguish was resolved by a spontaneous abortion, but her marital problems intensified to the point that she began taking amphetamines and was considering experimentation with LSD. It was at this juncture that her former therapist recommended analysis.

At the first session Fran complained of feelings of anxiety, depersonalization, and an inability to control her self-destructive behaviors. The latter included, by her own admission, promiscuity, drug abuse, and suicidal gestures. She reported a long history of self-inflicted injuries, beginning in early adolescence. She had cut her wrists several times during the latter part of her senior year in high school, when she was living in a home for delinquent girls run by nuns. On these and numerous other occasions the actual cutting was done deliberately and dispassionately, without pain but in response to an inner voice commanding her to so injure herself. She was aware of intense feelings as she observed blood appearing on her skin: the act of cutting was accompanied not by orgasm per se but by a sense of relief, release, and discharge.

The presenting picture was discouraging, to say the least. I nevertheless decided to see her five times a week on the couch, not fully aware of the depth of her pathology. My initial diagnosis of hysterical personality was influenced partly by the fact that she had come with a specific recommendation for analysis. Her condition seemed to exemplify what Glover (1954) and Ticho (1970) have described as the heroic indications for analysis. Though uncertain that she could be helped analytically, I believed that no other form of therapy held a better prognosis.

Background and History

Fran was born in the home of her maternal grandparents, devout Irish Catholics. The product of an unwanted and physically difficult pregnancy, she incurred the resentment of both mother and maternal grandmother even before her birth. She did not nurse and was weaned from the bottle at seven months. During her childhood her mother treated her as a virtual prisoner, rationing her food, restricting her activities, and meting out extreme punishment for minor infractions of family rules. She tied Fran's hands at night to prevent her from masturbating, forced her to use the toilet only at certain times of the day, and locked the kitchen cabinet to make sure that she had no food other than the portions allotted her at mealtimes. As Fran grew older these restrictions encompassed her playmates and play activities as well. In short, her mother spared no effort to humiliate the patient and to depreciate her every achievement.

When Fran entered puberty her mother actively discouraged her from taking any pride in her blossoming feminine appearance. She prohibited her from wearing a bra or stockings, from shaving her legs, and from wearing lipstick, although these same privileges were accorded her older sisters. On one occasion Fran's mother told her she was "deformed" because she had larger breasts than her sisters had. The mother was joined in these efforts of systematic degradation both by the older sisters and by the maternal grandmother.

At the beginning of analysis many of Fran's early memories concerned traumatizing visits to the maternal grandparents on holidays, when she had invariably been compared unfavorably with her older sisters, excluded from family dramatic and musical performances, and endlessly confronted by her grandmother with pictures of Jesus with a bleeding heart as testimony to the result of her various misbehaviors ("Look what you're doing to Jesus by being bad"). Fran often became sick, vomiting during these visits and eventually just before them. Fran's relationship with her immediately older sister, Cindy, fared no better. This sister adopted the sadistic bearing of the mother and grandmother, and Fran's envy and hatred of her were enormous. She recalled many battles, and was so furious that she had held a knife to her sister's throat. On one occasion the sister pushed Fran down a treacherous hill on a bicycle; on another she persuaded Fran to crawl into a pipe from which she would not help her extricate herself.

Fran's major solace amid all this suffering was her father's interest. Although he frequently traveled and was generally ineffectual in tempering his wife's abusive regimen, he did spend time with her, teaching her to swim when she was three and to play tennis when she was in grade school. In fact, the father's involvement with all his daughters shaded into unnatural intimacy. When home from business trips, for example, he gave all his daughters baths until they were quite grown. When the father was home, moreover, Fran recalled frequently joining both parents in bed in the morning. This behavior continued until she was eleven, when on one occasion she noticed that her father had an erection. On noting her awareness he told her to leave the bed and never to return to it. Fran's precocious development was the focus of considerable conflict with her mother. She constantly referred to her daughter as a "cow' because her breasts were large. Her sister Cindy reinforced the mother sadistic behavior, once giving Fran a ridiculously oversized bra as a birthday present. Predictably, social life and social appearance became sources of chronic conflict, especially after the family moved to another part of the country and Fran began high school. She remembered how her mother refused to allow her to act in a school play because of the "indecent" costume the part required. The mother placed a strict curfew on Fran, which she often violated. She had intercourse for the first time when she was sixteen and recalled coming home with blood on her shorts, which she believed her father noticed. On a subsequent occasion her parents discovered she had climbed out the bedroom window one night to join two boys. On returning, she denied having done anything wrong, but nevertheless begged her father to beat her. Shortly after this incident her father came home from work with a high fever; Fran called a friend and announced that she had made her father ill and was going to leave home. A fight with her mother ensued, the family doctor was summoned, and Fran ended up in the psychiatric ward of a genera] hospital.

She remained there for two months and, being very rebellious, was placed on what she called "solitary confinement." Though permitted to visit her parents at home, she would not speak to them on these occasions. On one such visit they took her to a nearby beach where she swam out so far that she eventually had to be rescued by a lifeguard. Once she ran away from the hospital, only to be discovered by her father and her doctor in a boyfriend's apartment. They dragged her back to the hospital, where she was physically restrained. At this point her psychiatrist recommended that she be placed in a home for delinquents in order to learn "discipline." She did well at this home in certain respects, teaching tennis, but her behavior remained provocative. It was at this time that she first cut her wrists in a suicidal gesture; in analysis she recovered a vivid memory of blood spurting over the white habit of the nun who discovered her.

After graduating from high school Fran was sent to a small college chosen by her mother. Her psychiatrist referred her to a psychiatrist in that area, and she began psychotherapy. Though she was expelled from this college under unclear circumstances, she continued to see her psychiatrist while auditing courses at a local university. This was her status at the time of her first pregnancy. She recounted her great surprise upon learning she was pregnant; she had never used birth control and yet had never before conceived, though by her estimate she had slept with fifty or sixty men, most of them much older than she. At first she denied the pregnancy, even to herself, but eventually she told her psychiatrist, who in turn informed her parents. Only her father came to see her, as her mother would have nothing to do with her. As the major parental objective was to prevent the rest of the family from learning of the pregnancy, her father made arrangements for a maternity residence. Fran could not understand why she was not permitted an abortion. Her father simply relayed her mother's decision that it was out of the question, that Fran must have the baby "to pay for her sins"; she heard nothing further from her father until he appeared at the maternity residence some time later to relocate her in a psychiatric hospital. During the interval he had apparently been advised to hospitalize her by a colleague whose son had recently committed suicide.

THE ANALYSIS

Although the later pregnancy that prompted Fran's referral for analysis was, as noted, resolved by spontaneous abortion, marital problems remained in the forefront for the first several years of the treatment. Extramaritally active during this time, she was now using birth control pills to prevent pregnancy. Shortly thereafter, when her husband, desirous of a child, urged her to discontinue the pill, she complied with his request despite her disappointment at having to forgo extramarital affairs. But in fact her own wish to have a child was increasing, seemingly in response to her growing insight into her relationship with her mother and a corresponding ability to feel less guilty about the hostility she felt toward her. This relationship was the major focus of the analytic work during this phase of the analysis and led to her decision to break off contact with her mother. Previously she had visited her occasionally and had spoken with her frequently by phone.

Shortly before going off the pill she had intercourse with a married college professor fifteen years her senior who, she volunteered, looked like her analyst. Within a matter of weeks she was again pregnant. Although she felt it unlikely that her husband was not the father, her single extramarital contact around the time of conception made her uncertain. She agonized over this issue, alternately considering having an abortion, killing herself, killing the baby, and confessing her indiscretion to her husband.

During this turbulent period of the analysis, Fran frequently expressed the wish to terminate, partly because she did not want me to see her pregnant. Pregnancy was a sign of sin, the very attitude evinced by her mother following her first pregnancy. But eventually Fran gave birth and returned to analysis with only a ten-day interruption. Her pleasure and relief at having given birth to a healthy baby boy, the very image of her husband, was diminished by her anger at my failure to visit her in the maternity ward. Although she had not asked me to visit her, on resuming treatment she confessed that she had assumed I would "read her mind," as her mother had. Her sullen anger at my failure to do so seemed to repeat her angry disappointment with both parents, who had likewise refused to see her during her first pregnancy and subsequent hospitalization. She transformed her passive resentment toward her mother into active measures to keep her from visiting her new grandson.

Her anger was compounded by postpartum depression, which she had attributed to her renewed use of birth control pills, her cessation of nursing after six months, and her continued dissatisfaction with her husband, who, while pleased with the baby, was emotionally unavailable.

Following an unsuccessful Caribbean cruise that was intended to save her marriage, Fran's depression intensified in the wake of my announcement that I would be away all of March. Her depression was accompanied by the return of self-mutilating propensities, which had been in abeyance during her pregnancy and the eight months following her delivery. More alarming still, she now expressed suicidal thoughts of sufficient intensity to make me contemplate hospitalization. As a less extreme expedient, I allowed her to sit up,

161

which she did for about five days before voluntarily returning to the couch. It was in the context of this distressing impasse in the analysis that she described a need to "act" rather than "talk." she acknowledged that this inability to talk about feelings embodied simultaneous wishes to reveal and to conceal. She added, however, that she wanted me to force her to confess.

It took some time to work through the layered meanings of the "secret" that she wanted me to drag out of her. Her first confession was that she enjoyed anal masturbation. In reply to my question, she indicated that she masturbated with her right hand even though she is left-handed. When I pointed out that she also used her right hand to cut herself, she volunteered that she was aware of masturbatory wishes preceding her self-mutilative activities, another of her secrets.

It was at this juncture that she came to a session telling me that she had cut herself again. This episode followed her breaking off the relationship with the professor. She reported that she had made a long cut just below the line of her pubic hair, although she had really wanted to cut a long circle under each breast and an "x" on each buttock. Her associations to these fantasied cuts went back to puberty, when her mother had ridiculed her breasts and prescribed an operation to remove "excess fat." she recalled in this connection that she had always been examined by the family doctor in the presence of her parents, and that this doctor, prior to administering an injection, would trace an "x" and a circle on her buttocks with methiolate, thus creating a bull's-eye for the needle. She remembered her father observing this ritual attentively and, from this memory, associated to her father's general interest in his daughters' pubescent bodies. She remembered that he once pulled down Cindy's pants and administered a spanking, though she was then in late adolescence.

It was now clear that memories involving both parents were implicated in her selection of desired sites for cutting, and it was the transference that provided the impetus for the revelant childhood associations. I had become the sexually prohibitive mother, raising questions about her recent affair, but I was also the father to whom she would expose the site of her fantasied and actual cuts, thereupon exhibiting breasts, buttocks, and pubic region. She acknowledged a wish to be naked on the couch, as well as occasional feelings that she actually was naked.

She reported the following dream. She was in a building that resembled a house or stockade that Indians were attacking. They penetrated the stockade through the back door, and a girl was pierced by an arrow. Ensuing association linked the location of the dream to a trip out west with her father during Easter recess her senior year in high school. He had taken her along on a business trip, to both the chagrin and the relief of her mother, who welcomed the opportunity to be apart from both of them. Fran's father was drinking rather heavily then; she recalled the several bottles of whiskey he had taken on the trip. Then she remembered that she had shared her father's bed in the motels they stayed in. Once she awakened in the middle of the night and "thought" her father was having anal intercourse with her. she was upset and accused him of doing something "bad" to her, but he assured her that she had only had a nightmare. The next morning, she continued, "it was as if nothing had happened." When I commented that anal intercourse represented "penetration" through the back door, as in the dream, she replied that her memory of anal rape must be untrue, that her father didn't do such things. But she proceeded to recall an occasion when she had entered her parents' bedroom and observed her father alone, fondling his penis. He permitted her to stay, but cautioned her not to tell her mother. She left this session visibly shaken.

The next day she reported that she had not wanted to come to her session. After the previous day's session she had become aware of her mother's voice instructing her not to talk to me and to cut herself. Overcoming great resistance, Fran returned to the events recounted the previous day. she remembered that after the trip west she had begun to "really sleep around in earnest." It was in response to this behavior that her parents had first hospitalized her and sent her to the reformatory.

Then, during the winter or early spring of her first year at college, her father came to visit her. He picked her up at her dormitory and took her to his hotel room, where he humiliated her with abusive interrogation regarding the boys she was sleeping with. As she associated to the details of the room, she recalled that she not only spent the night with him, but once again shared his bed. As her regression intensified, she recalled the following sequence of events. In the middle of the night she had had intercourse with her father (the dream image of the girl being pierced by the arrow came to her mind). She had been terrified at her father's initial sexual advance; what made matters "even worse," however, was the sequel. She had awakened later in the night and requested intercourse again. When her father refused to comply, she had become even more terrified, both at her own "wish" and at her father's "rejection." Her terror reached a peak when it occurred to her that her mother would discover everything. Fran reacted to these recovered memories with a mixture of amazement and disbelief; part of her believed it was "all a fabrication." Her mother, after all, had always accused her of making up stories. How could her father have done such a thing? It should be recalled that all this material emerged in the context of her mounting concern over my impending vacation. Her intense wish that I not abandon her was accompanied by a minor suicide attempt, the superficial cutting of a wrist. On my return she again expressed the desire to leave analysis. Why hadn't I canceled my vacation, given howtraumatically upsetting her recent memories had been? I was just as bad as her father: I had forced her to recover memories of "all these terrible secret things" only to go away, just as he had initiated intercourse with her only to decline her advances and then leave her. she recalled that for a week following the seduction she had fantasied that her father, having slept with her, would leave her mother and live with her. yet he had opted for her mother, just as I had opted for a vacation with my own wife and family.

The negative transference reached such a pitch thereafter that she obtained a referral from her husband's analyst. After a single visit with this senior consultant, she returned, reiterating her desire to quit despite the consultant's recommendation that she continue. When I informed her that the decision was hers to make, she proceeded to bewail her weakness and powerlessness with me. why couldn't she make me do what she wanted? When I suggested that her wish to leave analysis masked her wish to escape from painful material that remained uncovered, she acknowledged this to be the case. she had recently begun to have sexual fantasies about me, realizing full well that intercourse with the analyst would spoil the analysis. She felt doomed to frustration, feeling I could give her something but had elected to withhold it.

As she left one session she expressed the urge to kick me "in the balls." At the following session she reported cutting herself, but would not tell me where. When I surmised that she had cut her genitals, she admitted I was right. She was doing to herself what she had wanted to do to her father and now, in the transference, to me: cut off the penis and have it for herself. I suggested that having a penis would protect her from sex with her father and at the same time enable her to assume his role as frustrater rather than always being the frustrated one. Following this interpretation she recalled yet another incident of paternal abuse. Shortly after having given birth to her daughter she was in a motel room with her father. He said to her, "Okay, get undressed," and proceeded to inspect her genitals. She believed he wanted to "check her out" following the delivery. The details of this memory seemed quite vivid, but the patient had expressed amazement that she had complied with her father's demand in view of his previous behavior.

As we worked through again and again the events following her seduction by her father, her envy of the male genital and a corresponding dissatisfaction with her own emerged into consciousness and became the focus of our work. A penis became desirable because it was intrusive, enabling men to rape women. Women, she observed, could not rape men. She then recalled her childhood conviction that women did have penises, she alone being the exception.

These memories led Fran to a more realistic assessment of her father as sexually perverse and tragically weak. she recognized that intercourse with her father had preceded her first pregnancy, but was unable to entertain consciously the prospect that he may have fathered the little girl put up for adoption, although the stormy course of events that followed this pregnancy surely alluded to an unconscious awareness of this possibility. In fact, her anxiety about the identity of the father following her second pregnancy was a repetition of the anxiety that followed the first. The dynamic significance of the second pregnancy as a repetition of the first provides an explanation for her anxious concern lest the second child be a girl, i.e., lest it be like the first child, her father's child.

An episode of acting out at this point in the analysis proved illuminating. Having resumed her graduate studies, she was propositioned by a younger classmate. She acceded to his request despite herself, in the manner of a compulsion. But intercourse with him was unsatisfying. She felt that his penis did not "look right." Although she was upset by the encounter and had no desire to see him again, she felt cheated when the young man called her up to cancel a subsequent rendezvous. This transaction repeated yet again the events of her seduction at the hands of her father: initial disgust, unwilling arousal, rejection, and abandonment. But her promiscuity was by now beginning to diminish. She was propositioned by her thesis advisor and declined him. she told him that their collaboration should be in the classroom and not in the bedroom. She separated from her husband, avoided involvements with men, and concentrated her energies on her graduate work and on parenting her son. Her sexual interest henceforth focused on the analyst. Since I had cured her, I should marry her or, at the very least, initiate an affair with her.

Having previously been the bad father who had not only abandoned her for his wife (the vacation) but had refused to authorize the abortion that would have undone the possible consequences of his seduction, I now became the desirable father she longed for. Just as she had believed that but for the controlling mother her father would have chosen to live with her, so she now came to believe that but for our analytic contract I would have initiated an affair. If I would not seduce her because she was my patient, she would leave analysis. If, following termination, I still declined to have intercourse with her, it could only be because she was ugly, undesirable, physically repulsive, and misshapen. Her father had abandoned her because she was ugly and penisless; now I would do the same.

It was in this context that she again fantasized cutting herself and showing me her cuts. We understood this wish to make herself unattractive as a safeguard by which she defended against my sexual rejection of her. she would spare herself the narcissistic mortification of further rejection by seeing to it that she would never be sufficiently attractive to me; i.e., she would choose to make herself ugly rather than run the continual risk of being rejected by me or by her father because she was ugly. Ugliness produced by self-cutting was thus

167

overdetermined: it was a defense against the dangers associated with oedipal fantasies, a reenactment of their gratification in adolescence, and a punishment (by her mother or herself as her mother's surrogate) for both the fantasy and the reality.

Fran unconsciously identified with what she perceived as her mother's view of sex as sin. Menstruation was "horrible," large breasts were ugly, and pregnancy was a punishment for intercourse. In this context, blood and self-inflicted bleeding achieved overdetermined symbolic status. There was the bleeding heart of Jesus, menstrual blood, the blood on her shorts "exhibited" to her father after her first intercourse, and the blood "spurting" from her wrists on the nun's white habit. The arrow in her dream "drew blood." Piercing stood for incestuous intercourse genital or anal rape and castration. The spurting wound was the castrated genital (as suggested by her menstrual bleeding) or, when displaced elsewhere, stood for its opposite, the penis. Her "spurting" wrists defiled the nun's purity and allowed her a feeling of discharge akin to orgasm in which the passivity associated with incestuous victimization was reversed. In the termination phase, her exhibitionistic wishes not only served actively to repulse the wished-for sexual overtures from the analyst; in addition, these wishes to cut and to exhibit her cuts, to the extent that they remained mere wishes, evidenced symbolic mastery of her equation of penis activity with penis injury. A person without a penis, she learned, can be an active agent, not a mere victim, even one's own.

The case reported here presented an opportunity for follow-up approximately ten years after treatment. Following termination Fran had divorced her husband, remarried, and had a second child. She reported being very happy in her second marriage, with no further recourse to self-mutilating activities. She was on good if somewhat distant terms with her father, who has never commented on his sexual exploitation of her.

CONCLUSION

This case report presents the analytic treatment of a patient who both demographically and clinically qualifies as a practically perfect "model" self-mutilating patient with respect to age, sex, and other variables cited by Simpson and Porter (1981). The patient exhibited many characteristics of their subjects: drug abuse, suicide attempts, a history of parental physical abuse, and feelings of abandonment, isolation, and unlovableness. Many of the types of mutilation catalogued by Simpson and Porter arm or wrist cutting, the cutting of breasts and genitals, burning oneself with matches or cigarettes, the "aggravation" of existing sores and injuries were engaged in by this patient at various times. Moreover, the lack of maternal holding and physical stimulation during the first year of life reported by Graf and Malin (1967). Pao (1969). and Simonopoulos (1974) very likely typified her infancy. During psychoanalytic treatment, at a frequency of five sessions per week, the dramatic recovery of the memory of intercourse with her father during late adolescence, along with memories and reconstructions of other sexual experiences with her father, proved central to the understanding of her self-mutilative behavior and her eventual cure. This case therefore strengthens Simpson and Porter's finding of a significant link between self-mutilation in adolescent girls and earlier incestuous experiences.

REFERENCES

Asch, S. (1971). Wrist scratching as a symptom of anhedonia. *Psychoanalytic. Quart* 40:603–617.

Crabtree, L. (1967). A psychotherapeutic encounter with a self-mutilating patient. *Psychiatry* 30:91–100.

Friedman, M., et al. (1972). Attempted suicide and self-mutilation in adolescence: Some observations from a psychoanalytic research project. *Internat. J. Psycho-Anal.* 53:179–183.

Glover, E. (1954/1955a). The indications for psychoanalysis. *J Mental Science* 100:393–401.

Graf & Malin (1954). The syndrome of the wrist cutter. *Amer. J Psychiatry* 124:36–42.

Green, A. (1967). Self-mutilation in schizophrenic children. *Abst. Bull. Psychoanal. Med.,* 7:23–26.

Kafka, J. (1969). The body as transitional object: A psychoanalytic study of a self-mutilating patient. *Brit. J. Med. Psychol.,* 42:207–212.

Kwawer, J. (1980). Some interpersonal aspects of self-mutilation in a borderline patient. *J. Arner. Acad. Psychoanal.* 8:203–216.

Novotny, P. (1972). Self-cutting. Bull. Menn. Cain. 36:505–514.

Pao, P. (1969). The syndrome of delicate self-cutting. *Brit. J. Med. Psychol.,* 42:195–206.

Simonopoulos, V. (1974). Repeated self-cutting: An impulse neurosis. Arner. J. Psychother., 28:85–94.

Simpson, M. (1975). The phenomenology of self-mutilating in a general hospital setting. *Can. Psychiat. Assn. J.,* 20:429–434.

Simpson, C. A., & Porter, G. L. (1981). Self mutilation in children and adolescents. *Bulletin of the Menninger Clinic, 45:*428–438.

Clinic, 45, 428–438.Ticho, E. (1970). Differences between psychoanalysis and psychotherapy. *Bull. Menn. Clin.,* 34/3:128–138.

CHAPTER 9

The Evolution of Drive Theory in Contemporary Psychoanalysis: A Reply to Gill Bachant, J.L., Lynch, A.A., & Richards, A.D. (1995).

(1995). *Psychoanalytic Psychology, 12*(4), 565-573.

The Evolution of Drive Theory in Contemporary Psychoanalysis: A Reply to Gill," Merton Gill's (1995) commentary on our article, "Relational Models in Psychoanalysis" (Bachant, Lynch, & Richards, 1995) highlighted issues at the cutting edge of psychoanalytic thinking but evidences certain misunderstandings of the contemporary classical tradition that warrant clarification. Gill characterized the differences between the classical and relational points of view largely as attributable to differing hierarchical emphases on innate as opposed to experiential factors. What Gill calls the "innate" is not defined, however, with some resulting confusion of what he is trying to clarify. We believe his article leaves the reader with serious misconceptions of the way contemporary classical theory understands the concept of drive and its role in the systemic interaction of biopsychosocial forces.

Gill's article (1995) does raise the question of whether Mitchell has changed his view about drive theory's incompatibility with relational theory. Mitchell (1993, 1988) stated unequivocally that relational-model theories have abandoned the drive framework. Is the idea that was central in Mitchell's earlier work (1983, 1988) to be dismissed as "the exaggeration of early enthusiasm"?

Gill's comments, as well as a recent article of Mitchell's (1993) in which he discusses aggression, raises the question of whether Mitchell is moving, like Greenberg (1991) before him, to a position that integrates a drive component into his model. Is it now only Freud's drive theory, not drive theory in general, that Mitchell finds problematic? We need some clarification from Mitchell on this issue as well as on the status of the pleasure principle. Does Mitchell believe that people seek pleasure and avoid pain? Within his relational model, with its stress on humanity's preeminent motivational thrust of connection to others, is gratification a significant feature, a principle, or an occasional process?

Within the contemporary classical perspective, drives are basic motivational forces that prompt behavior. They are not the sole determinant of behavior but a component of it. Sometimes they inspire behavior and at other times they simply contribute to its form. Freud (1923, 1926) and later Waelder (1936) clearly described the multiple forces and functions that contribute to behavior. In his latest reformulations of theory, Brenner (1982, 1993) identified four major aspects in the formation of behavior and experience: drive derivatives, pleasant or unpleasant affects, defense, and superego functions.

Drives present in every person as childhood wishes and fears. These wishes and fears consist of passionate desires characterized by intentional themes to have something done to us and/or to do something to someone. The particular content and form of gratification sought through these wishes and fears are drawn from, and made relevant by, the individual's unique development (Brenner, 1982). Drive is the who-is-doing-what-to-whom impulse that organizes psychic structure.

In contemporary classical theory, the drives reflect one dimension of the dynamic unconscious.[23] Wishes and fears are formed in every phase of development. Throughout development, in combination with advances in cognitive capacities, moral value systems, complex emotional patterning, and defensive functioning, they are integrated into behaviors that fashion the child's maturing solutions to the inevitable frustrations of life. As development proceeds, earlier wishes and fears take on more primitive and frightening attributes and become unacceptable to consciousness. These wishes and fears gain expression in persistent unconscious fantasies that mature with development. In addition to the continuing influence of primitive wishes and fears, unconscious fantasies are patterned by important experiences, relationships, traumas, and conflicts of childhood. Unconscious fantasies provide a mental set that affects how we interpret the sensory data we perceive and how we choose among the options with which we can respond.

This redefinition of drive theory emphasizes psychological phenomena, but not at the expense of the biological or sociocultural contributions to the drives and mental functioning. Instead, it views these contributions as embedded within experience that is recorded and mediated psychologically. Central to this understanding is the belief that the mind develops in a dynamic unfolding processes determined by complex interactions between the child's innate,

---

23 As noted in Bachant et al. (1995), the crucial dimension of the interface between theory and practice is the clinician's understanding and use of the dynamic unconscious, because this understanding organizes the structure of the analytic situation. Indispensable to this concept is the idea that certain drive derivatives, specific wishes, and fears denied access to consciousness by various defensive actions have a profound impact on the development of psychic structure and a continuing influence on psychic life. This is exemplified by the endless transformations of fantasies that emanate from core unconscious issues that we see played out in the patient's life. The dynamic unconscious is the heart of transference, reflecting the individual's specific motivational imperatives and the way these are played out in the analytic situation.

biologically determined characteristics and influences from the environment.

Confusion about the nature of drive in contemporary classical thinking is rooted in Freud's continual reformulations of the concept and in later contributions that significantly changed the underlying assumptions about drives. Initially these contributions focused on the relation of the enhanced role of ego to reality. Nunberg's (1930/1960) elaboration of the ego's synthetic function, Waelder's (1930) principle of multiple function, and Anna Freud's (1936/1966) elaboration of defense and the role of conflict, in particular, changed the role of the ego from one helplessly driven by unconscious forces to an ego that worked to integrate and consolidate these forces.

Many of the issues being raised today were the subject of intense debate during the earlier part of the century. Hartmann in his early articles, and later in his collaboration with Lowenstein and Kris, worked to show that human beings were far too complex to be accounted for by a simple theory. To the existing dynamic, economic, and topographical–structural perspectives, he and his colleagues stressed the adaptive point of view. This perspective stressed the way in which individuals evolve and differentiate through interaction in an ecological system. It proffered a biopsychosocial integration:

Shifting the accent too exclusively either on maturation or on object relations or other factors gives a one-sided picture of development. Such seems to me to be the case in Melanie Klein's overemphasizing of the so-called "biological" factor, or in the opposite overemphasis of culturalism. (Hartmann, 1950/1964, p. 108)

Two key contributions from these theorists to a contemporary understanding of drive were the redefinition of aggression and the elaboration of the undifferentiated matrix. Hartmann, Kris, and Loewenstein (1949) suggested that aggression, like libido, fell within the pleasure principle and that the discharge of aggression is pleasurable and the inhibition of aggression is unpleasurable (Brenner, 1982). They also suggested that aggression may have multiple aims.

Hartmann et al. (1949) postulated the beginning of personal differentiation not from an id of instincts but from an undifferentiated matrix in interaction with the external world. This idea was developed by Fenichel (1945) and Jacobson (1964). Fenichel noted that "both ego interests and libidinal drives, which later certainly are often in conflict with each other, have evolved from a common source" (p. 58). Hartmann et al. (1949) showed that even as the individual individuates, the drives are fused and neutralized to fuel the activity of the psychic structure. This neutralization comes about to the extent that the individual is able, with the aid of the mother, to negotiate with the environment. These experiences lead to a transformation of the drives into object relations: "While the development of object relations is co-determined by the ego, object relations are also one of the main factors that determine the development of the ego" (Hartmann, 1950/1964, p. 105).

Jacobson (1964, p. 13) brought the theory of drives to another level. First, she suggested that instinctual energy, too, is undifferentiated at birth and separates into two kinds of drives *"under the influence of external stimulations"* (p. 13, italics added). Second, she restated that the pleasure principle is not based on the drive discharge concepts of the constancy principle, but on the experiences of pleasure and pain from infancy on. These experiences determine the balance of comfort and are maintained through a state of homeostasis. Jacobson's concepts of dispersion of undifferentiated drive, introjection and projection, the gathering poles of frustration and gratification, fantasies of merger and expulsion, structuralization of mind and representational world, all contributed to the evolution of drive theory.

We can see from this brief review of the evolution of the drive concept that contemporary psychoanalytic theory long ago abandoned the notion of drive as a tension–reduction, drive–discharge phenomenon. Today it embraces a psychologically based understanding of the concept that integrates biopsychosocial determinants. The contemporary understanding of drive stresses the fundamental motivational significance of the individual's unique history as expressed in a dynamic unconscious that is structured by an integration of biopsychosocial factors. There are two issues that distinguish between classical and relational models.

First is the notion that the unconscious is dynamic—it is more than a static entity lost to our consciousness for various reasons. It plays a pivotal role in structuring, organizing, and motivating experience. As opposed to Gill's (1995) characterization of the classical perspective as seeing "the present as a repetition of the past" (p. 129), it is more accurate to say that this perspective sees the past as alive in the present. We concur with Gill's characterization of the relational view as viewing the present as more independent of the past. There may be a real difference between relational theory and classical theory on the issue of the centrality of early childhood experience in development (see Bachant & Richards, 1993), which bears on the relational stress on new interpersonal experience over insight as mutative.

Second, Gill's (1995) statements that "it is uncontestable that the classical point of view emphasizes the innate over the experiential," and that in the classical framework "the innate is explanatorily superordinate to the experiential," (p. 120) are simply wrong. They obscure a fundamental difference between the models. Although Gill recognized that Mitchell's view of contemporary classical drive theory is "caricatured" (p. 177), he had difficulty acknowledging that contemporary classical theory has integrated drive and relational components. As outlined earlier, unconscious fantasies not only gain expression in the relational context but were constructed in the relational context of childhood. The classical analyst understands that an integration of biopsychosocial factors is always and inevitably at work in the construction of experience. Relational model thinking, on the other hand, although it gives a nod to what Gill calls the innate, substantially limits our understanding. Within this model, despite the liberal sprinkling of conflict references, despite Mitchell's characterization of his theory as a "relational/conflict theory," use of conflict is limited to relational considerations alone: to conflict between and among different relationships as well as within a single relationship. Gill, in fact, agrees with Zucker (1989) that the intrapsychic is too narrowly defined in relational theory. This is essentially the same point we made in our article (1995); it has also been emphasized by Bachant & Richards (1993), Hatcher (1990), and Hoffmann (personal communication, cited in Gill, 1994). Hoffmann warned that when bodily urges are understood by way of interpersonal relations, we may underestimate the importance of sexual interest and desire *in itself* rather than as a channel for something else not intrinsically sexual.

Perhaps the emphasis Gill refers to as "uncontestable" resides in the fuller appreciation of the body that exists in classical theory. Gill (1995) raised an important point about unconscious fantasy that deserves highlighting:

I refer to the kind of bodily fantasy like castration anxiety, penis envy, and other bodily ideas which so often seem bizarre to the uninitiated, even only as a metaphor. Classical analysts of course believe that while they may serve as metaphors, they are concrete as well. In my reading of the literature, such fantasies, even if only as metaphors, are underplayed in relational writing. (p. 95)

No one would deny that relationships with others play a central role in the structure and organization of the self, but there is another relationship that, although influenced by relationships with others, is also separate from them: the primary relationship with one's own body. Early in life, this relationship may dominate our experience. Although technically inseparable from interactions with others, many of our earliest experiences are intensely personal, reflecting primitive wishes, fears, and ideas connected with our involvement with our bodies. Our relationship with our own bodies involves processes that make demands, generate pleasure, and pain, and serve to connect us to our primary caretakers. At a moment in our psychoanalytic history when "the relationship" is in the ascendant, even when mind has been defined by some as social in nature (Mitchell, 1988), it is important to keep in mind that the child's relationship to the body, although inextricably linked with relational patterns and stimulation, is not limited to interactions with caregivers. As Pine (1990) reminded us, there are ample moments during child's maturation for different kinds of experience to be dominant.

The centrality of the relationship to the body that characterizes the Freudian perspective has been corroborated across a broad spectrum of contemporary understandings mental development. Piaget & Inhelder (1959) anchored cognitive development to the sensory motor phase, the formative phase of life in which learning is a type of bodily learning revolving around action. The importance and centrality of the body in psychological development is credited by some with a critical role not only in our individual consciousness, but also in the evolution of consciousness itself. In *A History of the Mind: Evolution and the Birth of Consciousness* (1992) Humphrey took as his task the problem of explaining how states of consciousness arise in human brains. Demonstrating that raw sensations are central to all conscious states, he reformulates Descartes assumption with the paradigm "I feel, therefore I am." Humphrey proposed that our sensory consciousness—our awareness of what it is like to be ourselves, arises out of bodily responses of pain and pleasure. Damasio (1994) built on Humphrey's work in the development of the somatic-marker hypothesis, positing that bodily feedback, particularly the accumulated record of what he called "dispositional representations," is an essential link in the development of consciousness and primary in the organization of reason and emotion.

A primary reason for the continuing influence of the body in mental life evolves from its centrality in organizing painful and pleasurable states. Gratification, or the lack of it, is a central experience, especially for the young child, whose experience is so largely mediated through the body. Some rendering of the bodily based pleasure–unpleasure principle is seen to play a decisive role in developing psychic structure and motivating behavior in contemporary cognitive, neurological, and classical psychoanalytic perspectives. The pleasure principle proposes that unsatisfied wishes of drive origin persistently seek gratification. Childhood wishes that remain ungratified because they arouse unpleasure and conflict are understood to remain active and to drive the person continually in the direction of gratification.

A fully adequate psychoanalytic theory of motivation must embrace the drivenness of human behavior, unconscious wishes and fantasies, and bodily experience. Contemporary classical analysis accommodates these factors while allowing for the shaping impact of early object relationships and resulting relational patterns. Classical analysis does not, in the manner of the interpersonal tradition, impute superordinate status to the quest (or drive) for relational intimacy. But it does not thereby devalue it. The notion that personality, normal or pathological, is a product of the relational matrix seems to downplay the way in which bodily experience fuels wishes and fantasies. Arguing, in the manner of Mitchell (1988, pp. 16–17), that biological and physiological factors are contained within relational configurations, seems to make such factors epiphenomenal to the creation and maintenance of human relationships.

As clinicians, we must always be alert to the fact that [the] other (from the perspective of the subject) can be understood in part as a symbolic representation of endogenous processes. Not only are we affected by our significant others, but we, in turn, affect those others and use them to carry and represent certain aspects of ourselves, just as during the preverbal era, we use our own bodies to carry inner urges and meanings in addition to relational ones. (Bachant & Richards, 1993, p. 442).

In this way the themes of penis envy and mutilation, as well as the metaphors that carry early bodily experience into adult interaction— the images of oral incorporation, anal expulsion, and urethral poisoning that may characterize our patient's analytic process—have concrete bodily referents in addition to symbolic meanings.

In sum, we feel that Gill's distinction between the innate and the experiential does not line up with the difference between contemporary Freudian and relational points of view. It is also not true to the structure of the psychoanalytic theory of Freud himself. In *Group Psychology and the Analysis of the Ego* (Freud, 1921c), he wrote:

In the individual's mental life someone else is invariably involved, as a model, as an object as a helper, as an opponent, and so from the very first individual psychology in this extended but entirely justifiable sense of the word is at the same time social psychology as well. (p. 69)

Gill's brief in his discussion for the relational point of view seems to be a continuation of his critique of Freud's metapsychology that he developed in the 1960s together with other colleagues and students of David Rapaport. This was the "psychology is not biology" position. In this body of work, the biological was the innate and the energic, which these critics argued fatefully organized Freud's theory of mental functioning.

It is of interest to us that the innate experiential distinction is not presented in Gill's last book in the same dichotomous way as it seems to us to be developed in his discussion of the articles in Volume 12, Number 1 of *Psychoanalytic Psychology*. In *Psychoanalysis in Transition* (1994), he presented his view of the dialectical relation between a series of pairs including innate–experiential, interpersonal–intrapsychic, drive–object, and one person–two person. He also asserted that, for him, what is essential for psychoanalysis is the concept of unconscious fantasy: "the great discovery peculiar to psychoanalysis, the internal factor in the sense of unconscious fantasy... [which] psychoanalysis must zealously protect." In a sense, Gill offers this as his credo, and it is ours as well. We would like to believe that our personal discussions with Merton in recent years and his consideration of our article contributed to this final formulation of his point of view. We certainly learned a great deal about psychoanalysis from him. Merton Gill was a towering presence on the psychoanalytic landscape, and his death this last November has left a gaping hole in the skyline. The continuing efforts of all of us to make sense of the complex issues of psychoanalytic theory and practice will long acknowledge his outstanding contributions and thereby honor him. He will be greatly missed.

REFERENCES

Bachant, J.L., Lynch, A.A., & Richards, A.D. (1995). Relational models in psychoanalytic theory. *Psychoanalytic Psychology*, 12:71–87.

———.& Richards, A.D. (1993). Review essay: Relational concepts in psychoanalysis: An integration by Stephen Mitchell. *Psychoanal. Dial.*, 3:431–460.

Brenner, C. (1982). *The mind in conflict*. New York: International Universities Press.

——— (1993). Mind as conflict and compromise formation. *Journal of Clinical Psychoanalysis*, 3:473–488.

Damasio, A. R. (1994). *Descartes' error: Emotion, reason, and the human brain*. New York: Grosset/Putnam.

Fenichel, O. (1945). *The psychoanalytic theory of neurosis*. New York: Norton.

Freud, A. (1966). The ego and the mechanisms of defense. *The writings of Anna Freud*. New York: International Universities Press. (Original work published 1936)

Freud, S. (1905). Fragment of an analysis of a case of hysteria. *Standard Edition* 7:1–123.

——— (1921). Group psychology and the analysis of the ego. *Standard Edition* 18:65–143.

——— (1923). The ego and the id. *Standard Edition* 19:1–59.

——— (1926). Inhibitions, symptoms and anxiety. *Standard Edition* 20:87–174.

Gill, M. M. (1994). *Psychoanalysis in transition: A personal view*. Hillsdale, NJ: The Analytic Press.

——— (1995). Classical and relational psychoanalysis. *Psychoanal. Psychol.*, 12:89–108.

Greenberg, J., & Mitchell, S. (1983). *Object relations in psychoanalytic theory*. Cambridge, MA: Harvard University Press.

Greenberg, J. (1991). *Oedipus and beyond: A clinical theory.* Cambridge, MA: Harvard University Press.

Hatcher, R. (1990). Review of S. Mitchell's 1988 Relational Concepts in Psychoanalysis. *Psychoanalytic Books*, 1:27–136.

Hartmann, H. (1964). Psychoanalysis and developmental psychology. In *Essays on ego psychology* (pp. 108–109). New York: International Universities Press. (Original work published 1950)

——— Kris, E., & Loewenstein, R. M. (1949). Notes on the theory of aggression. *Psychoanal. Study Child*, 3/4:9–36.

Humphrey, N. (1992). *A history of the mind.* New York: Simon & Schuster.

Jacobson, E. (1964). *The self and the object world.* New York: International Universities Press.

Mitchell, S. (1988). *Relational concepts in psychoanalysis: An integration.* Cambridge, MA: Harvard University Press.

——— (1993). Aggression and the endangered self. *Psychoanal Q.*, 52:351–382.

Nunberg, H. (1960). *The synthetic function of the ego. Practice and theory of psychoanalysis.* New York: International Universities Press. (Original work published 1930)

Piaget, J., & Inhelder, B. (1959). *The psychology of the child.* New York: Basic Books.

Pine, F. (1990). *Drive, ego, object, self.* New York: Basic Books.

Waelder, R. (1936). The principle of multiple function. *Psychoanal Q.*, 5:45–62.

Zucker, H. (1989). Premises of interpersonal theory. *Psychoanal. Psychol.*, 6:401–419.

CHAPTER 10

Commentary on Reisner's "Reclaiming the Metapsychology"
(with *Janet Lee Bachant, Ph.D., & Arthur A. Lynch, DSW)*

[(1992). *Psychoanalytic Psychology,* 9(4):563–569.]

Reisner's (1991) article and Holt's (1992) commentary promulgate serious misunderstandings of the place of relational considerations both in the Freudian corpus and in the writings of second- and third-generation theorists. Specifically, the contention that ego psychologists narrowed and systematized a rendition of Freud as a drive theorist for whom endogenous, biological, nonpsychological force is central and relational dynamics are peripheral is challenged. The contributions of these theorists are highlighted and compared with Reisner's and Holt's contentions.

To demonstrate that psychoanalysis considers real experience in general and social experience in particular to be determiners of behavior is to bang on an open door. (Rapaport, 1960p. 62)

Reisner's (1991) article "Reclaiming the Metapsychology: Classical Revisionism, Seduction, and the Self in Freudian Psychoanalysis" and Holt's (1992) commentary on it provide us with an opportunity to consider some prevalent views about contemporary psychoanalytic theory, theoretical diversity, and Freud's theoretical legacy, often referred to as his metapsychology. It is our contention that both Reisner and Holt have mounted a critique of what they consider the orthodox or classical Freudian position which is primarily political and not scientific and is based on important misunderstandings of the "establishment" psychoanalytic theoreticians they criticize.

Reisner attempts two specific tasks. First, he reviews Freud's metapsychology to show that it encompasses both relational and endogenous instinctual components. Second, he attempts to demonstrate how the "second generation" of analysts narrowed the scope of metapsychology so that it became a "pseudoscientific, monistic theory of endogenous drives blindly seeking discharge" (p. 449). Members of that generation, he argues, having accepted "Freud's idealized representation of psychoanalysis-as-science" (p. 457), rewrote metapsychological theory to explain away the seeming contradictions, especially those that were related to environmental influences. This has resulted in a division with some theorists rejecting classical theory and others maintaining it.

In his reexamination of metapsychology Reisner argues, rather as did Hartmann (1959/1964), that Freud developed different theoretical points of view by metaphorically applying multiple sources of knowledge (e.g., biology, anthropology, mythology) to psychic functioning. It is Reisner's contention that within these metaphorical constructions Freud encompassed both endogenous and exogenous sources of motivation, viewing them as leading to behavior that serves either to reduce tension or to promote human interaction. Reisner is correct that Freud never lost sight of the integration of drive and relational concepts, a feature most poignantly illustrated in his case studies. In making his point, however, Reisner consistently overlooks the evolution of theoretical ideas by Freud and his successors, as well as the relationship among the various metapsychological viewpoints in explaining human behavior. Holt (1992) correctly criticizes Reisner's confusion about metapsychology: "... he treats it as if it were just another term for the psychoanalytic theory of motivation, clinical as well as metapsychological" (pp. 111–112). Conceptually, metapsychology has continued to change from one generation to the next.

By 1923 Freud sought to understand what aspects of clinical phenomena could be accounted for by the dynamic, topographic, genetic, and economic models. Indeed, Freud was not consistent in what he considered the essence of psychoanalytic metapsychology, and he continually struggled to create a more comprehensive explanation of mental processes.

As the next generation of analysts set about making their contributions, they addressed many of the questions raised by Freud's inconsistency. Metapsychology, however, maintained its function as a set of abstract generalizations regarding both psychic functioning and its interactional focus. Hartmann (1959/1964) noted:

> ... still bearing in mind that psychoanalysis takes into consideration the interaction of the individual with his environment, as well as his so-called "innerpsychic" processes... "metapsychology"... signifies... those psychological investigations that are not limited to conscious phenomena, and that formulate the most general assumptions of analysis on the most abstract level of theory. Metapsychology is concerned also with the substructures of personality, the ego, the id, and the superego which are defined as units of functions. (pp. 324–325)

This brings us to Reisner's second task, which is to explain how the second generation of Freudian analysts, especially Hartmann,

Rapaport, Fenichel, and Anna Freud, narrowed and distorted the scope of metapsychology. Reisner would have us believe that through a selective representation of Freud's theory, metapsychology "became equated with a theory of endogenously arising psychic tension" (p. 440). Here we must strongly disagree with him. To support his point he presents the work of these theorists selectively and out of context.

An identification of Freud's metapsychology with tension reduction, and a drive theory which accords little importance to relational considerations, are assumptions not found in the works of Rapaport, Hartmann, Fenichel, A. Freud, or any of their collaborators. As early as 1939 Hartmann, in describing the reciprocal relationship between the environment and the individual, wrote: "I believe I am in harmony with Freud's conception when I stress simultaneously the primary importance of social factors in human development and their biological significance" (1939/1973, p. 32). Fenichel (1945) argued for a similarly balanced view of the relation between biological needs and external influences. Both Hartmann and Fenichel warned against the overestimation of either. Addressing those who reproach psychoanalysis as too biologically oriented, Fenichel (1945) maintained that Freud's writings are essentially descriptions of "how instinctual attitudes, objects, and aims are changed under the influence of experiences" (p. 6). Likewise, Rapaport (1960) viewed drive as "an organization of actualities and potentialities which limits and regulates the extent and kind of changes that experience can bring about" (p. 49). This is an active organization of experience as opposed to its passive registration. Rapaport spoke to the importance of the psychosocial dimension of Freud's metapsychology when he described society as:

[The]... necessary matrix of the development of all behavior. Indeed, the development and maintenance of the ego, of the superego, and perhaps of all structures are dependent on the social matrix: behavior is determined by it and is possible only within it. (p.65)

These passages represent the spirit of the contributions of this generation and are a far cry from what Reisner, Holt, and theorists like Greenberg and Mitchell (1984; Mitchell, 1988) would have us believe. In fact, the distorted and narrowed version of Freud's metapsychology—whether imputed to Freud or to his successors—is rejected by all of them, and more aptly describes the perspective of their critics than that of the larger body of second- and third-generation classical psychoanalysts. The characterization of Freud as a drive theorist for whom endogenous, biological, nonpsychological force is central and relational dynamics are peripheral ignores the complex interdependence of Freud's multiple perspectives and oversimplifies an extremely rich and multifaceted theory (see Bachant & Richards, in press).

Reisner has made an interesting "selective representation" of the literature from the second generation theorists for his review. Of particular note is the absence of the definitive work contributed through the collaboration of Hartmann, Kris, and Loewenstein, as well as the omission of any mention of such significant writers as Jacobson, Greenacre, Glover, Lewin, Nunberg, and Waelder. (Also of note is the absence of any reference to the evolution of object relations theory in the structural model.) All these authors worked to elaborate the domain of psychic functioning that was least clear in Freud's writing and of most contemporary interest. This of course involved the ego and the various psychic processes, structures, and functions serving to mediate the internal and external worlds. Reisner and others who exploit the literature to support their main arguments are far more guilty of rewriting history than those who have contributed to its development.

189

Similarly, Reisner's characterization of a group of third generation psychoanalysts (e.g., Brenner, Arlow) as espousing a nonrelational view of classical metapsychology and instinct theory involves the acceptance of Mitchell's dichotomy of drive theory and object relations theory, a dichotomy that psychoanalysts such as Brenner would not accept and that does not reflect an accurate understanding or careful reading of their work. To support his argument that these generations have selectively narrowed Freud's ideas, Reisner offers the following quote from Richard's tribute to Brenner: "... Brenner has been praised for his 'clarifying emendations to the psychoanalytic theory of the drives...amount[ing] to *Freud's own position refined and shorn of the extra-analytic presuppositions*'" (Reisner, 1991, p. 450, italics added by Reisner). This offers us an excellent opportunity to show, through the full quotation, how the selective presentation of ideas can narrow their meaning:

It is to Brenner's lasting credit to have shown how clarifying emendations to the psychoanalytic theory of the drives, which amount to Freud's own position refined and shorn of the extra-analytic presuppositions, culminate in a substantive revision of the structural theory. Rejecting Freud's speculations about the biological origins of the drives, Brenner is led to reassess the notion of the id, which Freud envisioned as the repository of the drives. Freud, and most analysts since him, viewed the drives as constitutionally determined and present from the very beginning of postnatal life. The clear implication is that drives are more independent of experience than are those aspects of mental functioning subsumed under the rubric of "ego." Brenner, however, drawing on all the available psychoanalytic evidence, suggests that drive-related activities, whether libidinal or aggressive, are from birth influenced by experiential factors that gain expression in ego development. In short, clinical analysis does not sustain the separation of ego development from issues of drive expression and drive gratification. It follows that a sharp distinction between ego and id, even a sharp heuristic distinction, must be brought into question. (Richards, 1986 pp. 9–10)

This is a relational view! It exemplifies an understanding of development which encompasses both drive and relational considerations from birth. Because it is written on a metapsychological level, the level of abstract concepts and generalizations, it lacks a certain clinical immediacy. That many writers of the second and third generations addressed metapsychological issues should not be construed as neglecting clinical or relational ones. To achieve a better understanding of the third generation's contributions one simply needs to review Arlow's (1974) ideas about unconscious fantasy in free association; Arlow and Brenner's (1964) elaborations on the dangers and calamities of childhood; or Brenner's definition of drive derivatives as unique, individual, and specific wishes and fears:

What is important with respect to each patient is to learn as much as possible about the libidinal and aggressive drive derivatives which are dynamically important at the moment, including their relation to childhood derivatives and to subsequent experiences and development. What is important, in other words, is to learn as much as possible about what a patient wishes, about who is involved in his wishes, and about how and why he has just those particular wishes about those particular persons. (Brenner, 1982 p. 26)

These contributions rest on profoundly relational concepts involving the centrality of childhood relational configurations and of wishes and fears regarding parents and siblings. The centrality of these concepts is evident in the theoretical and clinical contributions of Arlow and Brenner and other theorists of that supposed school. Reisner is correct in his insistence that Freud always included both endogenous and exogenous factors in his theoretical formulations. We would stress not only that they are both present, but also that they are always viewed as interactive.

Reisner's characterization of so-called second-generation classical revisionists as omitting "those driving forces which Freud consistently depicted as responsive to environmental or relational experience" (p. 441) is simply wrong. Here Reisner is right about Freud, Holt is wrong about Freud, but both Reisner and Holt are wrong about those analysts whom they characterize as Freudian. The acknowledgment of a complex interaction between drive-based and relationally based forces characterizes Freudian theory as well as second-and third-generation classical thinking.

Reisner is on shaky ground when he argues that Freud's theory was marred and distorted by his followers. In fact, the theoreticians to whom he refers have broadened rather than narrowed that theory and have attempted as well to render it less reified and experience distant. We would cite in this regard Arlow and Brenner's (1964) discussion of the advantages of using structural concepts rather than economic ones in regard to psychosis, Beres's (1965) paper on "Structure and Function in Psycho-Analysis," Rangell's (1986) work on the unconscious decision-making function of the ego, and Brenner's (1982) discussion of drive versus wish. All of these are examples of the direction of theorizing that to some extent parallels the efforts of some of the antimetapsychologists, such as Schafer. Further, Brenner's efforts to clarify the concept of defense mechanism, as well as his view of the superego as a compromise formation, involve a revision of Freud's theoretical terms and concepts precisely in the spirit advocated by Holt in his plea for the development of consistency and clearly defined terms in psychoanalytic theory.

These trends in psychoanalytic theorizing make Reisner's charges of conservatism, regressive tendency, and distortion in this group of psychoanalysts very puzzling. Both Holt's narrow understanding of

Freud and Reisner's efforts to restate Freud's original views seem to be in the service of attacking the so-called contemporary classical Freudians by erecting a straw man. It would seem that there is a search for a bad object here. As a result, the level of discourse is polemical, citations become ad hominem rather than scholarly, arguments political rather than scientific.

REFERENCES

Arlow, J.A. (1969). Unconscious Fantasy and Disturbances of Conscious Experience. *Psychoanal Q.* 38:1–27.

——— & Brenner, C. (1964). *Psychoanalytic concepts and the structural theory*. New York: International Universities Press.

Bachant, J., & Richards, A. (1993). Relational concepts in psychoanalysis: A comparative review. Psychoanalytic Dialogues, 3(3):431–460.

Beres, D. (1965). Structure and Function in Psycho-Analysis. *Int. J. Psycho-Anal.* 46:53–62.

Brenner, C. (1982). *The mind in conflict*. New York: International Universities Press.

Fenichel, O. (1945). *The psychoanalytic theory of neurosis*. New York: Norton.

Greenberg, J., & Mitchell, S. (1984). *Object relations in psychoanalytic theory*. Cambridge, MA: Harvard University Press.

Hartmann, H. (1964). Psychoanalysis as a scientific theory. In *Essays on ego psychology: Selected problems in psychoanalytic theory* (pp. 318–350). New York: International Universities Press, 1959.

Hartmann, H. (1973). *Ego psychology and the problem of adaptation*. New York: International Universities Press, 1939.

Holt, R.R. (1992). Some Problems Created by Freud's Inconsistency *Psychoanal. Psychol.* 9:111–114.

Mitchell, S. (1988). *Relational concepts in psychoanalysis*. Cambridge, MA: Harvard University Press.

Rangell, L. (1986). The Executive Functions of the Ego—An Extension of the Concept of Ego Autonomy. *Psychoanal. Study Child* 41:1–37.

Rapaport, D. (1960). The structure of psychoanalytic theory: A systematizing attempt. *Psychological issues*, 2(2, Monograph No. 6). New York: International Universities Press.

Reisner, S. (1991). Reclaiming the Metapsychology *Psychoanal. Psychol.* 8:439–462.

Richards, A.D. (1986). Introduction. In A.D. Richards & M.S. Willick (Eds.), *Psychoanalysis—The science of mental conflict: Essays in honor of Charles Brenner*, pp. 1–27. Hillsdale, NJ: The Analytic Press.

Psychoanalytic Theories of the Self
Ernst A. Ticho, Ph.D. and
Arnold D. Richards, M.D.[24]

[(1982). *Journal of the American Psychoanalytic Association* 30:717–733.]

Ernst A. Ticho presented the opening paper, "The Alternate Schools and the Self." In accord with his belief that the study of "alternate" schools of psychoanalysis is relevant to the evaluation of new psychoanalytic therapeutic approaches, Ticho discussed the approaches to the self of the schools of Adler, Jung, Horney, and Sullivan. Although their definitions of self vary considerably, these schools all emphasize the importance of the subjective, living, creative, experiencing, spontaneous aspects of the psyche in their theories, and criticize what they consider Freud's fragmenting and mechanistic approach to the self. They stress the unity of the self, its indivisibility (Adler) and individuation (Jung). In general, these theories share an optimistic and inspirational orientation with strong moralistic overtones. As a result of stressing the creative self and the meaning and purpose of life, Adler, Jung, and Horney all opposed theories (like Freud's) that stressed inner conflict. Nonsexual

---

24 Held at the Fall Meeting of the American Psychoanalytic Association, New York City, December 21, 1980. Panelists: Harold P. Blum, William I. Grossman, Otto F. Kernberg, Leo Rangell, Arnold D. Richards, Ernst A. Ticho.

meanings were emphasized at the expense of sexual meanings, and the dynamic unconscious was either downplayed, forgotten (Adler), or subordinated to the collective unconscious (Jung). For the alternate schools, synthesis proved more important than analysis. Freud, on the other hand, did not find it necessary to undertake a special synthesis after analysis; for him the unity of the self was, so to speak, self-understood. It should be noted, of course, that Freud's perspective antedates the "widening scope of psychoanalysis" and recent work with more regressed patients.

Ticho next turned to Freud's use of the term *Ich*, pointing out that the German noun *Selbst* (self) is used rarely and sounds awkward. Freud used the German *Ich* in three ways: first, to signify the individual, the person in contrast to other persons; second, as part of the psychic structure; and third, as the experiencing, subjective self. It is of interest that from the beginning of their development, the alternate schools, in contrast to Freud, focused on the subjective, experiential ego and therefore found the English word *self* very much to their liking. To the extent that they wrote German, however, they continued to use the term *Ich* to mean self. In current German psychoanalytic literature, *Selbst* is used a great deal, but primarily as a result of the translation of contemporary American and English literature into German.

Ticho considered in some detail the respective approaches of each of the alternate schools. Adler, who rejected Freud's topographical and structural points of view as arbitrary divisions of the psyche, stressed "style of life" as an overcompensation for inferiority feelings in his early writings. Later, when he found this concept too mechanistic, he spoke more of the "creative self." He felt it futile to base psychology on drives alone, and spoke instead of the creative power of the child that supplies the person with meaningful goals. He refused to regard a person as "other than a self-consistent being and thus as a goal-directed and purposeful whole."

Like Adler, Jung believed the individual's goals were central. For him the self was an archetype expressing the individual's need for unity and wholeness. Since unconscious material belonging to the self always exists, however, regardless of how much of it is made conscious, "there is little hope of ever being able to reach even approximate consciousness of the self." Ultimately, integration, harmony, and self-realization remain ideals to be pursued, but that are better left unachieved.

Karen Horney introduced the idea that the self is idealized to maintain a sense of pseudo unity. Her terms *ideal self* and *grandiose self* have been adopted by more recent theorists. She believed that idealization leads to increasing alienation from the real self. In Horney's theory, neurotic tension between the real self and the idealized self is expressed as a conflict between self-idealization and self-realization. The ideal self, though characterized as "a bit of psychosis woven into the texture of neurosis," nonetheless resembles Adler's conception of the individual's fictional goal. In treatment, according to Horney, the pathological idealized self must be uncovered so that the real self may emerge.

Sullivan developed the concept of a self-dynamism made up of reflected parental appraisals. Sullivan's self includes habitual thoughts about the world and about oneself, everyday perceptions (and misperceptions), more or less recognizable emotions and motives, attitudes about life in general, one's moral code, one's hopes and expectations about the future. This conception is similar to the self-concept of Jacobson, although Sullivan was primarily concerned with interpersonal relations rather than internal psychic organization.

In his concluding section, Ticho, citing Michael Polanyi's view that the thinking and discoveries of scientists are intimately connected with their personalities and are often based on ideas dating back to early childhood, considered the relation between Jung's and Adler's early development and their psychological theories. Does Jung's theoretical contention that early and deep fragmentations of oneself are part of human psychology possibly relate to his own early experiences? Jung's clinical emphasis on supportive measures and reality issues, in contrast to his theoretical concern with the profundities of the collective unconscious, may be related to the near-psychotic breakdown he suffered during a particularly intense period of self-analysis.

In Adler's case, Ticho suggests that the severe learning inhibitions he had to "train himself" to overcome might well connect with the educative thrust of Adlerian psychotherapy. Adler's patients typically remained in formal treatment for only a short time and then became members of his society for individual psychology, a wider family that may be significant in light of Adler's early feelings of rejection by his mother and lifelong feelings of inferiority to an older brother.

In a paper that concerned "Present Controversies Regarding the Concept of the Self," Otto F. Kernberg outlined three major issues related to the position and functions of the concept of the self in contemporary psychoanalytic theory: (1) the relation between the concept of the self and the theory of the ego; (2) the developmental model appropriate to the conception of the self in relation to the ego; and (3) the motivational forces determining ego and self-development.

The Ego and the Self. The theory of the ego and the concept of the self involve three related concepts. The first is the ego itself, the English translation of Freud's *Ich.* The term *ego* lacks the personal quality of the German, which encompasses both Freud's theory of the ego as a mental structure and his concept of the more subjective, experiential self. The second concept is that of the person, the "self" as differentiated by Hartmann from the intrapsychic representation of the person (the self-representation). Kernberg maintained that the apparent clarification of the difference between ego, self, and self-representation by Hartmann and Jacobson has in fact obscured a crucial problem. Freud, he argued, chose not to differentiate fully between these three concepts in his description of the *Ich* as a system; the translation of *Ich* as ego obscures this ambiguity, thereby sacrificing complexity and depth for terminological clarity. In Kernberg's opinion, Freud's ambiguous use of *Ich* reflects his view that the ego is the seat of consciousness, including consciousness of one's self. Hartmann, attempting to free the term ego from this ambiguity, in the end impoverished it.

The Ego and the Self from a Developmental Perspective. Kernberg proposed that we reserve the term self for the "developmental integration of early and later self-representations into an integrated concept of the self" and discard the concept of self as the "objective" person. The self thereby becomes an intrapsychic structure, embedded and originating in the ego, that evolves as the increasingly integrated precipitate of self-representations that arise in connection with the internalization of object representations. Kernberg went on to pose three broad questions relating to the origins of the self, particularly to the differentiation of self- and object representations and the task of integrating contradictory self-representations that reflect gratifying and frustrating experiences.

1. Does the infant have a capacity to differentiate itself from the mother at the beginning of life? Kernberg, in agreement with Jacobson and Mahler (but in disagreement with Melanie Klein, Bion, and Fairbairn), posits an initial stage in which self and object cannot yet be differentiated.

2. If the existence of an initially undifferentiated state of varying duration is accepted, does the early instinctual investment of the "ego-id matrix" reflect a "purely narcissistic" omnipotent primary self-representation, or does the fused, undifferentiated self-object representation contain the precursor of the self- and object investments found in later differentiated states? Kernberg addresses this question through the work of Jacobson, who proposed restricting the term *primary narcissism* to the stage of development that preceded ego differentiation, i.e., the stage of the "primary psychophysiological self." She viewed *secondary narcissism*, on the other hand, as referring to the libidinal investment of an undifferentiated self-object representation from which self- and object representations develop. According to Jacobson, object representations and external objects are invested simultaneously and mutually reinforce each other. Jacobson's formulations, although reinforced by recent infant observations that demonstrate the infant's early discriminatory reactions to environmental stimuli, do not settle the issue of the nature of early drive investments; by pushing back the state of "primary narcissism" to an assumed earliest phase of diffuse discharge onto the "psychophysiological self," she left the origin and development of drives and their relation to libidinal and aggressive investment of self-object representation obscure.

3. Does the self originate simply from blissful states of merger with the mother or from the integration of such states with contrasting states of merger of self- and object representations under the impact of painful, frightening, frustrating, or even catastrophic experiences in early development? Kernberg considered this question crucial because different responses entail different developmental schema and treatment approaches. If one answers that the normal self is directly derivative of the original blissful state, one must view frustrating experiences and the aggression triggered by them as part of the "not

me" experience rather than part of the original self. Thus, Kernberg believes that if Kohut formulated a comprehensive model of earliest development, his approach would necessarily exclude aggression from the structural analysis of the development of ego and self. The contrasting conception of the development of the self sees frightening, painful, or frustrating experiences as contributing to the build-up of merged self-object representations. With development of the aggressive drive, these representations are ultimately differentiated into aggressive self- and object representations. According to this view, shared by Kernberg, parallel investments of libidinal and aggressive self- and object representations lead to contradictory self-representations and contradictory object representations that pose a developmental challenge during separation-individuation that accounts for fixation between symbiosis and object constancy. Central to this conception is the belief that the self is invested with both libidinal and aggressive drive derivatives fused in the integrated self-representations. This is Kernberg's solution to the puzzling question of how psychic structure formation, self-integration, and drive development correlate.

Motivational Forces of the Self: Drives, Affects, and Object Relations. Kernberg claims that an insufficient reexamination of the relationship between drives and affects has tended to perpetuate uncertainty regarding the motivational forces of earliest development. An important question here is whether the primary motivational system consists of internalized object relations rather than affects or drives. More important, what implications follow from the assumption that affects themselves, like drives, are complex structures involving cognitive components?

The Self in Normality and Pathology. Kernberg outlined the implications of his developmental model of ego and self for the clinical understanding of normal and pathological narcissism.

201

Complementing Hartmann's view that normal narcissism reflects the libidinal investment of the self, Kernberg held that the normal self constitutes a structure of self-representations that has integrated both libidinal and aggressive components. The integration of good and bad self-representations is a prerequisite of the libidinal investment of a normal self, just as the integration of love and hatred is a prerequisite for the capacity of normal love. In narcissistic character pathology we see libidinal investment in a pathological self-structure rather than in a normal self-representation. This pathological grandiose self is a condensation of real self, ideal self, and ideal object representations, whereas devalued or aggressively determined self- and object representations are split off, dissociated, repressed, or projected. Psychoanalytic treatment permits the gradual integration of these contradictory self- and object representations and results in the consolidation of a normal self.

From the diagnostic point of view, in borderline conditions the self-concept is not integrated (the syndrome of identity diffusion), in narcissistic personalities a highly integrated but pathological self exists, and in neurotic patients an integrated normal self is present that is the superordinate organizer of key ego functions, including reality testing, ego synthesis, and ego identity.

Finally, Kernberg stressed that the normal self emerges naturally in the context of the integration of the tripartite intrapsychic structure. The self is embedded in the ego but derives from precursors that constitute the structural preconditions of the entire tripartite structure. At the same time, it is subject to repressed, internalized object relations that strive for reactivation through invasion of the self's intrapsychic and interpersonal field. Kernberg believes this concept of the self remains true to Freud's original conception of the *Ich*; it does not abandon Freud's appreciation of the *Ich* as related to, and dependent on, the dynamic unconscious as a constant underlying current influencing psychic functionings.

In a paper titled "The Self as Fantasy: Fantasy as Theory," William J. Grossman located the problem of the self at the intersection of two axes. The first axis is philosophical; it joins the everyday personal experience of self—self-awareness, self-consciousness, etc.—to traditional dilemmas concerning the relation between mind and body, free will and determinism, self and the world of things. The second axis is psychoanalytic, with theoretical concepts at one end and the events of the clinical situation and the patient's subjective experiences at the other. Grossman's basic position is fourfold: (1) there is an essential tension in psychoanalytic theory between the subjective and objective points of view regarding patients' experiences; (2) this tension is built into patients' experiences and is inherent in personal concepts of the self; (3) this tension cannot be avoided in the philosophy of the self or in any theory of the self; and (4) theories derived from direct infant observation attempt to evade this tension by assuming that the behavior observed is equivalent to mental activity, thereby blurring the distinction between objective and subjective by imputing subjective meaning to observed behavior.

The sources and nature of the subject-object duality evident along both axes were next examined with regard to psychoanalytic theory. Grossman considered three sources of this duality: (1) Freud's theoretical belief that man has a dual orientation as a biological organism and a person whose conflicts can be formulated in the nonbiological language of impulses and values; (2) the nature of the analytic stance whereby the analyst must recognize the unity of the patient's present and past while maintaining an "objective distance" from both his own subjective responses (psychoanalytic neutrality) and the patient's subjectively couched communications; and (3) the nature of analytic data whereby the patient's reports contain a subjective component—the expression of imagery, feelings, thoughts, emotions, along with a capacity for objective reflection.

Grossman argued that each source of the subject-object duality bears out the psychoanalytic model of mental activity in which personal accounts and descriptions of self-experience are, in a broad but fundamental sense, theories. Thus when Freud took the self-reflecting patient and the observing analyst and placed them in the mind as the system Cs.-Pcs., he was viewing all mental products as, in some sense, theories. Comparably, his contention that childhood memories are selected and formed with a purpose, his remarks on secondary revision as the first interpretation of the dream, his observation that myths are theories and theories are myths, and his view that fantasies constitute theories about sexuality all demonstrate this belief. For Freud, theory and fantasy are effectively seen as serving both subjective, conflict-resolving aims and objective, reality-oriented aims. Hence their similar form. Freud's willingness to acknowledge correspondences between prescientific cosmologies and psychoanalytic ideas is illustrated in his acknowledgment of the similar structure of Schreber's delusion and the libido theory.

Grossman formulates a definition of the self that follows from the idea that both Freud's libido theory and Schreber's delusion are partly self-state and partly object-relations descriptions. A self-state description, constructed in the same way as any mental product, can be viewed as a fantasy construction that expresses in everyday language feelings, impulses, and ideas about the "self." In other words, the "self" is a special fantasy with its own language and referents. It is anchored in, and derives a sense of immediacy with, bodily experience, activity, and emotional interactions with other people. Although it appears to be supremely subjective, it is nonetheless an objective organization discernible to others. In presenting this definition of the self, Grossman did not invoke a narrow concept of fantasy akin to the daydream, but a complex entity that organizes and directs behavior. His self-concept is a fantasy structure with a wide-ranging organizational and dynamic importance; it is synthesized and abstracted from self-representations regarded as nuclear fantasies of complex structure.

Grossman asked, "If the self is a fantasy, what is the fantasy about?" He answered that the self is the fantasied construction of an object of reflection and self-reference, the locus of self-defining experiences of continuity, and the initiator of self-control. Self-fantasies include in them the idea of self-reference, which, in turn, entails the issues of the self's connectedness with, similarity to, and differences from other people. Grossman noted the similarity between this "fantasy" view of the self and Spiegel's view that the self is a reference framework from which one gains perspective. Citing Mischel and Toulmin's analysis of the self-concept and some remarks by Stone, Grossman characterized the self as a personal myth which, except in borderline or otherwise narcissistic patients, is ordinarily outside awareness.

In closing, Grossman cautioned about the adultomorphic danger of using child observation in constructing a concept of the self in analysis. The self-experience of adults, especially disturbed adults, is too readily equated with infant behaviors of apparently similar form, and adult categories of experience are too easily imputed to infants as yet lacking the requisite discrimination between self and object.

Harold Blum next provided a wide-ranging, extemporaneous discussion that initially focused on definitional issues surrounding the self. Blum pointed out that self-concepts involve different frames of reference and levels of discourse. These concepts include, in addition to that of the self, "the global ego," the self-representation, the true and false selves (Winnicott), and identity (Erikson). The self is offered variously as (1) a substructure (a part of the ego); (2) a parallel structure; (3) a fourth component added to the tripartite system

(Lichtenstein and Eissler); and (4) a superordinate structure (Kohut). Blum offered his own definition of the self as an entity different from, but consonant with, the self-representation that has continuity over time (cohesiveness), is defined at least partly by contrast with other concepts (self versus object, self versus ego), and includes fantastic, magical, mythical, and realistic elements. Noting our debt to Hartmann, Jacobson, Spitz, and Mahler for their formulations regarding the development and function of the self and of self- and object representations, he addressed the tensions in psychoanalytic theory elaborated by Grossman between the different perspectives of the self, pointing out a similar tension between the observing ego and the experiencing ego (Sterba).

Anna Freud

The psychology of the self, Blum submitted, is offered not as a supplement, complement, or extension of our present theories, but as a competing paradigm. To illuminate historical antecedents for this perspective, Blum referred to August Aichhorn's 1936 paper, "The Narcissistic Transference of the Juvenile Imposter." In this work, Aichhorn contended that with many delinquents a narcissistic transference developed only when the therapist presented to the delinquent a glorified replica of his ego ideal. As Anna Freud pointed out, in Aichhorn's treatment of delinquents the transference was used, not analyzed. In the transference relationship, Aichhorn proposed that the delinquent underwent experiences that undid and compensated for deficiencies in early development, enabling him to complete structure formation that had been arrested at a primitive level. According to Blum, both Aichhorn and Anna Freud sharply distinguished this "corrective emotional experience" approach in the treatment of delinquents from the classical analytic treatment of neurosis, and Anna Freud never maintained that a structural deficiency could be repaired simply by utilizing the transference. Blum's implication was that the alternate schools, including the current school of self-psychology, take the opposite view. Self-psychology is "a theory which departs from instinctual conflict or at least sets deficit or developmental arrests alongside conflict at the heart of psychoanalytic work." Self-psychology offers a new mode of treatment for "tragic man" and limits the applicability of insight and structural theory to the treatment of "guilty man." Blum questioned this distinction, pointing out that for the great tragedians, notably Sophocles and Shakespeare, tragedy involved guilt and self-reproach, and both oedipal triumph and punishment.

Blum next considered the self-psychologists' empathic mode of "observation" in relation to their stress on the lack of maternal empathy as a single etiology of psychopathology. He observed that in self-psychology the empathy of the analyst as a selfobject is considered a curative agent; transmuting internalization, the building block of the infant's development, thereby becomes therapeutically central in the analysis. He questioned this broad view of empathy as an etiologic and curative agent, as well as its centrality as a mode of observation. Citing Brenner, he argued that 80 years of psychoanalytic data-gathering from free association have repeatedly demonstrated that empathy is regularly subject to falsification, self-deception, and disguise. Similarly, there are limits to the developmental role we can attribute to parental empathy. Self-psychology's focus on failures of maternal empathy presents us with a theory based on a single trauma that Blum compared to Freud's initial assumption regarding the role of seduction. The mother, Blum noted, brings more than empathy to her caretaking activities, e.g., she provides various cognitive and regulatory functions. She sets limits and disciplines the child, providing, as Kris has noted, an optimal balance between frustration and gratification. Blum doubted whether the complex mother-child interaction so necessary for optimal development could be captured by the "empathy" or "bipolar self" concepts of self-psychology. He further contended that self-psychology lacked a cohesive developmental framework, and contrasted it with the contribution to developmental theory made by Mahler's work on separation-individuation. He pointed up the importance of child observation in helping us avoid "the twin problems of genetic fallacy about later development and the adultomorphic myth about early development."

Leo Rangell stressed that for him the subject of the panel was not psychoanalytic theories of the self, but rather the psychology of the self in psychoanalytic theory. Alternative psychological theories of the self, he believes, generally entail alternative theories of mental functioning that affect the psychoanalytic process so profoundly that they bear no resemblance to psychoanalytic understanding or treatment as we know it. Rangell seriously questioned "Kohut's assertion that the typical modern psychoanalytic symptomatology is based on early deficits" rather than on intrapsychic conflict, as well as Gedo's declaration that oedipal or castration conflicts should no longer be considered central to psychopathology. He made the further methodological point that when analysts diagnose a deficit based on lack of parental empathy, accept the patient's defensive idealization, and attempt to supply what was missing, they employ a therapeutic technique that can only confirm the diagnosis; they cannot then claim that their clinical experience provides evidence that conflict was absent.

Rangell went on to note that narcissism was in fact central to Freud's original division of the mental apparatus into sexual drives directed toward preservation of the race and ego instincts directed toward preservation of the self. Rangell similarly argued that Freud's early division of psychopathology into transference neurosis and narcissistic neurosis cannot be maintained because clinical experience demonstrates that no transference neurosis occurs without narcissistic conflicts, whereas no patient with a "narcissistic neurosis" fails to form a transference.

Whereas Freud himself took care to include both inner and outer, self and object, in his formulations, alternate theories or "insistent new schools" have always stressed one side of the distinction at the expense of the other. An emphasis on either aspect as a whole, moreover, has characteristically been associated with the downplaying of intrapsychic elements in conflict.

"Advocacy of the self in the theoretical context is preservation of the self in a subjective sense." Rangell submitted that this dynamic applies to the whole person in Schafer's action theory, the self-schema of George Klein, the self-organization of Gedo, the power drive of the ego in Adler, and the person in the psychological system of Carl Rogers, as well as to Erikson's concept of ego identity and Kohut's self or self-object.

Rangell claimed that Freud's breakthrough was to dissect the whole into its parts. To abandon our knowledge of internal structure and return to a psychology of the composite whole (i.e., a psychology of the person or self) would represent a scientific regression; the explanatory reach of psychoanalytic theory, especially the parsimonious comprehensiveness afforded by the structural view, would thereby be lost.

Rangell felt that these issues had not been adequately discussed by the authors of the alternative schools. He submitted that Kohut's concept of separate lines of development for narcissistic and object libido was not new but rather intrinsic to Freud's first formulation in which ego instincts were directed toward self, sexual instincts toward objects. But the issue is still more complex because the libidinal trends are both separate and connected: connected in Mahler's symbiotic phase (which in fact corresponds to Kohut's self/selfobject stage), separated at separation-individuation (though after this stage they are still intrapsychically linked via projective and introjective mechanisms). Other questions of priority must be addressed. Can Kohut in fact be credited with formulating the need for tact, empathy, and a nonjudgmental attitude toward narcissistic patients or with recognizing the role of pregenital factors? All these concepts were central to psychoanalysis long before Kohut. More important, Rangell argued that conflicts over self-worth and self-esteem are more satisfactorily explained by internal conflicts than by structural deficiencies. He questioned whether Kohut's concept of self-fragmentation represents a contribution to anxiety theory that in any significant way differs from the existing analytic concept of the traumatic state.

Commenting on Kernberg's contributions, Rangell pointed out that whereas Kohut has become increasingly separatist, Kernberg has become progressively less so, retaining psychoanalytic metapsychology in his clinical descriptions and theories. However, he questioned whether Kernberg's self-object-affect units of internalized self and object relations carry sufficient theoretical conviction and exhibit sufficient cohesiveness and applicability to constitute a new paradigm. His feeling was that insofar as Kernberg substituted defects in these units for intersystemic conflict and, further, viewed the units as primary structures determining both instincts and affects, he veered toward the position of Kohut and was subject to similar criticism.

Shifting to developmental considerations, Rangell questioned the purported existence of infantile narcissism at a time when neither libido nor self can properly be said to exist. Narcissism, whether in its original infantile form or in the form it assumes as a result of regression, is "hardly the self-loving, secure state" that the term signifies in later life, nor is its regressive form tantamount to "the hypertrophied self-esteem traced back to early origins" of original psychoanalytic theory. What appears here as omnipotence is actually compensatory and defensive.

In conclusion, Rangell stated that although basic theory is still not settled, further advances will not necessarily come by discarding such inner psychic components as drives, defenses, and conflicts, as the new psychology of the self has advocated. The theoretical modifications he proposed constitute an expansion of ego psychology that stresses ego-motivational forces. These forces comprehend the self and can fully articulate its inner composition.

In the final prepared presentation of the panel, Arnold Richards contended that psychoanalysis does not need a psychology of the self and, furthermore, that the elevation of the self to the status of a superordinate concept places upon it a burden too heavy for it to bear. Richards proposed Alston and Rubinstein's working definition of the self: the self is the person a person is to himself.

Referring to Kernberg's discussion of the ambiguity in Freud's use of the term *Ich*, Richards suggested that this ambiguity might reflect Freud's belief that distinctions between mind and mental apparatus, between the person and the organism, encroached on philosophy and were therefore beyond the explanatory domain of psychoanalysis. He proceeded to endorse Hartmann's terminological distinction between personal and systemic organismic realms whereby "self" refers to the person and "ego" to the organism. This important distinction, Richards submitted, is lost in the psychologies of the self.

Richards reviewed briefly the self-psychologies of George Klein and John Gedo in order to demonstrate that the introduction of the self as a superordinate construct offers no conceptual, explanatory, or clinical advantages. Klein proposed replacing Freud's metapsychological constructs with the construct of the "self-schema" which he defined as "a central apparatus of control which exhibits a variety of dynamic tendencies, the focus of which is either integration of experience in terms of a sense of continuity, coherence, and integrity or its impairment as cleavages or dissidence." Klein, Richards, argued, intended "self" to be more personal and less subject to reification or concretization than "ego," but lost this intended personal quality when he included in his definition the word *apparatus*. He further questioned the central role Klein assigned in his theory to the need for personal autonomy and the need to be part of a larger social unit, while commending Klein for retaining the central role of unconscious conflict and for not recommending significant shifts in our clinical approach.

Gedo, like Klein, faults Freud's and Hartmann's metapsychological constructs for being too reductionist and abstract and offers the self as the antidote to the impersonal quality of ego-psychological constructs. Unlike Klein, however, Gedo attempts to bridge the hermeneutic/ natural science gap in theoretical conceptualization by including biological motivators. In Richards's opinion, however, Gedo does not convincingly demonstrate the superiority of his schema of the "self-organization" over Hartmann's ego concept, which includes both constitutional and experiential determinants. Gedo's system posits personal autonomy as the highest aim of the organism. Gedo expresses disapproval for usages of the self-concept that focus on it as a mental content or a content of thought, as in the work of Hartmann, Jacobson, and Sandler and Rosenblatt. Such usages "explicitly disavow" what he considers "the cardinal importance of the concept, the epigenesis of human motivations, i.e., of mental structure itself." Richards disagreed with Gedo's claim, arguing that both person and organism develop as a result of the complex interaction of developing biological givens and the environment and that this process is not adequately defined by affixing to it the noun *self*.

Turning to Kohut, Richards pointed out that Kohut's theory assigns the self a superordinate status that is only approached in the psychologies of Klein and Gedo. Kohut's psychology of the self is today presented as a theory able to explain human behavior and psychopathology more cogently than classical psychoanalytic theory. This claim represents a shift from an earlier position (1972), in which Kohut argued against making the self "the basic axiom of psychoanalytic theory," as this would lead to "an abrogation of the importance of the unconscious." Since 1972, however, moving along a road punctuated by a series of sharply dichotomous formulations on various clinical and technical issues, Kohut has evolved a model of the self in which the classical drive model is all but discarded and a "whole new concept of man" is promulgated. Richards believes that the outcome of this shift is a unidimensional view of human nature and psychopathology in which self-cohesion is the highest aim and loss of self the greatest danger. He did not contend that this position is inherently indefensible, but submitted that it is sufficiently different from the perspective of psychoanalysis, with its continuing emphasis on the importance of conflict, infantile sexuality, and oedipal determinants as to make the two approaches irreconcilable.

Richards next raised some questions about the term *grandiose self*, a term introduced by Kohut and adopted by Kernberg. For Kohut the grandiose self is so basic that it becomes one pole of his "bipolar nuclear self." Although the drive connotation was present in Kohut's original formulation, this aspect became less and less evident in his later writings. For Kernberg, on the other hand, the grandiose self represents a specific intrapsychic structure, a form of internalized object relation that organizes the patient's psychopathology and the transference. It is this structural point of view, this description in terms of internalized object relations, that Kernberg would add to our traditional formulation. Richards stressed that Kernberg's concept is an addition to, and not, like Kohut's grandiose self, a replacement for, traditional assumptions, and raised the following questions about Kernberg's use of the term. Is the grandiose self a characterization of a person or a pathological intrapsychic structure? Does the grandiose self represent the totality of the patient's personality or a single aspect of it? Do we have more than one self, i.e., a grandiose self and a normal self, or do we have a series of pathological selves and a series of normal selves? Does Kernberg's suggestion that the self is a psychic organizer, rather than an unconscious fantasy, mean that he is positing a difference between the grandiose self and a fantasy with grandiose features or content? Richards suggested that a sharp difference exists between Kernberg's view of the grandiose self as a pathological structure that has to be discovered and then altered or replaced, and a grandiose fantasy or a fantasy with prominent grandiose features that needs to be analyzed. He argued that a deficit issue is implicit in Kernberg's use of the term *grandiose self* but added that clarity would be better served by using "grandiose" as an adjective referring solely to mental content while including deficit aspects under the concept of an ego that embraces both fixation and regression, deficit and defense.

In conclusion, Richards observed that the concept of the self has been used in an attempt to solve the epistemological problems of what is subjective and what is objective, what is personal and what is organismic, as well as to bridge the hermeneutic and natural science approaches to psychoanalytic theory and experience. The self, he argued, is offered as "a kind of conceptual Valium for the philosophical and theoretical dualities inherent in our work."

Roy Schafer opened the general discussion by offering his view that the topic of the self requires a greater focus on theory construction than on theory reaffirmation; he attributed the latter emphasis to the contributions of Kernberg, Blum, Rangell, and (to some extent) Richards. Schafer viewed the attention given Kohut's self-psychology as symptomatic of the fact that the grip of traditional metapsychological models on psychoanalytic theory is not as tight as it once was. Attempts to discredit alternate psychoanalytic conceptualizations, frequently by misrepresentations, are made by those seeking to defend traditional theory.

Schafer viewed Ticho's contribution as addressing problems of theory construction, but faulted Ticho for not applying the psychobiographical approach to Freud's theory construction as well as Adler's and Jung's. He credited Grossman's contribution with a similar concern, but questioned Grossman's distinction between objective and subjective standpoints. He pointed out that any set of formulations has to be made within a certain framework or point of view and that no theory can therefore embody an objectivity that is truly free and can be contrasted with subjectivity.

Paul Ornstein complimented the panelists for "rather lucid, forceful, and explicit presentations" but felt that certain issues required further clarification. For example, he considered incorrect the notion that Kohut stresses empathy to the exclusion of interpretation. For Kohut empathy is a mode of observation on the basis of which an interpretive hypothesis can be constructed. With reference to Ticho's presentation, Ornstein asserted that self-psychology's focus on the transference, especially the selfobject transferences of all types, makes it vastly different from all other alternate schools. He considered the paucity of discussion of these transferences a serious deficiency of the afternoon presentations. Finally, Ornstein felt that Kohut was misunderstood with reference to the definition of the self and the issue of whether or not it is a superordinate concept. It is not true that Kohut offers no definition of the self. In fact, he offers multiple definitions in his description of the genesis of the self, its dynamics, structure, and functions in health and illness. Furthermore, Kohut has offered an alternate formulation of drives that should be examined for its merits, weaknesses, and complications.

Responding to Schafer, Grossman elaborated his understanding of the difference between objectivity and a purely personal or subjective position: the patient lacks the kinds of information about the analyst that the analyst has about the patient. This information allows the analyst to assume a position that is in a certain sense objective.

After comments from the floor, the discussion was continued by several panel members. Speaking first, Rangell observed that formulations about the development of the self are often confused by a failure to distinguish between three separate developments: that of the self-representation, the "mental self," and the "body self." He added that he was not persuaded by Ornstein's contention that both empathy and interpretation are considered in Kohut's system. Empathy is given vastly more attention than interpretation, an emphasis that Rangell

216

considered unwarranted. Furthermore, Kohut's stress on the empathic stance in the analytic situation removes an important nonjudgmental aspect of analysis and results in a significantly different kind of transference that makes it more difficult to discover the patient's past. Rangell also believes that Kohut has eliminated conflict from its central place in psychoanalysis.

Ticho, responding to Schafer's charge that he had failed to consider the personal determinants of Freud's psychology (as he had those of Adler's and Jung's), affirmed his belief that Freud's convictions could be traced to roots in his early past. Responding to Ornstein's assertion that a focus on the transference distinguished self-psychology from the alternate schools, Ticho referred to Jung's concentration on the transference. Finally, in regard to Ornstein's belief that Kohut is often misunderstood, Ticho felt that this misunderstanding partly resulted from Kohut's lack of clarity of definition and conceptualization.

Speaking at some length, Kernberg commented first that both Grossman and Schafer had introduced to the issues at hand a philosophical perspective that stresses motives over causes. For Kernberg this is but one philosophical position; other positions are also tenable, including one that holds it possible to develop a scientific, causal approach to psychology. For him, the combined analysis of the subjective communication of the patient's behavior and the interaction between patient and analyst provides objective knowledge.

Turning next to his definition of the self, Kernberg reaffirmed the usefulness of the concept of structure, which he defined (citing Rapaport) as (1) stable configurations of psychic functioning with a slow rate of change; (2) channels of organization of psychic functioning that determine specific behaviors or experiences; and (3) a dynamic organization of these configurations (which are determined by conflicts) in, for example, the form of a fantasy. For Kernberg, however, the self, as the integration of the self-representations, is not simply a fantasy as Grossman and to some extent Richards suggest, but an intrapsychic structure with significant organizing qualities. At the same time, Kernberg agreed with Rangell's correction that an integration of self-representations results in a composite self-representation, not in the self. Kernberg maintained that Richards had misunderstood his concept of the grandiose self. To Kernberg, the grandiose self is an important structure that includes highly specialized ways of dealing with self and others. He stressed, however, that his view of structure is conflictually determined, and any suggestion that he supports a deficit theory of psychopathology is totally incorrect.

The last speaker was Grossman, who asserted that Kernberg was incorrect in contending that he (Grossman) underestimates the importance of observing behavior. Kernberg and he were simply addressing themselves to different issues.

CHAPTER 12

Unconscious Fantasy: An Introduction to the Work of Jacob A. Arlow, M.D., and to the Symposium in His Honor

[(1992). *Journal of Clinical Psychoanalysis,* 1(4):505–511.]

The notion of unconscious fantasy is central to psychoanalysis in the 1990s. The contributors to this issue of the *Journal of Clinical Psychoanalysis* will be clarifying the degree to which this notion is grounded in Freud's pioneering work; and they will be clarifying, in turn, the ways in which this notion has evolved, both theoretically and clinically, in the half-century following his death. Since the New York Psychoanalytic Society's 1991 symposium, "The Clinical Value of the Concept of Unconscious Fantasy," was the occasion for these papers, it is fitting that we begin the issue by reviewing the contributions of Jacob Arlow, who was honored at the symposium. For it is Arlow who has placed the understanding and interpretation of unconscious fantasies at the heart of the psychoanalytic endeavor, and his work significantly informs the contributions to follow.

For me, Jack Arlow is the Richard Feynman of psychoanalysis. Like the brilliant theoretical physicist acclaimed for his ability to solve the problems of engineers and applied scientists (his demonstrating the cause of the failure of the space shuttle Challenger's O rings is a recent example), Arlow is the analyst called on by colleagues and candidates when an analysis is intractable or when efforts at clinical formulations have left lesser heads spinning. His confident ease in approaching problems rests on an utter mastery of psychoanalytic theory and method, though to the undiscerning this mastery may be obscured by his consistent use of jargon-free and experience-near terminology. These qualities typify his papers and in large measure account for their immense popularity among students. Almost all of his many contributions to the literature contain extensive case material well-integrated into the text. If there has been some neglect of Arlow's status as a theoretician of psychoanalysis, it is only because of his accessible writing style, his clinical directness, and the fact that his considerable body of work has up to now appeared primarily in the journal literature, making difficult its assessment as a coherent whole. In contradistinction, Charles Brenner, his frequent collaborator, approaches metapsychological issues more directly, and his work has long been accessible in two volumes, *Psychoanalytic Technique and Psychic Conflict* (1976) and *The Mind in Conflict* (1982).

The publication of *Psychoanalysis: Clinical Theory and Practice* (1991), a volume containing 22 of Arlow's most important papers, provides us with ready access to the seminal contributions that account for Arlow's pervasive impact on our field. Selected by Arlow himself, the papers are arranged chronologically, beginning with "Anal Sensations and Feelings of Persecution" (1949) and ending with "The Dynamics of Interpretation" (1987). Since that time, Arlow has published approximately 25 additional papers, so that we can probably look forward to the publication of a second volume.

In the state of theoretical diversity that characterizes contemporary psychoanalysis, these papers are recommended to readers on all sides of current debates. They are especially recommended to adherents of the various schools that now range themselves against what they consider an outdated "classical" psychoanalysis, of which Arlow and

Brenner are the representatives most frequently mentioned. That in fact (if not intention) the two figure in these debates as straw men is evident from the typical absence of any substantive discussion of their work and its development over several decades. In one recent dialogue between adherents of contemporary classical psychoanalysis and the relational school of analysis, the representative of the latter approach acknowledged that his discussion may well have been impeded by his having inadequately studied the contributions of contemporary classical Freudians. This new volume gives everyone an opportunity to immerse themselves in Arlow's work. There is now even less excuse for neglect.

In *The Science of Mental Conflict,* a Festschrift for Charles Brenner, a case was made for the innovative if nonrevolutionary aspects of Brenner's work (Richards and Willick, 1986). Two years later, Yale Kramer (1988) made a similar case on Arlow's behalf, arguing in the Festschrift *Fantasy, Myth, and Reality* that Arlow's contributions have "gradually transformed our understanding of the human mind and of what psychoanalysis is" (p. 11). Kramer identified three transformations in particular. The first involves the conceptual and linguistic shift from instinct theory and economics to conflict theory and dynamics. This shift was first elaborated in the book Arlow coauthored with Charles Brenner in 1964. The linguistic and theoretical yield of this study is that it allows analysts to dispense with concepts such as cathexis, decathexis, and hypercathexis. These experience-distant terms, Arlow and Brenner hold, prevent the analyst from coming to grips with the specific childhood determinants of the patient's symptoms and behavior. A new appreciation of the dynamic unconscious allows the elucidation of motivations to replace a simple naming of processes. Kramer paraphrases an Arlow formulation that has transformed work with patients:

Each individual has a hierarchy of fantasy formations in his mind and this hierarchy reflects the vicissitudes of his experience

221

and psychic development. Furthermore, these fantasies are grouped around universal infantile wishes, and the same wish may be expressed in different fantasies as the individual matures and the integrative capacity of the ego changes [p. 18].

The beauty and the utility of this formulation rest in its balanced depiction of the relation between environmental and endogenous forces in psychic development and pathogenesis. It helps the analyst avoid dichotomous thinking through misplaced emphasis on one aspect of experience, whether environmental or intrapsychic, to the exclusion of the other.

A second major transformation for which Arlow is responsible concerns the way analysts think and do clinical work. I refer to the shift of emphasis from unconscious content to the analysis of defense. This shift was prepared for by Freud's theoretical reformulations of the mid-1920s, which were then extended by his collaborators in the mid-1930s, and by his successors over the ensuing two decades. Arlow and Brenner's emphasis on the technical precept that analysis cannot succeed by simply uncovering the unconscious/suppressed has provided the foundation for many of today's most important contributions. For Arlow, the concept of defense is central to the entire range of normal and pathological phenomena. The latter are represented in this collection by papers on depersonalization, derealization, and déjà vu.

Arlow's third and most significant transformation is to have made the concept of unconscious fantasy central to clinical thinking and practice. The central idea is that the lives of patients and analysts alike are affected for better or worse by childhood wishes expressed in fantasies having both individual and universal features. This notion is complemented by a theory of memory that avoids the fruitless debates between relativists and realists. In it, proper place is given both to external reality and psychic reality, to fantasy and trauma/seduction.

A dynamic relation is posited between childhood wishes and childhood trauma, childhood imperatives and childhood experience; this relation is maintained throughout development and is seen to underlie what is observed in the analytic situation. In "Theories of Pathogenesis" (1981), Arlow, evoking Freud, contrasts the *recovery* of memories with their *reconstruction,* noting "how rare it is for the memory of a primal scene experience, for example, to be recovered... even in... instances in which patients had been exposed... repeatedly and for long periods of time to parental activities in the bedroom" (p. 333). He invokes Ernst Kris's comments challenging the "pathogenic significance of a specific memory" (p. 333). Reconstructive work, Kris had suggested in 1966, would be hopeless were its aims to reconstruct exactly "what had happened." Instead he wrote, "Its purpose is more limited and much more vast. The material of actual occurrences... is constantly subjected to selective scrutiny of memory under the guide of the inner constellation.... They are molded into patterns and it is with these rather than with the events with which the analyst deals" (p. 333).

Nevertheless, Arlow notes the persistence of the "appeal of specificity" in authors such as Kernberg and Kohut. He argues, "The quest for specifics... has been transposed from the domain of individual memories" to that of certain very specific pathogenic object relations that seem "independent of... the usual conflicts over childhood instinctual wishes" (pp. 333–334). Even in his own work the appeal is not muted. But for Arlow, it serves principally as a reminder that the possibility of a real trauma or its actual recovery in memory is not to be foreclosed, even if it is the reconstruction of psychic reality, which is never made up out of whole cloth, that affords therapeutic leverage. In "Affects and the Psychoanalytic Situation" (1977), Arlow tells of a patient who, in response to a severe disappointment, had fallen into a trancelike state. She reported this in the next session and associated to a severe bout of eczema at the age of 6 months. Here Arlow stops to reflect:

Did she regress to the actual experience and relive it as a motor memory in the context of fresh disappointment and helpless, frustrated rage? Or had she reactivated some fantasy connected with being told about her childhood trauma? While I am much tempted by the former explanation, parsimony inclines me toward the latter [Arlow, 1991, p. 276].

Kramer, in his appreciation of Arlow's work, claims: "In psychoanalysis, we are no longer interested in the individual's objective history because there is none.... All memory is screen memory" (p. 34). Here Kramer falls, momentarily at least, into the extreme relativism that Arlow is careful to avoid. Interestingly, Kramer's remark is a gloss on a page from Arlow that appears in the ellipsis: "What constitutes trauma is not inherent in the actual real event, which in any case is posited, but rather in the individual response to the disorganizing, disruptive combination of impulses and fears integrated into a set of unconscious fantasies" (p. 34). Here we discern an ample corrective to Kramer's misplaced emphasis, which on balance seems mainly verbal.

This more nuanced view of fantasy, memory, and experience is part of a more general move beyond the ego psychology formulated by Hartmann and his colleagues, a body of theory that Arlow views as having drawn too sharp a distinction between the conflictual and conflict-free spheres of mental functioning. In a broader sense, what Arlow has elaborated is consistent with Freud's idea that there is no sharp distinction to be made between the normal and the abnormal in mental life. This has allowed Arlow to accomplish what Kramer rightly praises as "conceptual streamlining of our clinical and technical theory." One of the main strategies for achieving such streamlining has been Arlow's insistence that every practitioner of psychoanalysis be able to articulate the theory of pathogenesis on which treatment is based. Since for Arlow symptoms are caused not by memories but by intrapsychic conflicts, what is curatively central is knowledge of conflict and the patient's "understanding of how his mind works" (Kramer, 1988, p. 27). Thus Arlow brings about a shift in emphasis from structure to meaning. Although Arlow refers frequently to the structural model and structural change, there is a pronounced hermeneutic aspect to his conceptualization of the psychoanalytic process and a diminished role for the concept of mental agency. Arlow himself does not appear to have elaborated this shift in a self-conscious fashion. Brenner has recently attempted this elaboration in an unpublished paper that might aptly be titled "The Deconstruction of the Structural Model."

Arlow's elevation of the concept of metaphor ("Psychoanalysis is essentially a metaphorical enterprise" [Arlow, 1979, p. 373]) suggests that his approach may be viewed as a sophisticated communications theory in which the rules and procedures by which unconscious is translated into conscious, latent into manifest, and vice versa, hold a central place. The role of context and contiguity in determining latent meaning is also emphasized in this context. Viewed in this way, psychoanalysis is very much a cognitive psychology. It is also important to note that Arlow's emphasis on metaphor allows him to transcend any narrowly phasic or zonal focus. It is an error to read into his work a clinical focus on the oedipal and genital-phallic stages; wishes and their attendant conflicts from earlier and later phases often play important pathogenic roles. In this regard, there is an affinity between Arlow's approach and that of other schools, particularly the Kleinians, inasmuch as he shares with them an emphasis on the centrality of conflict.

Kramer is correct in asserting that Arlow, like Brenner, has abandoned the use of a structural model with reified psychic agencies.

This can be confirmed by means of a simple experiment. Go through the pages of his volume of papers and eliminate the terms *id, ego,* and *superego* wherever they appear. It will be found that this can generally be done with little sacrifice of meaning and content; one sees as well that the frequency with which the terms are used diminishes over time. Often their use seems to occur simply through habit or by way of afterthought. Even in the case of the most apparent exception to this finding, the 1982 paper on the superego, structural theory seems in the process of dissolution as this erstwhile agency becomes simply one outgrowth of the "calamities of childhood" catalogued by Brenner and occasioning conflict, defense, and compromise formation.

"Id, ego, and superego," Arlow has remarked, "exist not in the patient but in psychoanalytic textbooks" (personal communication). And even there, where they once served as useful shorthand for processes that are now better understood, they seem to be losing ground. "At the moment," Kramer notes, "we seem to be in a transitional period, one in which we cannot do without the structural theory and yet seem to have transcended it" (p. 36). Contemporary classical analysts like Arlow and Brenner have been in the forefront of this movement, refining psychoanalytic theory as they have rendered its concepts more experience-near. Arlow's work in particular can be viewed as an expression of Wallerstein's concept of clinical "common ground." It is, after all, shared clinical practices and experiences that have held our field together.

REFERENCES

Arlow, J.A. (1949), Anal sensations and feelings of persecution. *Psychoanal. Q.*, 18:79–84.

——— (1979). Metaphor and the psychoanalytic situation. *Psychoanal. Q.*, 48:363–385.

——— (1981). Theories of pathogenesis. *Psychoanal. Q.*, 50:488–513.

——— (1987). The dynamics of interpretation. *Psychoanal. Q.*, 56:68–87.

——— (1991). *Psychoanalysis: Clinical Theory and Practice.* Madison, CT: International Universities Press.

——— & Brenner, C. (1964). *Psychoanalytic Concepts and the Structural Theory.* New York: International Universities Press.

Brenner, C. (1976). *Psychoanalytic Technique and Psychic Conflict.* New York: International Universities Press.

——— (1982). *The Mind in Conflict.* New York: International Universities Press.

Hale, N.G. (1971). *Freud and the Americans: The Beginnings of Psychoanalysis in the United States.* New York: Oxford University Press.

Kramer, Y. (1988). In the visions of the night: Perspectives on the work of Jacob A. Arlow. In: *Fantasy, Myth, and Reality, Essays in Honor of Jacob A. Arlow.* Madison, CT: International Universities Press.

Kramer, Y. (unpublished). Modern conflict theory or beyond the ego and the id, 1992.

Richards, A.D., & Willick, M., eds. (1986). *Psychoanalysis: The Science of Mental Conflict. Essays in Honor of Charles Brenner.* Hillsdale, NJ: Analytic Press.

CHAPTER 13

Book Review of: *The Human Core. The Intrapsychic Base of Behavior.* Vol. I: *Action Within the Structural View;* Vol. II: *from Anxiety to Integrity*

By Leo Rangell, M.D. Madison, CT: International Universities Press, Inc., 1990. 959 pp.

[(1993). *Psychoanalytic Quarterly* 62:281–287.]

Leo Rangell

Like Arlow and Brenner, who have effected major revisions in Freudian theory, Leo Rangell extends psychoanalytic theory into new areas. His contributions, like theirs, are not patchwork jobs for an ailing theory but rather proposed solutions to important psychoanalytic problems. In the present collection, 35 papers are selected from the more than 300 Rangell has written over the course of four decades.

In Volume I, *Action within the Structural View*, Rangell re-examines the problem of anxiety in psychoanalytic theory and considers problems of choice, responsibility, and integrity. He provides a set of concepts and constructs dealing with aspects of human behavior that very few psychoanalytic theorists have even considered. As in all his works, his solutions to problems are grounded firmly in the work of Freud and his successors, chief among them Heinz Hartmann, Otto Fenichel, and David Rapaport. Rangell argues that his "postulation of unconscious choice conflict and the contiguous concept of unconscious ego decision-making... is... quite different from the conventional type of oppositional conflict which leads to a solution by compromise formation" (p. 14). To Freud's concept of signal anxiety and of thought as experimental action he appends four additional concepts: "intrapsychic process" as against intersystemic conflict between, for example, ego and id; a new ego function referred to as unconscious decision-making; the syndrome of the compromise of integrity; and the exercise of will as an aspect of ego autonomy.

In "Psychoanalysis, Affects, and the 'Human Core,'" written in 1964, Rangell introduces his concept of "the human core," which is marked by "the unconscious rather than conscious, the intrapsychic rather than internal-external, and the conflictful rather than the conflict-free and autonomous..." (p. 61). This harks back to Ernst Kris's definition of psychoanalysis as human behavior seen from the point of view of unconscious conflict. Of interest in this paper is Rangell's discussion of the then hot concept of identity; he remarks that the concept had encountered "less resistance than has almost any other psychoanalytic formulation..."; he argues that this was so because the concept "dynamically act[s] like an inexact interpretation" (p. 65). Identity is rather "an intermediate formation,... as much the result of pre-existing intrapsychic conflicts and their derivatives and resolutions as a node from which further conflictful or adaptive constellations eventuate" (p. 65). Nearly thirty years later, the identity concept has arguably been replaced by the concept of the self. Rangell's point is that explanations based on identity disturbance or the vicissitudes of self-esteem are "not erroneous, but incomplete and unidimensional" (p. 67).

In "Structure, Somatic and Psychic," Rangell comments on the way direct child observation complements inferences made from adult analyses. One of the myths about "classicists" is that they filter all their formulations through the lens of oedipal dynamics. This chapter illustrates that with Rangell this is not the case. He is concerned with the first year of life, the oral phase in particular. He states that classical analysis has always been concerned with understanding preoedipal phases and that it has always employed both direct observation and psychoanalytic inference. The concept of psychobiological unity is introduced to bring together Freud's two theories of anxiety; Rangell relates the first to biological and physiological aspects of anxiety and the second to its psychological components. His point is that both are relevant and must be included in any comprehensive theory. This au courant concept allows the integration of recent biological studies of anxiety into a psychoanalytic frame of reference.

Rangell's unitary theory of anxiety is presented succinctly: "The anxiety reaction is always set in motion by an existing traumatic state, either one which has invaded the ego involuntarily from outside of its control (as in Freud's first theory); or one which has been brought about by the ego under its control in a minimal and experimental way (from Freud's second theory)" (p. 305). Rangell contrasts his position with that of Brenner, who would limit anxiety to signal anxiety, requiring an ego capable of anticipating danger. There would seem to be some semantic confusion in Rangell's claim that he retains Freud's concept of actual neurosis. "Actual neurosis" is not simply the equivalent of a traumatic state; "actual" has here the meaning of "everyday" and involves Freud's idea that anxiety stems from unsatisfied sexual needs and the attendant damming up of the libido, which is then converted into anxiety. Rangell, however, seems to take "actual" as meaning automatic. He then insists that the concept be retained, as for him "automatic" does not entail the absence of psychological meaning, but is used simply to mean "occurring involuntarily" (p. 259). Rangell and Brenner would likely agree that anxiety as the presence of a traumatic state is in essence a signal of danger. The danger in trauma, according to Rangell, is in its continuing or getting worse or never stopping.

In "The Psychoanalytic Theory of Affects," Rangell sharpens his critique of Brenner's position that depressive affect is on a par with anxiety as a cause of defense. Rangell asserts that for him anxiety "occupies a supraordinate position since, in contrast to any of the other affects, anxiety is never absent in the intrapsychic sequence of events prior to the institution of the defensive activity" (p. 319). He also refers to Brenner's suggestion that ideation is included within the concept of affects. By contrast, Rangell sees ideation and affect as "separate derivatives of instinctual drives as modified and influenced by ego and superego activity" (p. 321). The connection between affect and instinctual drive is part of Freud's earliest formulations. Brenner would likely argue that the connection moves in the direction of an energy transformation view of affect, energy being either libidinal or aggressive, which has limited clinical usefulness as compared to a theory that replaces the concept of instinctual drive with psychological wish, libidinal or aggressive.

In *From Anxiety to Integrity*, the second volume of *The Human Core*, the emphasis shifts "from the intrapsychic core of human behavior to the core of psychoanalysis itself, as science and as a technical procedure" (p. 471). Rangell is deeply concerned with psychoanalytic dissidence, which he views as fueled by irrational forces and unresolved conflicts in the minds of those dissenting. These have resulted in a series of linkages, of groups and theories, built around different points of emphasis in repetitive succession. In each there has been the fallacy of either *pars pro toto* or the selection of one pole of what in life is a duality. The external environment at the expense of the internal was selected by Horney, the interpersonal by Sullivan, downplaying the intrapsychic, object relations rather than drives by Fairbairn. Pregenital determinants are pointed to exclusively, without the role played by the oedipal; the "here-and-now" is sought instead of reconstruction, deficiency rather than conflict, empathy over interpretation, new experience rather than insight into the past (p. 836).

He goes on to comment on the overemphasis by some theoreticians of one phase of development over another: the moment of birth for Rank, the first year of life at the expense of all that follows for Klein, Fairbairn, Bowlby, and Winnicott.

Clearly, Rangell cannot accept Wallerstein's notion of common ground. As the distance between competing schools increases, "The lines of cleavage are not semantic but substantive, with definitive consequences for the conduct of analysis" (p. 865). Finding the common ground approach inadequate to meet this situation, he advances his notion of total composite psychoanalytic theory. For Wallerstein, clinical theory, unified and universal, is the common ground; different explanatory views are simply metaphorical. Rangell views that distinction as dovetailing nicely with Waelder's view of experience-near clinical theory versus experience-distant abstract theory, but the distinction is not at all that clear-cut, as many clinical concepts are theoretical and abstract, even that of transference. Rangell's response to the question "One psychoanalysis or many?" is a belief in what he calls diversity in unity, multiple phenomena under the umbrella of a single integrated theory. He points to an interesting difference between Wallerstein and Fenichel. Whereas Wallerstein posits a diversity of theories but a single clinical method, Fenichel's view, which is in essence Rangell's, is that there "are many ways to treat neuroses, but… only one way to understand them" (pp. 867-868). A third position, which Rangell fails to note, is that of Arlow, for whom the treatment of neurosis is tied closely to the analyst's theory of pathogenesis. As there are more ways than one to understand neuroses, so there are more ways than one to treat them.

Rangell finds no basis of commonality with self psychologists, who have built a theory founded on childhood deficits and failures to the exclusion of the intrapsychic and the conflictual, or with Melanie Klein, who stressed the first year of life and de-emphasized the role of later experience. Against Fred Pine's federation of "four psychologies" Rangell asserts that we have but one theoretical country and thus no need to bring into it secessionist theoretical provinces with no justification for having seceded in the first place. Unfortunately, this political metaphor works all too well and suggests that our theoretical differences are often more political than scientific.

Volume II begins with a paper from 1953 that discusses similarities and differences between psychoanalysis and psychoanalytically oriented psychotherapy. Rangell defines psychoanalysis as "a method of therapy *whereby* conditions are brought about [that are] favorable for the development of a transference neurosis, in which the past is restored in the present, *in order that*… there occurs a resolution of that neurosis (transference *and* infantile) *to the end* of bringing about structural changes in the mental apparatus of the patient to make the latter capable of optimum adaptation to life" (p. 479). Important to his view is that the differences between psychoanalysis and psychotherapy are not based on differing concepts of psychopathology and the mind at work.

The next chapter, "Psychoanalysis and Dynamic Psychotherapy," was written twenty-five years later. The difference he notes in his technical views is in the direction of flexibility. Now he presents himself as willing to see patients sitting up as well as lying down, to conduct hours on the telephone, to schedule sessions back-to-back or irregularly, etc. He contrasts his position with that of Gill, especially on the issue of transference. For Rangell, transference is "the central lever of the therapeutic process," but it is also "a means, not an end, a way station through which the infantile neurosis and its derivatives are incorporated into the analytic procedure" (p. 493).

In "The Psychoanalytic Process," Rangell offers an account of what happens in psychoanalysis:

Only in psychoanalysis, under the protection of the analytic situation, is the patient motivated and willing *to produce* voluntary psychic disequilibria in a regressive path toward such original nuclear etiological situations. In other psychotherapies only anxiety which is already present... is accepted to be faced by the patient... only [in psychoanalysis] does interest transcend the structure of the symptom and concern itself in depth with the genetics, dynamics, and structure of the basic surrounding and underlying character (pp. 540–541).

He points out the dangers of an excessive concern with transference.

Patients treated with excessive, even compulsive concentration on transference can emerge looking and feeling analyzed but with a pathetic and clonelike quality of dependence. They cling to their analysts, can become devotees, even benefactors of analysis, but with a shallow defensiveness through which the opposite can break through (p. 551).

As for Kleinians, they

generally present interpretations beyond data and below defenses, memories, or preconscious readiness... Analysts backed by ego and structural theory who also give priority to transference phenomena generally impart interpretations of intrapsychic conflict in principle connected with associative data (p. 553).

But, he acknowledges, "Structural concepts can of course also become reified and irrational" (p. 553). "What causes change," he asks, "and—where it occurs—cure?" (p. 562). The factors include a quantitative one connected with the severity of trauma in a given case and with the changes in signal anxiety as a result of psychoanalysis. The result is a wider choice for the ego of what it can safely do, an increase in the area of the patient's "active though unconscious choice." The central idea here is that interpretations given by the analyst can diminish automatic or signal anxiety. This leads to an increase of capacity for active choice. Choices, however, "even with neurotic anxiety sharply diminished, may still not be as free as the analyst thinks or the patient would like" because of "internal limitations which mitigate equally against the expansion of life" (p. 568). Limited ego capacities; a paucity of learning, information, or developed channels of discharge; excessive passivity; a low level of instinctual strength—all are factors that hinder the movement from insight to change.

In "Defense and Resistance in Psychoanalysis and Life," Rangell describes what he considers a characteristic common to Freud's thinking and that of his successors: namely, the tendency to divide larger categories into their component parts. Freud, he reminds us, divided instincts into subtypes and dissected symptoms into "components of which they are the vectors" (p. 582). Anna Freud divided defensive behavior into specific defense mechanisms. Rangell notes that today there is opposition to "differentiating part processes within the whole" (p. 582) due to a concern that "the process of differentiation... does violence to the subjective integrity of the individual" (p. 583). Rangell, however, insists that mainstream psychoanalytic theory retains an important place for integration as "a parallel process and principle alongside the process of differentiation... " (p. 584). Relevant here is the synthetic function described by Nunberg, the organizing and integrating function described by Hartmann, and, not least, the unconscious decision-making executive function described by Rangell himself.

In "Rapprochement and Other Crises," Rangell warns against the overuse of some Mahlerian concepts, "rapprochement crisis" in particular. He points to a similar tendency, one having even less felicitous results, as regards the concept of projective identification, a term that "has come to be used to explain indiscriminately almost all interpersonal phenomena... " (p. 617). As for rapprochement, Rangell is concerned about its use as a specific etiological point of pathology. Socarides, for example, has used it in regard to the etiology of perversion, while the Tysons have used it to explain what they call pseudo-narcissistic personality. Rangell writes that the term *rapprochement* takes its place alongside all such universal tools of insight. But its enlistment as a distinct memory, or as a developmental year or few months of specifically experienced anxiety, trauma or depression cannot be automatically pointed to, or taken for granted from universal knowledge, as an individually exposed and remembered event or condition or series of experiences (p. 623).

He concludes, aphoristically, "Psychopathology stands on a base, not a point."

It is in remarks such as this that Rangell, who so often is taken as the representative of an outdated and ossified classical theory, reveals an outlook that preempts the criticisms of would-be revisionists. In these papers he has elaborated the developed body of Freudian thought in a way that highlights its longstanding attention to both wholes and parts. While he rejects any easy dichotomy that would identify a psychology of the whole as humanistic and a psychology of the parts as mechanistic, he insists that "the self, and the object, as whole entities, have always had a firm place in central unified psychoanalytic theory" (p. 6). That theory is for him not ego psychology but a total composite psychoanalytic theory, embracing id, ego, and superego, as well as the external world. Resisting the widespread tendency to characterize the classical position narrowly as drive theory or ego psychology or structural theory, Rangell presents an approach whose aim is to render unnecessary a plurality of competing theories.

CHAPTER 14

Review of: *Practice and Precept in Psychoanalytic Technique. Selected Papers of Rudolph M. Loewenstein: With an Introduction by Jacob A. Arlow.*

(New Haven & London: Yale University
Press. 1982. pp. 240. £17.50.)

[(1984). *International Review of Psycho-Analysis*, 11:369–372.]

Rudolf Loewenstein

Practice and Precept in Psychoanalytic Technique brings together 13
papers written by Rudolph Loewenstein between 1951 and 1972,

12 of which deal with technique and the theory of technique.[25] The remaining paper included in the volume concerns the psychodynamics of masochism, "A contribution to the analytic theory of masochism." Excluded from this collection are the five landmark papers Loewenstein co-authored with Heinz Hartmann and Ernst Kris, his *Christians and Jews: A Psychoanalytic Study* (1951), his "In Memoriam" essays, and a number of brief contributions and review essays. Grouping these papers on technique in a single volume makes a certain amount of repetition perhaps unavoidable. But though one cannot read the collection cover to cover with any sense of continual discovery, Loewenstein's major arguments retain their importance and so bear repeating. The book clearly establishes the value of the insights and technical recommendations which issues from Loewenstein's ego psychological perspective. The first paper in the collection, "The problem of interpretation" (1949), is a treasure trove of useful dos and don'ts exemplifying the balanced viewpoint Loewenstein brought to the major issues of psychoanalytic technique. His major contribution to the problem of interpretation, as Arlow observes in his excellent introduction to the volume, was to emphasize that "interpretations do not represent the sum total of the analyst's interventions" (p. 5), and to describe, accordingly, the range of interventions necessary if interpretations are to have their desired dynamic effect. Confrontation, clarification, and questioning of the analysand are among the dimensions of the analyst's activity that are addressed in these pages. Loewenstein's sensitivity to the various constituents of the interpretive process serves as a necessary counterweight to the tendency of analysts to "define" analysis as a therapeutic modality in which the transference neurosis is resolved by "interpretation" in

---

25 The remaining paper included in the volume concerns the psychodynamics of masochism, "A contribution to the analytic theory of masochism."

the narrow sense of the term. Indeed, Loewenstein's papers are of particular value for the very reason that they help us steer between the Scylla of psychoanalytic rigidity and the Charybdis of wild analysis.

Within the context of Loewenstein's treatment of interpretation several topics are worthy of mention. His reconsideration of Freud's analogy between psychoanalytic and archaeological investigation (chapters 1 and 7) is noteworthy for clarifying anew the limits of the comparison: "even the best preserved relic of antiquity may remain unnoticed until the curiosity of some searcher uncovers it; only then can it become capable of influencing the present. By contrast, the buried remains of an individual's past may influence his present not only during but because of their concealment and it is precisely due to this indirect influence they exert on the patient's actual behavior that they become subject to investigation and thus can be uncovered at all" (p. 129). Of special note is Loewenstein's attentiveness to "the nature and development of defense mechanisms against superego demands"; he reminds us that frequently it is not drives but superego concerns (guilt) that are repressed. This insight is particularly relevant to patients with so-called narcissistic personality disorders, whose impulsive, drive-oriented behaviour frequently masks unconscious guilt. We should mention as well the fruitful yield of Loewenstein's continued interest in speech and language as they impinge on psychoanalysis. This topic—which is the subject of an entire paper (chapter 4) and figures in two others (chapters 7 and 10)—is of continuing importance. Loewenstein was a pioneer in efforts to relate issues of speech and verbalization to a theory of cure. Drawing on Karl Bühler's classification of speech functions (1965), Loewenstein conceptualized the analyst's role as "transforming the appeal function of the patient's speech into the expressive function by showing him, through interpretations, how he expresses or describes something about himself when he speaks of persons or things outside himself"

(p. 56). Loewenstein's conclusion that "in the formation of analytic insight verbalization is an essential step" (p. 61) anticipates a great deal of subsequent research in this area. His discussion of speech and language does not, of course, exclude consideration of the importance of non-verbal communication and unconscious communication. Loewenstein himself was certainly aware of these dimensions. "To be sure," he observed, "not all relevant processes during an analysis occur on the level of consciousness; nor have all of them been verbalized. And yet, without verbalization on the part of the patient, without interpretations, without gaining of insight, there would be no analysis and thus no such processes" (p. 65). This last point is an important analytic principle, as relevant now as in 1952, the year Loewenstein presented the paper from which it is drawn (chapter 4).

Loewenstein's papers on technique can be viewed from a broader perspective as embodying the corpus of technical recommendations and modifications derived from the ego psychological contributions of Anna Freud and Heinz Hartmann. Anna Freud's work on ego defense and Hartmann's work on autonomous ego functions are indeed acknowledged by Loewenstein as the theoretical basis for his technical recommendations. At the time of their publication, Loewenstein's papers sought to bring psychoanalytic practice up to date with the theoretical advances of ego psychology. However, there is some question as to what extent significant changes in the psychoanalytic theory of mental functioning over the past 80 years have led to commensurate changes in basic psychoanalytic technique and the psychoanalytic theory of therapy. I have noted elsewhere (Richards, 1982) that proponents of major alterations in technique (Adler, Jung, Ferenczi, Alexander) have not remained within the psychoanalytic mainstream, which suggests that psychoanalysis is more receptive to revision of its theory of mental functioning than to modification of its technical procedures and the theory of therapy underlying them. There is agreement that Hartmann in his papers on autonomous ego functions and the conflict-free sphere proposed a significant change in the psychoanalytic theory of mental functioning then current. There is less agreement as to how substantive were the technical changes which followed from Hartmann's theoretical contributions, which make up an important part of what we refer to as "ego psychology." In the first paper in the volume Loewenstein writes, "Important though this influence of ego psychology has been, it has brought about no fundamental change in psychoanalytic technique, but rather a shift of emphasis which, however, has had significant consequences" (p. 43). Of what does this "shift in emphasis" consist? In "Some remarks on defenses, autonomous ego, and psychoanalytic technique" (chapter 3), Loewenstein delineates three indices of the shift: analysts (1) pay increasing attention to events and conflicts in later life and the present; (2) "dwell... more deliberately and more persistently... on the resistance and on the ego aspect of the patient's production" (p. 43); and (3) "accord greater attention to the patient's autonomous ego functions and the role they exert on conflict solution, and on the choice of pathways of gratifications, and, possibly, on the choice of defense". I think there is a consensus regarding these shifts, particularly (1) and (2), though to some extent the id analysis that Loewenstein disowns could be seen as a misapplication of Freud's psychoanalytic principles by some of his early disciples rather than as a direct consequence of "prestructural" psychoanalysis. In regard to the third index ("greater attention to the patient's autonomous ego functions and the role they exert on conflict solution"), Loewenstein points out that this 'shift' is 'but the systematic elaboration of Freud's advice that analysis of resistance should take precedence over analysis of id derivatives" (pp. 43–44). It was Freud, Loewenstein reminds us, who in his early papers on technique offered the general advice that analysis should proceed from the "surface" to the "depth," just as it was Freud who warned against "so-called 'deep' interpretation at the beginning of analysis" (p. 44). Nevertheless, it was not until the publication of Anna Freud's *The Ego and the Mechanisms of Defence* that defence analysis was placed upon a solid foundation. There are some in fact who assert that "a technical lag" with regard to defence analysis persists to this day (Gray, 1982).

For me the most problematic and the least useful part of Hartmann's contribution to analytic theory is his positing of ego autonomy, i.e. of autonomous ego functions operating in a *conflict-free* sphere. I do not find it surprising, then, that throughout these papers Loewenstein repeatedly indicates his ambivalence regarding the relevance of the conflict-free sphere to questions of technique. In the first paper of the collection, "The problem of interpretation" (1949), he claims that interventions which foster 'the analytic atmosphere" contribute "to the strengthening of the conflictless sphere of the ego" (pp. 18–19), only to add in a footnote that "as a matter of fact, the strengthening of the conflictless sphere of the ego is mainly brought about by interpretation" (p. 19n), i.e., by the interpretation of *conflict*. In contending that the analyst's alliance is with the conflict-free sphere of the patient's ego, Loewenstein is referring to "the patient's perceptions, memory, thinking, reality testing, capacity for self-observation and understanding of others and his faculty for verbal expression." His point, it seems, is that the analyst allies himself with the patient's autonomous ego functions. But Loewenstein seems to have had some doubt as to the theoretical wisdom of using a conflict-free sphere in this way. In a paper of 1965 he writes, "Intrasystemic conflicts probably exist only in conjunction with intersystemic ones" (quoted by Arlow in his introduction, p. 10). However, in the final paper in this collection, "Ego autonomy and psychoanalytic technique" (1971; chapter 13). Loewenstein remains intent on emending, on the basis of Hartmann's contribution, Freud's classic dictum regarding the effect of psychoanalysis: "Where there is conflictual ego," runs the paraphrase, "the autonomous ego should acquire increased control" (p. 226). Nevertheless, one should consider the following points in evaluating Loewenstein's attempt to derive technical implications from Hartmann's postulate of the conflict-free sphere: (1) Regarding the analytic alliance, might it not be theoretically preferable to say that the analyst allies himself with ego functions that have not been *seriously impaired* by conflicts than to say that he allies himself with ego functions operating in a discretely conflict-free sphere? Loewenstein was aware, as we all are, that unconscious wishes and fantasies play a significant role in the initial therapeutic engagement of the analysand. The analysis is often initially fuelled by unconscious wishes and magical fantasies which the patient brings to the analytic situation; these wishes and fantasies are only gradually supplanted by the patient's "work ego" (see Olinick et al. (1973)). (2) Regarding the theory of therapy, using "conflictual" and "autonomous" as adjectives characterizing the ego tends to (needlessly, I believe) reify it in a counter-productive way (Schafer). I would argue that at this point it makes better sense, both theoretically and clinically, to think in terms of ego functions that may be altered by conflict in various ways, and to various degrees, than to posit an "autonomous" ego oblivious to conflict.

In summary then, Loewenstein's papers on technique exemplify the cautious, evolutionary development of technique that has characterized the history of psychoanalysis. They are transitional in nature; they hark back to certain aspects of Freud's technical writings, aspects insufficiently appreciated and not firmly grounded until the work of Anna Freud and Heinz Hartmann in the 1930s and 1940s, even as they look ahead to issues (e.g. the status of non-interpretive interventions in analysis, the relationship of speech to psychoanalytic insight) that are of major importance to analysts of the current generation. And though one might raise questions regarding the theoretical status and usefulness of Hartmann's concept of the conflict-free sphere and remain sceptical as to its serviceability as a basis for technical recommendations, Loewenstein's technical insights, especially those bearing on matters of defence and resistance, have retained much of their power to illuminate, sometimes quite strikingly, the practice of psychoanalysis.

REFERENCES

Buhler, K. (1965). *Sprachtheorie: Die Darstellungs-funktion der Sprache* Stuttgart: Gustav Fischer.

Gray, P. (1982). "Developmental lag" in the evolution of technique for psychoanalysis of mental conflict J. *Am. Psychoanal. Assoc.* 30:621–655.

Loewenstein, R.M. (1951). Christians and Jews. A Psychoanalytic Study New York: Int. Univ. Press.

Olinick, S. et al. (1973). The psychoanalytic work ego: process and interpretation *Int. J. Psychoanal.* 54:143–159.

Richards, A.D. (1982). The superordinate self in psychoanalytic theory and in the self psychologies *J. Am. Psychoanal. Assoc.* 30:939–957.

CHAPTER 15

Review of: *The Second Century of Psychoanalysis: Evolving Perspectives on Therapeutic Action.*

Edited by Michael J. Diamond and Christopher Christian. London: Karnac Books, 2011, xxxii + 362 pp., $59.25 paperback.

[(2013). *Journal of the American Psychoanalytic Association* 61(1):157–165.]

The Second Century of Psychoanalysis is the fourth book in the Confederation of Independent Psychoanalytic Societies series The Boundaries of Psychoanalysis. The editors of this volume are members of the Los Angeles Institute and Society for Psychoanalytic Studies (LAISPS), the fourth society admitted to the IPA after settlement of the antitrust lawsuit against APsaA, the IPA, and the New York and Columbia institutes. That suit reversed decades of exclusion of psychologists from APsaA, gaining nonphysicians the right to train in APsaA institutes, and non-APsaA societies in the United States the right to become societies in the IPA. All of the thirteen contributors are faculty members at LAISPS, and all, with the lone exception of Leo Rangell, are psychologists. American psychoanalysis lost a great deal when it decided to follow A. A. Brill rather than Sigmund Freud in the matter of lay analysis. What is done cannot be undone, but at least the contributions of those once excluded can now be disseminated widely, both in the North American psychoanalytic community and worldwide.

This book, a collection of original papers on the therapeutic action of psychoanalysis, addresses questions often raised but seldom answered satisfactorily, at least not to the point that anything approaching consensus has been reached. In 1920 a prize was offered for the best paper on the topic, but it was never awarded: no paper was deemed good enough. Since then, the discussion has repeatedly become bogged down in false dichotomies, such as the vexed question "Is interpretation or relationship the true curative factor in psychoanalysis?"

In his preface to the volume at hand, Fredric Perlman reframes that question, rendering it far more productive: "How do... the curative factors interact to promote cure?" He concludes that "on leaving the volume it, is self-evident that insight and relationship are inseparable, mutually facilitating forces, each potentiating the other, each moving the mind towards awareness of its own operations and towards the recognition of the other as separate and distinct from rigid and preformed representations, and alive with new potential" (p. xv).

It is hard in a review to do justice to a volume as rich as this. But I will begin with Rangell's "The Aims and Method of Psychoanalysis a Century Later," because in some ways Rangell exemplifies the path that medical psychoanalysis followed to bring us to where we are today. He was for me a friend, a mentor, a role model, and an adversary. We shared a radical political past and a love of Yiddish. He was a great mime and joke teller, especially of Jewish jokes. A couple of years ago, Arthur Lynch and I wrote a paper presenting an overview of his work, "The Journey of a Developed Freudian" (Lynch and Richards 2010) that was published in *Psychoanalytic Review*. But Rangell was

248

not at first an advocate for lay analysis; on the contrary, he embraced the view that psychoanalysis should remain part of medicine. Still, after settlement of the lawsuit, he accepted without reservation the contributions of nonmedical analysts and forged strong friendships with many. At the end of his life, he and the psychologist Janet Bachant were working together on a book on psychoanalysis for young mental health professionals. About the lawsuit, he wrote there that it resulted in an "influx of multiple societies of analysts such as LAISPS and others which were to enrich psychoanalytic activity, both theory and practice, from a vast nonmedical direction." In his contribution here, Rangell's central point is that while the American psychoanalytic mainstream referred to itself as representing ego psychology, in fact it was dedicated to what he calls "total composite theory." Ego psychology, he says, was really "id-ego-superego-internal world-external world-psychoanalysis-psychosynthesis psychology" (p. 29). He positions himself as a "developed" Freudian, working in a theoretical framework in which original discoveries have been added to, not replaced, by subsequent ones, and rejects the idea that there is authoritarianism, hegemony, or arrogance in this view.

I agree with him as far as theory goes. He rests his position on therapeutic action on the contributions of Edward Bibring (1954), who referred to five technical procedures and the creative principles corresponding to each: suggestion, abreaction, manipulation, clarification, and interpretation. This is in my view a felicitous typology. But Rangell's disclaimer fails to hold, I think, when it comes to psychoanalytic organizations, particularly our educational gate-keeping bodies. It was arrogance that accounted for APsaA's original position on lay analysis. Richard Simons (2003) wrote in a *JAPA* supplement that it was not antitrust violations but arrogance that caused APsaA to lose (more precisely, to have to settle) the lawsuit (p. 269). And even Rangell himself refers to the "noxious and deeply divisive medical requirement of the American Psychoanalytic Association" (p. 30).

He has written in painful detail about the theoretical turf wars he has witnessed, from Klein to Kohut to Winnicott to Bion. But he writes from his vantage point in Los Angeles, and it appears to me that theoretical warfare must have been much more personal and acrimonious there than in New York, where most fights have occurred over training analyst appointments (see Kirsner's *Unfree Associations* [2000, p. 324]). How can we account for that fact? My theory is that APsaA institutes in New York have a closer connection to the European analysts who immigrated here in the 1940s and were so influential in the New York Institute. The main theoretical conflicts in New York were not about Klein or Kohut, who never gained much traction, but about Arlow and Brenner's revisionism with regard to Freud's structural model.

There was also a political division between the Europeans, many of them Austro-Marxists, and their American supporters and Americans such as Arlow and Brenner with a more radical Marxist past (Richards, Brent, and Szajnberg 2012).

Rangell's paper is in the first section of the book, "Conceptualizing Therapeutic Action," which it shares with two other chapters: the editors' "A Brief History of Therapeutic Action: Convergence, Divergence, and Integrative Bridges" and Morris Eagle's "Classical Theory, the Enlightenment Vision, and Contemporary Psychoanalysis." Christian and Diamond recognize that any conceptualization of therapeutic action requires a theory of mind, a theory of pathogenesis, and a theory of development (to which I would add a theory of symptom formation and a theory of cure or change).

They point out that the Dora case was pivotal for Freud because it revealed to him the analysand's experience of transference. (It is noteworthy how much Freud learned from his female patients.

Before Dora was Frau Cecilie, whom Freud referred to as his "Lehrmeister," who taught him about the use of the couch and free association.) Then followed the march from id analysis to ego analysis and superego analysis and then to the interaction of all three agencies in the mind of the analysand. Sterba and Strachey came next, Sterba emphasizing the analyst's interpretation of the analyst's observing ego and Strachey emphasizing the superego's role in mutative interpretation leading to change.

Christian and Diamond contrast this view with its old rival: the idea that the curative aspect of psychoanalysis lies in modification of the patient's internal object relations via a new relationship with the analyst. This view, epitomized by Max Gitelson's pronouncement that a human relationship must be established before change through interpretation can occur, is the subject of many of the book's other chapters, and is a source of ongoing controversy in psychoanalysis. (Christian and Diamond consider Gitelson a precursor to Kohut's thinking about selfobjects and empathic connection between analysand and analyst.)

Christian and Diamond also delineate what they see as the major trends in analysis today. They understand these schools to differ in identifying what they call "nodal points," by which they mean a school's characteristic strategies for dealing with anxiety, its understanding of the relative importance of unconscious fantasy as opposed to reality, and how it handles patient resistances to change and countertransference. The task, of course, is to bridge all these approaches and develop integrative models. For Christian and Diamond, that is the challenge of psychoanalysis in the twenty-first century.

Morris Eagle connects the emphasis on the therapeutic action of interpretation with the Enlightenment vision and the admonition to "know thyself." Certainly the Enlightenment was very much part of Freud's makeup, from both his German and his Jewish (Haskalah) sides, and he described himself as having submitted his life to the "soft dictatorship of reason." His commitment to reason and the intellect was central to his secular Jewish identity. I agree with Eagle that it propelled his efforts to understand and advance a theory of therapeutic action and a theory of cure; I also agree that these, along with his theories of development, symptom formation, and pathogenesis, constitute the theoretical edifice of psychoanalysis that remains central today. But as Eagle (and many others) have noted, that is only half of the story. Eagle invokes the postmodernists, particularly Richard Rorty, in support of the idea that truth (that is, interpretation) will not necessarily set one free. But many contributors to psychoanalysis have advanced this view, beginning with Freud himself and continuing through Zetzel, Gitelson, and a host of others; I'm not sure that postmodern philosophy adds much to the argument.

Nonetheless, that half of the story does have to be addressed, and several chapters in this volume do just that, elaborating the idea that the care and concern of the analyst for the analysand is crucial for a successful therapeutic process. The best account of the therapeutic action of "analytic love" is provided by Peter Wolson in "The Seminal Therapeutic Influence of Analytic Love: A Pluralistic Perspective." In the book's third section, "Relational Experience and Mutative Dynamics," Wolson considers his topic from the standpoint of eight distinct models—topographic, structural, ego psychological, developmental, object-relational (Klein and the British Independents), intersubjective, relational, and self psychological. He maintains that analytic love "pervades everything that an analyst does that is therapeutic" (p. 166); he believes strongly "that analysts need to know, accept, and embrace analytic love as a core mechanism of therapeutic action in order to achieve the best results" (p. 184).

Wolson makes the point that it is the analyst's job to meet the patient's wish for analytic love. But I would apply two caveats to that assertion. One is that a well-timed and accurate interpretation can also confirm that wish and contribute to the growth of a therapeutic alliance. The other is that some analysts regrettably justify boundary violations as an expression of analytic love, and that therefore any fruitful discussion of analytic love requires close attention to the parameters within which it can be said to exist.

In the book's second section, "Conflict, Fantasy, and Insight in Therapeutic Action," Stephen Portuges and Nancy Hollander discuss Paul Gray's technique in the chapter "The Therapeutic Action of Resistance Analysis." They point out that Gray argues against an authoritarian analytic stance—a view of the analyst as "the only one who knows." They quote his caution against using the positive transference "as a vehicle for influencing the patient's participation in the analytic process... [retaining an] authoritarian element" (p. 81). They cite his encouragement that analysts "integrate their own self-reflective observations into their therapeutic practices" (p. 91) and make a strong case for considering the role of social factors and "social reality" (cultural and ethnic biases) in psychoanalytic investigation.

A point here. As I've said in other contexts, some of our disagreements over therapeutic action probably have as much to do with analytic personality as with the outcomes of our treatments. The Richards and Richards (1995) theory of the theory of technique is that a psychoanalyst develops a theory of technique to counter his or her own antitherapeutic proclivities. Freud was an activist and stressed abstinence; Kohut was unempathic and stressed empathy; Kurt Eissler, an interventionist, stressed parameters. The authoritarian Gray wanted to diminish the impact of the superego; the intuitive Arlow looked for evidence. Brenner, who was a very kind man, cautioned that the analyst must not offer condolences. Fenichel, who was something of an obsessional and clearly as much a product of the Central European Enlightenment vision as Freud, stressed in his textbook the centrality of emotion, urging us to "go for the affect." I have a colleague who was in analysis with Gitelson, the oracle, as I have mentioned, of the importance of establishing a relationship with the patient at the beginning of the treatment. According to my friend, Gitelson did not say a word for the first fifteen sessions.

Christopher Christian's chapter, "From Ego Psychology to Modern Conflict Theory," offers an overview of the movement from ego psychology to conflict theory, particularly Brenner's radical elision of the Freudian structural agencies. Christian writes that Brenner credits Yale Kramer and me with pointing out to him how far he was moving away from the structural model in his views that the id has to do not with drive but with wish, that there are no special ego defenses, and that the superego is a compromise formation. (My statement, for anyone interested, appears in my introduction to the Brenner festschrift, *Psychoanalysis: The Science of Mental Conflict* (1986), which Martin Willick and I edited. Christian's chapter is an excellent overview of the structural model and of the way it evolved in Brenner's hands into what Sander Abend has called modern conflict theory. But I fault Christian for what he leaves out—for example, Brenner's view of analytic change, which I find quite useful. According to Brenner, the goal of psychoanalytic treatment is to help the patient achieve better adaptation in his life: that is, to experience less anxiety, aggression, and guilt, and more pleasure. I also wish that Christian had included an explication of the role of unconscious fantasy, particularly as presented by Arlow. Paul Gray and Fred Busch have sometimes called it "deep-sea diving" to offer patients interpretations of unconscious fantasy, considering it too quick a move from the surface. But for Brenner and Arlow such movement is allowed "because it fits in with the proper expert authoritarian role of the analyst" (p. 114). Christian's chapter might also have included some mention of the therapeutic optimism of the modern conflict theory of Brenner and his associates, particularly Arlow, Rangell, and David Beres. When I was a candidate and then a recent graduate at the New York Institute, I was struck by the fact that Brenner and his colleagues rejected a number of concepts that many European analysts and their acolytes understood as realistic limitations of psychoanalysis: for example, developmental deficit, ego weakness, and unanalyzability.

I was pleased to recognize that some of the contributors to this volume are not reluctant to think outside the box and to break new ground. A good example is the chapter by Beth Kalish, "Movement Thinking and Therapeutic Action in Psychoanalysis," which makes us aware of an important aspect of nonverbal communication: the patient's movements in the session provide clues to what is going on in the patient's mind, and so deserve the analyst's attention.

It is fitting that this volume should end with an interview of Hedda Bolgar, whose life spans almost the entire twentieth century, and who now, well into the twenty-first, is still vigorous and productive at 102. She was a pioneer, the first candidate without a medical degree to graduate from the Chicago Institute for Psychoanalysis. In Los Angeles she founded the Wright Institute, a nonprofit mental health training and service center. Its Hedda Bolgar Psychotherapy Clinic even now provides low-cost treatment, continuing the early Austro-Marxist psychoanalytic tradition of providing treatment for those who cannot afford private fees. Bolgar shares Rangell's view that new orientations are creative expansions of, rather than replacements for, traditional points of view. At the end of the interview, Michael Diamond, the interviewer, asks her what analysts can most usefully learn and do to become better analysts. Bolgar's response stresses the value of life experience and a liberal arts education, which, she feels, is "really much more important than the medical background" (p. 303). What Bolgar is talking about is *Bildung*, the process of personal and cultural maturation so important to the German view of character

255

development. Freud's cosmopolitan education had given him a much clearer sense of the value of *Bildung* than the more provincial Brill ever had (Wang 2003), and this vision of a fully developed personhood is what American psychoanalysis lost when it narrowed itself and became just another medical specialty.

The papers in this book, and the varied responses to them that its readers are bound to discover in themselves, reflect yet again Ludwik Fleck's idea that science is always influenced by historical, cultural, sociological, and psychological factors (see Richards 2006). There is no immaculate scientific conception. There is no immaculate clinical or technical conception either, a point elaborated by several other contributors to this volume, including Diamond in chapter 10 ("The Impact of the Mind of the Analyst: From Unconscious Processes to Intrapsychic Change") and Peggy Porter in chapter 9 ("The Analyst's Subjective Experience: Holding Environment and Container of Projections").

These observations return me to where I began: celebrating the fact that most of the contributors to this volume are not physicians. It would appear that psychoanalysis is alive and well in the hands of these LAISPS psychoanalysts, and that their future (and ours) is bright as psychoanalysis moves deeper into its second century.

REFERENCES

Bibring, E. (1954). Psychoanalysis and the dynamic psychotherapies. *Journal of the American Psychoanalytic Association* 2:745–770.

Kirsner, D. (2000). *Unfree Associations: Inside Psychoanalytic Institutes.* London: Process Press.

Lynch, A.A., & Richards, A.D. (2010). Leo Rangell: The journey of a developed Freudian. *Psychoanalytic Review* 97:361–391.

Richards, A.D. (2006). The creation and social transmission of psychoanalytic knowledge. *Journal of the American Psychoanalytic Association* 54:359-378.

Richards, A.D., Brent, J., & Szajnberg, N. (2012). Panel: Psychoanalysts on the Left and the Far Left. YIVO Institute for Jewish Research, [http://www.yivoinstitute.org].

Richards, A.D., & Richards, A.K. (1995). Notes on psychoanalytic theory and its consequences for technique. *Journal of Clinical Psychoanalysis* 4:429–457.

Richards, A.D., & Willick, M.S., eds. (1986). *Psychoanalysis, the Science of Mental Conflict: Essays in Honor of Charles Brenner.* New York: Routledge.

Simons, R.C. (2003). The lawsuit revisited. *Journal of the American Psychoanalytic Association* 51(Suppl.):247–271.

Wang, W.-J. (2003). Bildung or the formation of the psychoanalyst. *Psychoanalysis & History* 5:91–118.

CHAPTER 16

Book Review of: *The Revolutionary Ascetic. Evolution of a Political Type*

by Bruce Mazlish. New York: Basic Books, Inc.,
1976. 261 pp.

[(1979). *Psychoanalytic Quarterly*, 48:149-152.]

The Revolutionary Ascetic is Professor Bruce Mazlish's third major attempt at psychoanalytically-informed historical exegesis. The first, *In Search of Nixon,* was straight psychobiography, clear in focus, but limited by the lack of data about Nixon's formative years. The second, *James and John Stewart Mill,* benefitted from access to considerable biographical data about both father and son, as well as information about their interaction. In that work, however, his extrapolations from the psychobiographical findings to broader historical trends, including speculations about the shape of the industrial revolution and the rise of nineteenth century liberalism, are less convincing. In his third book Mazlish's focus is primarily psychohistorical rather than psychobiographical; although Emerson's dictum about the understanding of man leading to the understanding of events is an appealing and perhaps theoretically incontrovertible principle, Mazlish's attempt to explain the revolutionary process by generalizing about the personalities of those who make revolutions requires great logical leaps to achieve credulity.

The historical theses of the book are: 1) that asceticism is a central dynamic of the two major modern revolutions, namely, the Russian and the Chinese; 2) that there is a link between revolution and puritanism; and 3) that there is a developmental line from a) religious asceticism to b) worldly asceticism to c) nineteenth century capitalism and industrialization to d) the revolutionary ideologies which transformed the Chinese and Russian societies in the twentieth century. Mazlish defines a "revolutionary ascetism" that links Mao's and Lenin's applications of Marxism to nineteenth century liberalism and utilitarianism. He makes the point, which I think is well taken, that both the Chinese and Russian revolutions were essentially modernizing upheavals in which fostering industrialization was at least as important as eliminating an oppressive regime. The most recent events in China—their new constitution, for example, which stresses the importance of the promotion of technology and scientific thought—clearly reflect this order of priorities.

Professor Mazlish's psychological theses are that "ascetics" make revolutions and that the revolutionary ascetic is an ideal personality type to which modern revolutionaries will partially correspond. However, here one may ask: Do ascetics make revolution, or does successful revolutionary activity require a certain amount of self-denial and self-discipline as well as a singular sense of purpose and devotion to a cause? In other words: Is there a trivial connection which might hold true as well for reactionary or counter-revolutionary leaders as it might for revolutionary ones?

According to Professor Mazlish the revolutionary ascetic has two major characteristics: first, he abhors "wine, women and song," and second, he has "few libidinal ties" and is therefore able to "deny the normal bonds of friendship feeling and affections and [to] eliminate all human consideration in the name of devotion to the revolution" (p. 6). Drawing from Freud's *Group Psychology and the Analysis of the Ego*,

Mazlish develops the thesis that the revolutionary leader has displaced his libido from individuals onto an abstraction, namely revolution. Mazlish uses his case studies of Lenin and Mao to establish this thesis, but in both instances he is handicapped by the relative paucity of childhood developmental data, autobiographical material, etc.

Unfortunately, Mazlish's approach to the data that he does have is often superficial and facile. For example, he makes much of Lenin's relationship with his mentor Plekhanov. Mazlish finds it significant that Lenin began to sign his articles in Iskra with the pseudonym "Lenin" directly after he broke with Plekhanov over policy. Mazlish says, "the Ulyanov given to sentiment has been replaced by the hard, unloving, unyielding Lenin" (p. 116). We are now in the presence of the prototypic leader "with few libidinal ties." Mazlish fails to consider the alternative that Lenin's pseudonym was taken from the River Lena possibly in emulation of Plekhanov who took his pseudonym "Volgan" from the name of the River Volga. Thus Mazlish has not proven his conclusion that the name change signaled a significant break in Lenin's capacity for libidinal investment.

Solzhenitsyn's portrait of Lenin in his *Lenin in Zurich* has a very moving account of Lenin's subsequent relationship with his mistress Inessa, which, although partially fictionalized, rings true. It establishes convincingly that even after his break with Plekhanov there was nothing strikingly deficient in Lenin's capacity to relate to people. The important issue is how to account for Lenin's success. Mazlish links it to his personality; this reviewer attributes it to his genius as a theoretician. Within the realm of personality, Mazlish focuses on asceticism and constricted object relations, but fails to give due weight to Lenin's opportunism and his consummate skill as a politician in small group meetings which, on the face of it, would seem more directly related to his success.

Similar objections could be made to Mazlish's inferences about Mao. Since he had three wives and several children who seemed, at least from Snow's account, to have meant a great deal to him, Mao probably did not lack objects. His reputation as a singer and dancer is evidence against asceticism. More important, he probably succeeded as a revolutionary because he was able to adapt his Marxist ideology to the particular Chinese situation, and especially to the role of the peasants. Through all the years of the war against the Nationalists, his policy of keeping the Red Army honest and paying peasants for supplies instead of taking them by force helped win the peasants to his side. He made the long march into the most successful propaganda road show in history. Mao's mastery of public relations seems to have contributed more to his success than his putative asceticism or his hypothetical deficiency of libidinal ties.

In summary, *The Revolutionary Ascetic,* although at times lively and interesting, is not convincing as historical or psychological argument. It can be faulted for being based on inadequate data and for a lack of logical rigor which limit its value for historians and psychoanalysts.

CHAPTER 17

Book Review of *Psychotherapy of the Borderline Adult: A Developmental Approach*

by James F. Masterson, M.D.
New York: Brunner/Mazel, Inc., 1976. 377 pp.

[(1979). *Psychoanalytic Quarterly,* 48:514–517.]

Engaged for more than twenty years in clinical research on personality disorders, the author focused, in his earlier work, on adolescents, particularly those seen in an inpatient setting; his more recent findings come from his experience in treating adults in his private practice, using the theoretical and therapeutic model he had developed in treating borderline adolescents. This is the same theory and technique he reports having taught to over a hundred psychiatrists with excellent results. Masterson's present study contrasts a technique derived from a developmental model and "object-relations theory" with one derived from a conflict-drive psychoanalytic model. Favoring the former, Masterson further dichotomizes the issue by focusing on preoedipal as opposed to oedipal issues and on an active technique involving confrontation and limit-setting, as opposed to a more passive "analytic" stance. Masterson views his own clinical experience and that of the more than one hundred psychiatrists trained in his technique as a

263

successful clinical trial. "Widespread application," he maintains, "is now-warranted." In making his case, he pays particular attention to his successes with patients who had previously been treated by adherents of other approaches with little or no improvement. In order to evaluate these claims, a closer look at this theory and the technique is needed.

Masterson states that the borderline patient suffers from an arrest occurring at the separation-individuation phase (rapprochement subphase) of development, due to the mother's withdrawal of "libidinal availability" when her child attempts to separate and individuate. He feels that these mothers are themselves borderline (an opinion based on observing their visits to their adolescent children in the inpatient setting). While imputing to these mothers a "defensive need to cling" to their children, he never precisely states what this need defends against. The child reacts to the mother's withdrawal with an "abandonment depression" (a term never adequately defined), defensively denies the depressive feelings and the separation, and clings to his mother. The child is rewarded by the mother for regression or punished with withdrawal for any progress toward separation and individuation. This results in a "split object relations unit," a rewarding part unit, and a withholding part unit. These units, abbreviated RORU (reward object relations unit) and WORU (withholding object relations unit), are the central constructs of Masterson's theoretical model. The RORU develops an alliance between itself and a part of the ego (it is not ever made clear whether the object relations units are parts of the ego or whether they exist apart from the tripartite psychical structure); this part of the ego is considered pathological in that it has failed to "undergo the necessary transformation from the pleasure principle to the reality principle." The RORU is seen as the borderline patient's principal *defense* (does this indicate that the RORU is an ego function?) against the painful affective state associated with the WORU, namely, the abandonment depression. Both object relations units become transferences (presumably through the operation of the repetition compulsion) in which the therapist is viewed as alternately rewarding and withholding.

Masterson states that psychotherapy "compensates for the two key developmental defects of the borderline intrapsychic structure—i.e., in object relations and ego structure." To this end, two therapeutic techniques are employed: (1) support from the therapist, a real person, for the patient's attempts at individuation; and (2) confrontation of the patient's denial of the destructiveness of his pathological ego. A new alliance is forged between the therapist's healthy ego and the patient's embattled reality ego. To quote Masterson,

A new object relations unit develops with the therapist as a positive object representation who approves of separation-individuation plus a self-representation as a capable developing person plus an affect (good feelings) which ensues from the exercise of constructive coping and mastery rather than regressive behavior. Working through impels progressive externalization of the RORU and WORU units (together with the latter's rage and depression) and sets the stage for the coalescence of good and bad self and object representations which is a prelude to the inception of whole object relations (p. 340).

In evaluating Masterson's approach to borderline patients, I would raise just two questions, although others do come to mind as well. First, although conflicts relating to separation, autonomy, and independence are clearly important in human development, what evidence is there that these issues are exclusively related to the pathology of one definable diagnostic group? Second, is a treatment approach based on a consistent focus on separation-individuation themes more helpful and effective in treating some patients than a more open-ended, investigative therapeutic approach?

In the second (and largest) section of the book, Masterson provides us with his own data, which he feels support a positive answer to the second question. He presents an account of his treatment of four adult patients diagnosed by him as borderline. Two cases are given as examples of what Masterson calls supportive psychotherapy aimed at helping the patients to control their "pathological egos" and to make their motivations "more reality oriented than fantasy oriented." Two other cases are presented as examples of reconstructive psychotherapy aimed at the "reconstruction of the patient's intrapsychic state by working through the abandonment depression associated with the separation-individuation arrest." Confrontation of the destructive value of the pathological defenses and interpretation of the object relations unit transference are the significant therapeutic techniques.

Psychoanalysis seems contraindicated for Masterson's borderline patients, but one feels disquiet that he never makes it clear why he believes conflicts relating to separation, loss, autonomy, and individuation cannot be dealt with in psychoanalysis. In this regard the book lacks an explicit classification of treatment approaches that are based on clear clinical and theoretical criteria; and psychoanalytic psychotherapy is not differentiated from psychoanalysis. While Masterson's clinical material in the book is detailed and carefully presented, the overall impression is unidimensional, with a skew toward the separation-individuation developmental arrest which Masterson maintains is central. A paucity of clinical evidence supporting Masterson's formulations rather than other, equally possible constructions is a major shortcoming of this book. I am concerned that Masterson's formulae may lend themselves to adoption as a "cook-book" approach to therapy which can be particularly stifling for psychiatric residents and other beginning therapists looking for ways to "organize" bewilderingly complex clinical phenomena. Psychoanalytic psychotherapy, as well as psychoanalysis, is diminished when it ceases to function as what Milton Horowitz has called "an investigative tool." This book does, nevertheless, merit attention by virtue of its focus on important clinical issues.

CHAPTER 18

Book Review of: *Forty-Two Lives in Treatment. A Study of Psychoanalysis and Psychotherapy*

by Robert S. Wallerstein. (New York: Guilford Press. 1986, 784 pp,

[International Journal of Psycho-Analysis 69:140–144.]

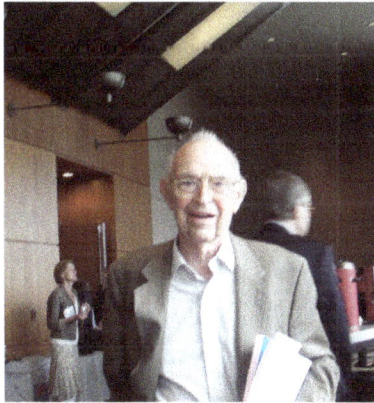

Robert Wallerstein

Robert Wallerstein's *Forty-Two Lives in Treatment. A Study of Psychoanalysis and Psychotherapy* is the final account of the 30-year (1954–1985) psychotherapy research project conducted at the Menninger Foundation. The last of a series of books about this project (Kernberg, 1972); (Voth & Orth, 1973); (Horowitz, 1974); (Applebaum, 1977), *Forty-Two Lives* is formidably comprehensive (784 pages), encompassing not only a huge amount of clinical data but also Wallerstein's own painstaking consideration of process and outcome issues. It may not be an exaggeration to say that the clinical portions of the book "read like a novel," for it should be noted that the comprehensive case summaries (Wallerstein had several hundred typescript pages available for each of the 42 patients) enliven this report in an altogether unique way. Here is a research report to which serious readers can devote themselves entirely.

Before I address the yield of this massive research effort, a few preliminary remarks on the study population and setting are in order. Subjects were selected from the Menninger Foundation waiting list for psychoanalysis and psychotherapy on a random basis, albeit with certain exclusion criteria. It was intended that the sample be evenly divided between men and women and between those in analysis and those in psychotherapy. This goal was approximated, with 22 patients recommended for analysis (12 women and 10 men) and 20 for psychotherapy (9 women and 11 men). Subjects ranged from 17 to 50 years of age, with a mean of 31 (33 for the men and 30 for the women). Individuals undergoing concomitant group or family treatment were excluded, as were individuals for whom hospital management was the major therapeutic instrument. It should be stressed that hospitalized patients *per se* were not excluded from the sample and that over half the sample, 22 of the 42 patients, were in fact hospitalized at least once during the course of the treatment. Also excluded from the study sample were patients for whom brief therapy was indicated, patients who had had previous treatment at the Menninger Foundation, patients who could not be readily available for follow-up, and patients deemed "professionally/socially selected cases" (i.e., patients drawn from the Menninger professional community). This final exclusion criterion, by eliminating among others the spouses and children of Menninger staff personnel, further skewed the population in the direction of not only "sicker" patients but of patients more likely to be treated by relatively inexperienced members of the Menninger staff. Wallerstein acknowledges that this implicit skewing of the study sample could have created an "unhappily more negative overall results effect" (p. 58). At the same time, the systematic exclusion of members of the professional community presumably skewed the comparison of analytic and psychotherapeutic outcomes to the advantage of the latter: study analysands were generally treated frequently as control cases by the least experienced analysts, whereas the psychotherapeutic cases were frequently assigned to more experienced therapists.

If, owing to these exclusions, the study population contained a disproportionately large number of patients for whom analysis or even analytic therapy was truly an "heroic indication" (Glover, 1954); (Ticho, 1970), it nonetheless remains a population amenable to the analytic effort in the unique setting of the Menninger Foundation. During the three decades of the study, the Foundation achieved international recognition for its comprehensive treatment approach, from the evaluative process through the range of treatment options and extensive support services for families. This approach reflects the spirit of Karl Menninger, whose many-sided consideration of patients as also persona strongly influenced the ambience, including the research spirit of the Foundation. Everyone working there, from residents to senior staff (I was myself a resident at the Foundation from 1960 to 1963), was vitally imbued with Dr Karl's approach to psychiatric case study, an approach that eschewed diagnostic labels in favor of co-ordinated assessment of the patient along intrapsychic interpersonal, social and biological axes. This "ecology" of the Menninger Foundation, to which Wallerstein refers, was undoubtedly responsible for the willingness of the study organizers to provide treatment to patients whose serious psychopathology would in all likelihood have disqualified them for participation in research studies conducted by psychoanalytic centers (see Weber & Bachrach, 1985); (Erle & Goldberg, 1984); (and Firestein, 1978). In Topeka, Leo Stone's "widening scope of psychoanalysis" (1954) was not merely a slogan but a day-today reality.

As a test, under optimal sanatorium conditions, of the true breadth of the "widening scope," the Menninger Psychotherapy Research Project (PRP) has a cautionary import. One of its most important findings is that, despite the "unparalleled comprehensiveness" of the Foundation's evaluation process, major psychopathology was concealed during the initial diagnostic evaluation in 24 of the 42 subjects. This finding bears on 18 instances of substantial underdiagnosis, 14 of which were the result of concealment during the initial evaluation. Of the 22 patients assigned to analysis, only 12, Wallerstein informs us, appeared in retrospect to have been suitable for such treatment. Of the 10 deemed unsuitable, six seemed unanalyzable, being drawn from the rank of the 'sicker' patients, the "alcoholic, the addicted, and the paranoid borderline" (p. 569). Of the 12 for whom analysis was judged in retrospect to have been the appropriate treatment choice, 10 achieved reasonably good outcomes, one was equivocal, and one was an outright failure. Of 20 patients assigned to psychotherapy, 12 appeared to have been appropriately selected and 11 of these had reasonably good outcomes. Of the remaining eight, six had problems for which outpatient therapy proved inadequate while two had poor outcomes, owing to 'totally inadequate social casework with the families'. For two of the 20 therapy patients, analysis appeared to be the treatment of choice but could not be undertaken, owing to financial limitations.

These findings and retrospective judgements are explored in the section entitled "Heroic indications for psychoanalysis considered."

Citing the pioneering articles of Glover and Stone, Wallerstein offers a two-pronged rationale for the Menninger Psychotherapy Research Project attempt to determine just how far the reach of psychoanalysis can be extended: (1) for many severely disturbed patients analysis is justifiable and even desirable simply because no other available therapy promises comparable help, and (2) for such patients analysis promised the greatest benefit when it is provided in a controlled sanatorium setting such as the Menninger Foundation. It was this "*double* set of convictions," Wallerstein writes, 'that PRP was in an excellent position to try to put to empirical test" (p. 670).

What were the results of this test? In supplying empirical referents for PRP patients who might qualify for the "heroic indications" category, Wallerstein mentions 15 who were severely alcoholic, eight who were severely drug-addicted, 18 who suffered severe sexual dysfunction (beyond potency and orgastic disturbance), 14 who showed strongly paranoid characters, and 20 who had borderline or otherwise precarious ego organizations. Citing 11 patients who fell into at least three of these five groups, Wallerstein submits, plausibly enough, that we have here "a group of extremely ill patients for whom psychoanalysis would indeed be a heroic treatment choice" (p. 671).

And what were the treatment outcomes for these 11 patients? Of the six recommended for analysis, three ultimately died of causes related to mental illness, drug abuse, suicide, etc. Another three were either taken out of analysis or removed themselves; five were in the overall group of six for whom analysis was to prove inappropriate. For four of these six treatment failures, Wallerstein notes, the "salient issue" was the emergence of a psychotic transference reaction that "threatened to be totally unmanageable." Five of the 11 "extremely ill" patients received psychotherapy. Of these, four were total treatment failures, including two deaths from causes related to mental illness. Only one of the five, a sexual masochist, who may be the sickest patient in the entire sample, managed to evince some moderate improvement after 30 years of almost continuous treatment. Reviewing these findings, Wallerstein concludes that, "Clearly, even with all of the availability of hospitalization within a psychoanalytically oriented sanatorium setting, and all of the historical clinical precedents for this course within this specific Menninger Foundation setting, psychoanalysis on the basis of these 'heroic indications' has been found tragically wanting as a treatment course" (p. 678). Referring specifically to two "heroic indications" patients who died in the absence of concomitant hospitalization, as well as to two other patients in this category who evinced significant improvement but were hospitalized for lengthy periods, he joins earlier commentators on the PRP in arguing for the necessity of concomitant hospitalization of severely disturbed individuals with whom analytic treatment is undertaken heroically.

A collateral issue of great interest is the relationship between insight and structural change in the study population. After duly noting the ambiguous meaning of such terms as "structure" and "structural change," Wallerstein goes on to observe that in 19 of the 42 subjects, changes brought about by treatment "substantially outstripped their developing insights" (p. 704). The preponderance of these 19 received therapy rather than analysis. By contrast, of the 10 patients for whom insight was coordinate with treatment change, nine were in analysis, six of whom were diagnosed as having hysterical character structure. For at least some of the PRP patients in analysis, then, change seemed related to achieving insight, whereas for virtually all of those receiving therapy it did not. This finding dovetails with Applebaum's earlier assessment of the PRP (1977). Using psychological test data, he found that structural change was positively correlated with degree of conflict resolution, but that structural change could and did come about in its absence. For Wallerstein, the overall asymmetry between insight and structural change in the PRP population was strongly suggestive of both the valence of the "analytic relationship in the psychoanalytic change process" and the efficacy of supportive, if analytically inspired, therapy.

With the patients treated via primarily supportive modes (of all the varieties specified), changes have been substantially in excess of concomitant achieved insights; furthermore, they have seemed over the course of follow-up observation to be just as stable, as enduring, as proof against subsequent environmental vicissitudes and as free (or not free) from the requirement for supplemental post treatment contact, support, or further therapeutic help as the changes in those patients treated via a centrally expressive mode (psychoanalysis). Moreover, in the arena of clinical assessment at follow-up contact, when changes in psychological functioning and well-being were being assessed, it was by no means necessarily clear whether the adjudged structural changes reflected underlying conflict resolution or not. Certainly, from all the data, "conflict resolution cannot be considered essential to structural change and may be independent of it in some instances" (Applebaum, 1977, p. 208); that is, structural change appears to occur independently of (without) conflict resolution in those instances (p. 719).

A monumental study, *Forty-Two Lives in Treatment* defies any such easy distillation. Its 30-year span, extensive documentation of every study case, and 100 per cent follow up set a standard that may never again be equaled. A critical appreciation of the yield and implications of the Menninger PRP would require something longer than a review. Let me then restrict my evaluative remarks to the two which I have focused on in the issues above: that involving the "heroic indications" for analysis and that involving the relation between, and the differing indications for, analysis and psychotherapy.

The question of "heroic indications" tests the practical limits of what Leo Stone, in his classic paper of 1954, referred to as the "widening scope" of psychoanalysis. Wallerstein cites Glover's "the indications for psychoanalysis" (1954) as the clearest statement of the case for "heroic indications," although it was, in fact, Ticho (1970) who introduced the term. Glover, in arguing for the defensibility of a recommendation for analysis in the absence of diagnostic indications, and Ticho, in citing cases in which "nothing else but psychoanalysis would make any dent," both equate "heroic indications" with virtually hopeless prognosis; nothing else will help so why not try analysis? The problem with this position is that it offers no criterion for differentiating the types and degrees of hopeless prognosis. Frequently, very good reasons exist for *not* undertaking analysis in the face of contraindications, not the least of which are monetary considerations and the time and energy to be extended by patient and analyst alike.

Now, with respect to the PRP population, one can only agree with Wallerstein that analysis on the basis of heroic indications was found "tragically wanting." But are the 11 PRP patients whose outcomes are the basis of this verdict truly representative of all patients for whom analysis might "heroically" be undertaken? Some "very sick" patients *do* benefit from analysis and the determination of those who can relies on a number of factors, the nature of their symptoms (alloplastic *v.* autoplastic), the extent to which alcoholism and drug dependency can be controlled early in treatment, and so on. It would seem, then, that Wallerstein's verdict that the PRP experience tends to support a "narrowing scope" and a retreat from heroic indications is unwarranted. Rather, the data suggest that the terms "widening scope" and "heroic indications" exceed their usefulness if they are meant to encompass both patients with severe autoplastic psychopathology and those suffering from alloplastic pathology, sociopathy, drug addiction, and so on. Analytic efforts with patients who are perhaps not so incapacitated as the PRP "heroic" sample but who still fall within the rubric of the "widening scope" continue to be successful (Richards, 1980), (1987). By the same token, cocaine addicts who as a group are less disturbed than patients with borderline disturbance and severe ego pathology remain virtually inaccessible to analysis and frequently to therapy: such treatments cannot compete with the chemical release afforded by their habit.

In short, the PRP data point to the need for further refinement of the notion of heroic indications, particularly with respect to those aspects of the analytic situation that can sustain an "indication" in the face of seeming unanalyzability. Here I refer to such phenomena as the ameliorative impact of frequent sessions and the neutral analytic atmosphere (as regards the containment of intense transference demands) and the organizing and salubrious effect of the analyst's mere decision to treat a patient analytically. Tyson & Sandler's proposal (1971), seconded by Firestein (1978), that we sharply differentiate criteria for indications from criteria for suitability might well help us specify the range of circumstances that make heroic indications *legitimate indications*. Certain patients may fail to meet the criteria of suitability (by virtue of absence of "ego strength," inability to confine regressive transference behavior to the analytic hours, etc.) but still meet the criteria for indications owing to the organizing and ameliorative aspects of the situation. Others may meet the criteria for suitability (as regards diagnostic category) but not the criteria for indications owing to such non-diagnostic factors as motivation, psychological-mindedness, and the primary or secondary gains offered by their illness. Glover's caveat (1954) that indications for psychoanalysis "should not be determined exclusively by prognosis" must be balanced by our recognition that hopeless prognosis is not itself an indication.

Wallerstein's conclusions regarding the overall absence of a correlation between insight and structural change in the PRP patients and his derivative claim as to the efficacy of supportive psychotherapy invite similar qualifications. Wallerstein takes the study to contradict the belief that only through psychoanalysis can the patient achieve changes that are stable, enduring, and reasonably proof against subsequent environmental vicissitudes. This verdict is true as far as it goes, but it glosses over the problem inherent in conceptualizing treatment outcome in terms of a single variable, i.e., type of treatment: psychoanalysis *v.* psychotherapy. In making no systematic allowance for patient variables and situational variables, this viewpoint resembles that of an economic monitorist who ignores the balance of trade and the productive capacity of industry, in the belief that the state of the economy reflects the vicissitudes of a single variable, the money supply. Patient variables in particular should be kept in mind when considering the study findings regarding outcome. It is possible that with less sick patients supportive psychotherapy would not have led to the same degree of positive change. Likewise, a healthier study population might have evinced a more significant correlation between insight and change. After all, the notion of "change" implies movement from one point on a scale to another: it says nothing about where on the scale one begins. A very sick patient might well change quite dramatically and yet still fall short of the point at which insight becomes effective.

Granting these caveats and restricting our purview to the PRP patients, we can only read with admiration Wallerstein's judicious consideration of the yield of the PRP. With respect to the PRP patients, certainly he is correct in finding the distinction between structural and behavioral change "questionable." Similarly incisive are various verdicts that echo Horowitz (1974) to the effect that conflict resolution is not a necessary condition for certain types of change and that a variety of changes can be brought about via the more supportive therapeutic modes and techniques. But when Wallerstein calls attention to the finding that supportive psychotherapeutic approaches, mechanisms and techniques so often achieved far more than were expected of them (p. 725), one is led to ask why, exactly, supportive psychotherapy was *not* expected to lead to a successful outcome. Does the value of psychoanalysis hinge on demonstrating the limitations of psychotherapy? In the absence of control studies involving comparable patient populations and taking into account cost effectiveness, time investment, and so forth, can we even begin to assign relative "value" to the two enterprises? The Menninger PRP does not study such crucial matters, but it is consistent with the long-held therapeutic assumption that "healthier" patients derive far less from supportive psychotherapy than do "sicker" patients.

Evaluation of the verdict that "psychoanalysis... was more limited in the outcomes achieved than had been predicted or anticipated—*with these patients*" (p. 727) requires equal attention to the PRP study population. Only 10 of the 22 analytic patients received relatively unaltered analysis, and by the "usual stricter criteria of customary outpatient psychoanalytic and psychotherapy practice." Wallerstein adds, "just about every single one of our PRP psychoanalytic cases would be considered substantially altered in varying supportive directions" (p. 726). This finding, then, must be qualified by a simple recognition of the fact that many if not most of these 22 patients might not have been accepted for analysis in either private practice or institute treatment center settings. This fact does not vitiate Wallerstein's claim that supportive treatment requires more specification in all its forms and variety than has usually been recorded in the psychodynamic literature. It does call into question the generalizability of the specific PRP finding. The PRP organizers, working in the halcyon days of the 1950s, are probably overly optimistic in their expectations of the efficacy of analysis with sicker patients, just as they were unduly pessimistic about the efficacy of supportive, albeit analytically-inspired treatment with this same population.

Wallerstein concludes *Forty-Two Lives in Treatment* with a section entitled "Tasks for the future: psychotherapy research." Ever attentive to the limitations as well as the strengths of the Menninger study, here he discusses projects that might take up where the PRP leaves off, e.g., a project in which randomized groups of hysterical patients would be treated via traditional and "augmented" analysis. Looking further down the road, he raises the possibility of a study involving comparative assessments of the major therapeutic approaches. Recognizing that such a study would require what is not currently available, that is mutual agreement among psychotherapy researchers 'on all of the relevant categories, criteria, instruments, and methods" (p. 742). That the PRP is a monument of such systematic application *a propos* psychoanalysis goes without saying. In the depth and scope of the observational data presented to the reader, it responds to the justified complaint of Arlow (1981), quoted by Wallerstein, that "In the literature of psychoanalysis, the production of theory far outstrips the supply of pertinent observational data". Given the "naturalistic" setting of the study, which is mentioned several times by Wallerstein, the PRP data may be limited in its potential for scientific validation. Any generalizations we draw from the outcome data remain tentative. And yet, as a reservoir of data about life in the therapeutic "real world," the study has no equal. For the gift of these data, let alone the probing and balanced discussions that accompany them, the profession owes Robert Wallerstein its gratitude.

REFERENCES

Appelbaum, S. (1977). The Anatomy of Change New York: Plenum Press.

Arlow, J. (1981). Theories of pathogenesis *Psychoanal. Q.* 50:488–514.

Erle, J. & Goldberg, D. 1984 Observations on the assessment of analyzability by experienced analysts *J. Am. Psychoanal. Assoc.* 32:715–737.

Firestein, S.K. (1978). Termination in Psychoanalysis New York: Int. Univ. Press.

Glover, E. (1954). The indications for psychoanalysis *J. Mental Science* 100 393–401.

Horowitz, L. (1974). Clinical Prediction in Psychotherapy New York: Jason Aronson.

Kernberg, O. et al. (1972). Psychotherapy and psychoanalysis: Final Report of the Menninger Foundation's Psychotherapy Research Project *Bulltn. Menninger Clinic* 36:1–275

Richards, A. 1980 Self theory, conflict theory and the problem of hypochondriasis *Psychoanal. Study Child* 36:319–337.

——— (1987). Fantasy or reality? Self-mutilation and father-daughter incest. In *Unconscious Fantasy, Myth and Reality: Essays in Honor of Jacob A. Arlow.* Hillsdale. NJ: Analytic Press.

Stone, L. (1954). The widening scope of indications for psychoanalysis *Psychoanal. Q.* 20:215–236.

Ticho, E.A. (1970). Differences between psychoanalysis and psychotherapy *Bulln. Menninger Clinic* 34:128–138.

Tyson, R. & Sandler, J. (1971) Problems in the selection of patients for psychoanalysis: comments on the application of the concepts of "indications," "suitability" and "analysability" *Brit. J. Med. Psychol.* 44:211–228.

Voth, H. & Orth, M. (1973). *Psychotherapy of the Environment* New York: Behavioral Publications.

Weber, J., Bachrach, H. & Solomon, M. (1985). Characteristics of psychoanalytic clinic patients: Report of the Columbia Psychoanalytic Research Project (I) *Int. J. Psychoanal.* 12:13–26.

CHAPTER 19

Review of *Psychoanalytic Treatment: An Intersubjective Approach*

by Robert D. Stolorow and Bernard Brandchaft.
Hillsdale, NJ: Analytic Press, 1987, x + 188 pp., $24.95.

[(1992). *Journal of the American Psychoanalytic Association,* 40:256–260.]

This is the fourth collaborative volume by Stolorow and his colleagues. With Atwood, he has coauthored *Faces in a Cloud: Subjectivity in Personality Theory*(Stolorow and Atwood, 1979) and *Structures of Subjectivity: Explorations in Psychoanalytic Phenomenology*(Stolorow and Atwood, 1984). A third volume, *Psychoanalysis of Developmental Arrests: Theory and Treatment*(Stolorow and Lachman, 1980), was written with Lachman, who has also coauthored the chapter on transference in the present work. Brandchaft, coauthor of the other chapters, has collaborated with Stolorow on a paper on borderline concepts (Brandchaft and Stolorow, 1984) and has on his own contributed a number of articles to the self psychology literature.

Psychoanalytic Treatment sets for itself the most ambitious of goals: to "formulate the basic theoretical constructs for a psychoanalytic science of human experience" (p. 132). To this end, the authors offer "two fundamental ideas" as "central guiding principles": (1) the concept of an intersubjective field, by which they mean to denote the idea of a "system of differently organized, interacting subjective worlds [as] invaluable for comprehending both the vicissitudes of psychoanalytic therapy and the process of human psychological development" (p. ix); and (2) the concept of concretization, defined as "the encapsulation of organizations of experience by concrete, sensorimotor symbols" (p. 132).

Although the authors observe that their notion of psychoanalysis as a science of the intersubjective evolved over 15 years of collaborative work, they did not introduce the term "intersubjective" until 1984, in *Structures of Subjectivity*. Prior to that, they were more closely aligned with Heinz Kohut's self psychology, as augmented by their own emphasis on the representational world. Chapter 2 of the present book, "Reflections on Self Psychology," is an excellent summary of what the authors consider the major conceptual and theoretical problems in Kohut's approach.

Overall, the strengths and weaknesses of this book emerge clearly in the four chapters (4, 5, 8, and 9) that contain detailed clinical material. Here we have an opportunity to test whether the authors achieve their central aim: "to flesh out the implications for psychoanalytic understanding and treatment of adopting a consistently intersubjective perspective" (p. 2). Since the authors stress throughout this work the advantages of such a viewpoint over that of classical psychoanalysis—which in their view attributes pathology "to the operation of intrapsychic mechanisms located solely within the patient"—we may put the relevant questions thus: (1) Does the case material demonstrate any difficulties in understanding and treatment consequent on the adoption of traditional points of view? (2) Does the theoretical approach suggested by the authors evince a superior understanding and yield more effective therapeutic strategies?

In suggesting that the answer to both questions is no, I am questioning not the usefulness of the author's conceptualizations, but rather any claim that they constitute a distinct and original clinical theory. *Psychoanalytic Treatment* propounds a sound clinical approach to rich clinical material, but misses the mark in attempting to present this approach as illustrative of an "intersubjective" viewpoint differing radically from that of traditional psychoanalysis. In point of fact, what Stolorow and his colleagues construe as emblematic of traditional theory—the unempathic analyst whose objectivist stance causes him repeatedly to miss the intersubjective truth—is a caricature of contemporary analytic technique.

Even if the authors presented a more balanced assessment of the traditional approach, their comparison of intersubjective with traditional psychoanalysis would be questionable owing to the treatment modalities through which they exemplify the former. Indeed, the very inclusion of the term "psychoanalytic" in the book's title is controversial. Several of the patients discussed at length would not be considered analyzable; critics would maintain that the intersubjective treatment they received was, at most, analytically informed therapy, and that the word "psychodynamic" should therefore have replaced "psychoanalytic" in the book's title. There is, be it noted, a countervailing point of view, of which Merton M. Gill is one influential proponent, that would sustain the authors' characterization of these cases as "psychoanalyses," especially given their emphasis on transference interpretation.

Another general criticism concerns the insularity of the authors' argumentation. Although some effort is made to locate the intersubjective viewpoint within the evolution of self psychology, there is consistent failure to consider relevant contributions outside this tradition. Consider the second of the authors' two guiding principles: that "sensorimotor symbols" can encapsulate "organizations of experience" was Freud's fundamental insight regarding neurotic symptoms. In hysterical symptoms, that is, traumatic memories gained expression as sensory experience, an idea Freud (1900) then applied to dream formation in Chapter 7 of *The Interpretation of Dreams*.

In the chapter on the treatment of borderline states, Otto F. Kernberg and his ideas about primitive defenses, splitting, and pregenital aggression are cast in the role of villain, but little mention is made of the substantial literature criticizing Kernberg's formulations. The authors' questioning of the clinical evidence for the operation of primitive defenses, for example, is anticipated by Willick's (1983) lengthy discussion of this issue. The authors admit that their understanding of borderline phenomena as arising in an intersubjective field "consisting of a precarious, vulnerable self in a failing, archaic selfobject bond" (p. 116) is consistent with other reported analyses of borderline patients, but they refer only to the work of J. Adler and M. Tolpin, making no reference to Abend, Willick, and Porder's *Borderline Patients: Psychoanalytic Perspectives*(1983), a book that presents four analyses of patients considered borderline; its authors, be it noted, join Stolorow and his colleagues in opposing Kernberg's viewpoint, but formulate their critique from the standpoint of classical analysis.

As regards the treatment of psychotic states, Stolorow and Brandchaft, in a final chapter devoted to the topic, make no effort to locate their intersubjective conceptualizations within the abundant literature on psychosis. Certainly, work in recent decades on family pathology and the double bind connects to their idea that psychotics fail to develop a sense of the validity of their own experience as a result of the early absence of validating responses from caregivers. In positing that a "core of subjective truth" (p. 134) inheres in the psychotic patient's delusional ideas, they mention neither Freud, who first referred to the kernel of truth in delusions, nor John Frosch, a classical analyst who, in *The Psychotic Process* (1983), elaborates this issue precisely in relation to psychotic states.

It is in this final chapter, moreover, that the authors' penchant for erecting and demolishing straw men is clearest. In reporting the case of Malcolm, who developed delusional ideas in response to sexual frustration and sexual overtures, the authors proffer their intersubjective approach as if the traditional analyst treats psychotics only from the standpoint of the analyst's own reality, attempting, through reassurance or alternative explanations, to bring the patient to accept the analyst's reality. It is only via the intersubjective viewpoint, they insist, that Malcolm's analyst, "somehow decenter[ed] from his own structuring of Malcolm's reality," began to understand that Malcolm desperately needed someone to affirm the validity of his own perceptual reality, and subsequently became able to "grasp and interpret the kernel of subjective truth that had been symbolically elaborated in Malcolm's persecutory delusions" (p. 143). They chide proponents of the traditional approach for reacting to "the literal content of ... delusions rather than their symbolic meanings" (p. 135).

Now what good therapist, psychoanalytically informed or not, responds "to the literal content of delusions"? Stolorow and his colleagues opine that therapists without the benefit of the intersubjective point of view are forever "invoking the concepts of objective reality and distortion" (p. 135), effectively telling psychotic patients that they are crazy. Such therapists attempt to "persuade their patients to admit they are mad, projecting or distorting in order to fortify the therapist's own endangered psychological world" (p. 136). One must wonder about the source of the authors' misunderstanding of the ordinary practitioner's approach to psychotic patients. *Any* good therapist responds to delusional ideas by recognizing their adaptive value for the patient. Within a classical framework, this recognition is tantamount to saying that psychotic delusions, like other mental products, are compromise formations, the most adaptive solutions available to particular patients at a given time. Likewise, the authors' plea that therapists try to comprehend the patient's "psychic reality" speaks to the widely accepted requirements for timing, tact, and compassion in treating all patients, not just the severely disturbed. The authors' provisos on these various counts cannot be faulted, but do they amount to a new theoretical approach? I think not.

To this reviewer, the obvious truth to the plaint that classical analysis, in its inception, tended to "view pathology in terms of processes and mechanisms located solely in the patient" does not entail the very different claim that the contemporary classical analyst necessarily "fails to decenter from the structures of experience into which he has been assimilating his patient's communications." In fact, a great deal of literature in the classical tradition addresses the intersubjective dimension of analytic treatment; the authors' failure to engage this literature suggests a failure to decenter from their own theoretical commitments.

As a result, their sound clinical approach and often insightful appreciation of treatment interactions are marred by what they take to be their signal contribution: the elaboration of a theoretical approach revolving around the terms "subjective" and "intersubjective." For this reviewer, these terms obfuscate rather than illuminate. The authors' continual use of the phrase, "intersubjective transactions" would read much better as "personal interactions," and, at many points in the book, the word "experience" seems more apt than either "subjectivity" or "intersubjectivity."

Finally, when the authors assert that subjective reality is the only reality accessible to, and relevant for, psychoanalytic inquiry, they advance a view that is as questionable as what they take to be the classical analytic position, i.e., the equation of pathology with processes and mechanisms located solely within the patient. The distinction between subjectivity and objectivity is an epistemological issue that cannot be resolved by fiat any more than can the distinction between realism and idealism apropos the physical world. The authors of *Psychoanalytic Treatment*, who have much to say that is clinically helpful, would strengthen their case by tempering their philosophical pretensions and wrestling more open-mindedly with what A. Goldberg, whom they cite, has noted as a longstanding *tension* within psychoanalysis: realism on the one hand, relativism on the other.

REFERENCES

Abend, S., Porder, M. & Willick, S.M. (1983). *Borderline Patients: Psychoanalytic Perspectives.* New York: Int. Univ. Press.

Atwood, G. & Stolorow, R D. (1984*). Structures of Subjectivity: Explorations in Psychoanalytic Phenomenology.* Hillsdale, N.J.: Analytic Press.

Brandchaft, R. & Stolorow, R.D. (1984). The borderline concept: pathologic character or iatrogenic myth In *Empathy Vol, ,2* ed. J. Lichtenberg. Hillsdale, NJ: Analytic Press.

Freud, S. (1900). The interpretation of dreams *Standard Edition* 4 & 5.

Frosch, J. (1983). *The Psychotic Process.* New York: Int. Univ. Press.

Stolorow, G. & Atwood, R.D. (1979). *Faces in a Cloud: Subjectivity in Personality Theory.* Hillsdale, NJ: Analytic Press

——— & Lachman, F. (1980). *Psychoanalysis of Developmental Arrests: Theory and Treatment.* Hillsdale, NJ: Analytic Press.

Willick, M.S. (1983), On the content of primitive defenses. *J. Am. Psychoanal. Assoc.* 31:175–200.

CHAPTER 20

Politics and Paradigms

[(1998). *Journal of the American Psychoanalytic Association* 46(2):357–360]

The appearance in this issue of papers by Charles Spezzano, Dianne Elise, and the team of Lewis Aron and Annabella Bushra is worthy of note. The fact that these writers are members neither of the American Psychoanalytic Association nor of the International Psychoanalytical Association marks a departure from the status quo as recently as four or five years ago. For example, in 1993 *JAPA* 41/4 included only one paper by a nonmember of those groups, and that contributor was Martin Bergmann, who subsequently became a member of the IPA and, in Toronto this May, an honorary member of the American. That the interpersonalist/relationalist schools, of which Spezzano and Aron are prominent representatives, are only now finding a place in this journal is evident from a cursory study of the bibliography of the Aron-Bushra paper. A search using the PEP CD-ROM reveals that John Fiscalini, a prominent interpersonal analyst, is cited for the first time in *JAPA*, although he was cited twenty-eight times in *Contemporary Psychoanalysis* through 1994. Gerard Chrzanowski, another prominent interpersonally trained psychoanalyst, is cited for the first time in *JAPA* since a single citation in 1965 in an article by Rudolf Ekstein. By contrast, there are no fewer than fifty-nine references to Chrzanowski in *Contemporary Psychoanalysis*.

291

The question for us to consider is the extent to which the development of psychoanalysis has been affected by organizational and political schisms over the years. Aron and Bushra cite some unexpected convergences between authors who seemingly have developed similar ideas independently of one another. A case in point is the approach to anxiety in the analytic situation developed by Paul Gray and Harry Stack Sullivan. The similarity in their views is unexpected and remarkable, and not at all consistent with a dichotomous drive/relational view of their respective schools. It is interesting to ponder how their theories might have developed had the Washington School of Psychiatry and the Baltimore-Washington Institute maintained an organizational affiliation.

In any consideration of contemporary psychoanalytic pluralism (a fact reflected in the range of books reviewed here under the rubric of pluralism), the personal and political roots of theory change and theory affiliation must be taken into account. A cardinal instance in this regard is the strikingly different courses taken by of the Columbia Center for Psychoanalytic Training and Research and the William Alanson White Institute.

In the late 1930s Sandor Rado, first education director of the New York Psychoanalytic Institute, rejected libido theory and began to develop his own theoretical approach, which eventually he would call "adaptational psychodynamics." That placed him at odds with important members of the institute's education committee, including Lawrence Kubie, Gregory Zilboorg, and Bertram Lewin. In 1940 the position of education director was abolished, and Rado, declining to remain on the Executive Council, went on to found the Association for Psychoanalytic Medicine in 1942 and the Psychoanalytic and Psychosomatic Clinic for Training and Research in 1945, which he succeeded in affiliating with Columbia University. Interestingly, however, once Rado established the Columbia Center he did all he could to have the new institute accepted into the American Psychoanalytic Association, a goal achieved the very next year. In this endeavor he went so far as to enlist the support of Zilboorg, his erstwhile rival, who helped him in having Columbia exempted from the association's standing rule of one institute per city. Thus, despite Rado's heresy—his culturalist, neo-Freudian theoretical posture—he succeeded in his efforts to remain within the mainstream.

Now consider the very different trajectory of the William Alanson White Institute. Clara Thompson left the New York Institute in 1941, along with Karen Horney. The latter, stripped of training analyst status, organized the American Institute of Psychoanalysis, which Thompson, the Riochs, Frieda Fromm-Reichmann, and Erich Fromm left when Fromm's training analyst status was also revoked. Joined by Harry Stack Sullivan, they formed a new institute affiliated with the Washington School of Psychiatry. In 1945 the Washington connection was severed, and the institute was given the name it bears today. In 1952 the institute withdrew its application for recognition by the American, it having become clear there was no possibility of its being accepted so long as Sullivan remained prominent and psychologists were trained. But the fact is that after this separation the Sullivanian interpersonalist point of view gained ascendancy at the White Institute and to this day remains its dominant theoretical orientation.

My point is to emphasize the interesting parallels between Rado's adaptational approach at Columbia and the White Institute's interpersonalist inflection. Both institutes shared an important interest in cultural determinants. Within the Columbia group, Abram Kardiner, Aaron Karush, and Lionel Ovesey produced vigorous critiques of libido theory which, rejected by mainstream psychoanalytic journals, were published in the *Journal of Nervous and Mental Diseases*. These papers resemble in many respects the critiques of drive theory written by the first generation of White interpersonalists.

Yet, despite these theoretical similarities during their early history, the Columbia Center and the White Institute have pursued very different paths. The White Institute retains its autonomy as the leading center of interpersonal psychoanalysis, while at Columbia Rado is forgotten, the center having become an integral part of the American Psychoanalytic Association mainstream. But here, I think, is what we should reflect on: had Rado not exerted himself to keep Columbia within the American, we might even now find ourselves engaging a Columbia-based adaptational psychoanalysis, much as we are now discussing interpersonal and relational theory. This is not to offer a judgment as to which historical path is to be preferred. Rather, I mean simply to underscore the way in which politics and personalities enter into our attitudes toward theories, often influencing the decision to pursue a separatist or an integrationist strategy in the face of theoretical difference.

There is an interesting postscript to this piece of history. In 1948, shortly after the White's founding, a group of social workers left the new institute, saying they felt excluded by the psychiatrist/psychologist ruling elite there. The social workers approached Harry Bone, a psychologist analyst, and asked him to be the "draw" at yet another new training institute. When Bone refused, they approached Theodor Reik, a lay analyst who, denied full membership in the New York Society/Institute in 1938, had organized a private study group active in the forties. Reik accepted the invitation, and NPAP, the National Psychological Association for Psychoanalysis, was established.

Later a group of ten, dissatisfied with what they regarded as the lax training standards at NPAP, broke away to form IPTAR (the Institute for Psychoanalytic Training and Research), while a second group, led by Gisela Birenbaum, left NPAP to organize the New York Freudian Society.

These groups, influenced by Reik, whose quarrel with New York was over lay analysis and not analytic theory, remained solidly Freudian. Many of their early members were in fact analyzed and supervised, sub rosa, by members of the New York Institute.

Aron and Bushra, as well as Spezzano, point in this issue of *JAPA* to interesting and unexpected convergences between contributors from different schools. Most striking is the similarity they note in the views of states of unconsciousness in the analytic situation held by Philip Bromberg, a relationalist, and Sheldon Bach, a Freudian. Is it not possible that whether a shift from a so-called "drive" paradigm to a relational one is viewed as revolution or evolution is a question determined in large measure by political considerations? There are even those who maintain that the shift itself is a political artifact. My own sense is that these theoretical distinctions will become less clear-cut (and will be advanced less insistently) as dialogue between the various schools continues. I am pleased that this journal can contribute to that process.